المفوض الرسمي
Commissioned by

مؤسسة سلامة بنت حمدان آل نهيان
SALAMA BINT HAMDAN
AL NAHYAN FOUNDATION

بدعم من
Supported by

وزارة الثقافة
MINISTRY OF CULTURE

الجناح الوطني لدولة الإمارات
بينالي البندقية

National Pavilion UAE
La Biennale di Venezia

La Biennale di Venezia
19. Mostra Internazionale di Architettura
Partecipazioni Nazionali

# Pressure Cooker Recipes: *An Architectural Cookbook*


Edited by
***Azza Aboualam***



Co-Publisher
KAPH
ART BOOKS FROM THE ARAB WORLD

National Pavilion
***United Arab Emirates***

# Contents

## COOKING TECHNIQUES



03

## MEAL KITS & PREP



04

## SEASONAL & LOCAL



05

## EPILOGUE

# *Prologue*



Illustrations by Khalid Mezaina

*Chapter* **00**

# Commissioner's Foreword: *Right Plant, Right Place*

**Salama bint Hamdan Al Nahyan Foundation**

Commissioner of the National Pavilion UAE – La Biennale di Venezia

Growing food in the desert climate presents unique challenges and opportunities demanding innovative approaches to architecture. Emirati architect Azza Aboualam developed a growing fascination around food production and set out to examine how the United Arab Emirates (UAE) has adapted greenhouse structures from their original cold-climate vernacular forms to respond to local needs such as shading, water retention, and crop type.

Documenting her investigation and experimentation in this project, Aboualam invites readers to explore her research and discover the transformative power of the greenhouse as a method for sustainable food production. Her work presents models for newly imagined archetypes that are customizable in scale and requirements for specific locations within arid climates. In the pavilion, the exhibition highlights the innovative practices that intertwine art, science, and agriculture, reflecting a growing consciousness about our relationship with the environment.

Greenhouses are more than mere structures; they are sanctuaries of growth and sustenance. They also serve as a metaphor for growing other initiatives, including ideas and ventures, nurturing the seeds of change in our urban landscapes and communities. Through the lens of these greenhouses, we delve into the future of food, sustainability, and community resilience. As we contemplate the vital role these spaces play in addressing global challenges, we are inspired to envision a world where food is not just a necessity but a source of creativity and connection.

Urban agriculture is transforming cities and improving residents' quality of life. By producing fresh food within urban areas, it strengthens food security and minimizes the distance from farm to table. This practice also encourages community engagement, as residents come together to cultivate shared spaces, build relationships, and promote social cohesion. Moreover, urban agriculture can contribute to environmental sustainability by invigorating green spaces, improving air quality, and promoting biodiversity. In addition, it serves as a powerful tool for education, inspiring future generations to embrace sustainable practices and understand the importance of local food systems.

As commissioners of the National Pavilion United Arab Emirates at La Biennale di Venezia, these are the types of research projects that we are excited to share with the world. They show the creativity and development of ideas that materialize into practical solutions. By engaging with real-life issues that tap into areas of necessity, they also take into account the environmental and cultural context in which we live, an important facet of our world and humanity. As always, there is an enormous amount of energy that goes on behind the scenes to produce this work and we are immensely grateful for the enthusiasm, commitment, and diligence of all the people who take part. In particular, we would like to thank the Ministry of Culture for its continuing partnership on this journey in the spirit of inquiry, synthesis, and a forward-thinking vision of the future.

# Supporter's Foreword

**His Excellency Sheikh Salem bin Khalid Al Qassimi,**
UAE Minister of Culture

Since 2009, the exhibitions presented by the National Pavilion United Arab Emirates at La Biennale di Venezia have driven conversations regionally and internationally. We are proud of what our cultural practitioners have achieved over the years, and that they continue to ensure that research, collaboration, and creativity contribute to the UAE's growth in both the culture and creative industries.

The UAE's contribution to the 19th International Architecture Exhibition of La Biennale di Venezia, entitled *Pressure Cooker Recipes* reflects our nation's steadfast commitment to fostering innovation in addressing critical global challenges. The curator, Azza Aboualam, investigates the intersection of architecture and food security, demonstrating how sustainable design can contribute to the nation's goal of climate resilience and enhanced resource management.

Using the UAE as a case study, this thought-provoking, heavily researched exhibition exemplifies the UAE's leadership in advancing architectural solutions for arid environments and provides a model for other nations facing similar challenges within their communities. Concurrently, the exhibition and the accompanying publication put forth the opportunity to expand the dialogue on sustainability and self-sufficiency in food and its production.

As the UAE continues to transform, each edition of the National Pavilion UAE reflects and shares that growth with a global audience. This would not be possible without the vision and unwavering commitment of the Salama bint Hamdan Al Nahyan Foundation, Commissioner of the National Pavilion UAE. Special thanks to the team at the pavilion who worked tirelessly with Aboualam to bring this exhibition and publication to fruition. The Ministry of Culture is proud to support this initiative and is committed to ensuring that the most effective framework is in place for creatives in the UAE.

It is heartening to see our nation's brightest minds and their compelling narratives continue to resonate and engage with people worldwide. As with past exhibitions, this year's contribution delivers a narrative that tackles a myriad of possibilities for the future.

# Curator's Note:
## *Where Do the Blueberries Come From?*

Azza Aboualam

## Origin Stories

Fig. 01: Locally produced blueberries. Photo by Ola Allouz.

"من وين هذا؟"

"Where are those blueberries from?" (Fig. 01) my mother asked one day after lunch as we nibbled on our usual fruit plate. I was often asked this question whenever I came back from the grocery store. "They're locally grown," I answered, as I pointed to the Made in UAE sticker. She looked at me in disbelief, responding mid-bite, "Really? They must be grown in greenhouses."

This conversation was the spark that instigated this project as my interest in local food infrastructures piqued. Walking around Spinneys, for example, or other local grocery stores, the signs that used to proudly display internationally sourced produce have transformed, in recent years, into labels that boast the terms "local" or "Made in the UAE." These labels began to proliferate in designated areas in the produce, dairy, meat, and poultry aisles with Emirati flags on them. Currently, The National Food Security Strategy 2051 aspires to transform the United Arab Emirates (UAE) into a world-leading hub for innovation-driven food security. It aims to elevate the country's ranking on the Global Food Security Index (GFSI) to number one and plans for half of its food to be produced locally by 2051.

At a time when over half of the world's population lives in urbanized areas, removed from sites of food production, the "local" label attempts to frame a shared understanding of the sources of our sustenance. Despite most peoples' distance or removal from the practice of agriculture, or food production by and large, this designation provides a semblance of comfort, albeit not painting the full picture that comes with those practices.

*Pressure Cooker* started as a documentation of local food production techniques and their overlap with architectural spaces, ranging from the rudimentary to the technologically advanced, shedding light on the UAE's strides toward its food security goals. As time went by and after visiting over 150 local farms, this project transformed into one that provides an alternative mode of knowledge production, documenting, analyzing, and learning from the UAE's local knowledge when it comes to the notion of sustenance. Seeing the desiccating farms in Al Dhaid and Ras Al Khaimah and the abandoned greenhouses in Umm Al Quwain and Al Ain was a stark reminder of what could be lost if those structures and techniques were not documented.

### Ongoing Questions

When it comes to the research provocation, *Pressure Cooker* proposes that architectural form can help facilitate an alternative mode of food production, creating a systemized output for the UAE and countering the unstructured proliferation of greenhouse structures in its agricultural lands. This project relies on architecture to help mitigate some of the existing challenges that occur in the face of traditional food production methods. Those challenges include climate change with unpredictable weather patterns and soil degradation, as well as shrinking

*National Food Security Strategy 2051,* ***The United Arab Emirates' Government portal****, 2023.*

*Within the context of the UAE, the "local" label is often seen as "Made in UAE". In June 2017, the UAE's ruling cabinet, chaired by Sheikh Mohammed bin Rashid Al Maktoum, ruler of Dubai and vice-president and prime minister of the UAE, approved the standardization of the "Made in UAE" label, with the aim of strengthening the country's manufacturing sector. The move forms part of a larger push to promote manufacturing in the UAE. The label applies to a wide range of products from foodstuff to ceramics and appliances.*

*Abir Ahmar, "UAE oil power farms the desert in quest for food security," in* ***Reuters****, February 16, 2023.*

*Peter Rogers, "Water Security: Supplies, Resources, and Uncertainty," in* ***Water and Food Security in the Arabian Gulf*** *(Abu Dhabi: Emirates Center for Strategic Studies and Research, 2013), 170.*

*FAO Agricultural and Development Economics Division,* ***Policy Brief: Food Security****, Issue 2, June 2006, http://www.fao.org/es/esa/.*

farmland as a result of expanding cities and loss of traditional knowledge. The newly formulated architectural language ultimately frees food production from its dependence on traditional methods, producing an architectural typology that takes the UAE one step closer to its food security goals and puts a portion of food production into the hands of the members of the community. At the moment, the world is undergoing a significant transition that has adverse implications for both current and future global food security. Intensifying climate change threatens to disrupt the already fragile supply of food and water, especially in the Middle East. While trade has provided an option to overlook local obstacles when it comes to food security, the UAE's strength in economic success with its exceptional transport and logistics infrastructure has proven helpful. This resulted in an arid country, such as the UAE, importing 90% of its food while only around 1% of the UAE's land is used for agriculture. Despite having heavily invested in overseas land acquisition for food production, the pandemic in 2020 was a stark reminder of the importance of its inclusion within Emirati borders. This project associates food security with agency in a rapidly changing climate, as it bridges three aspects: local techniques in food production, architectural form, and space making.

This leads us to the main research question, which is: Using the UAE as a case study, how can architecture be mobilized toward greater food security?

Some of the sub-questions include:
Seeing that the architectural form, supporting the UAE's agenda for food security, still remains unexplored, can its exploration identify and address existing challenges in food production, taking the UAE one step closer to its food security goals?

And, how will the growth of these newly designed models add to the architectural identity of the country by 2051?

At the intersection of local knowledge, producing new forms of space, and celebrating the act of building in arid environments, *Pressure Cooker* investigates the role architecture can play in bolstering food security. Here enters the greenhouse: the architectural typology that was explored and redesigned for arid environments within the context of the project.

**Dated Concepts**

Food security, as a concept, originated to reflect a global concern that was raised at the World Food Conference in 1974, at a time when widespread shortages and mass starvation threats seemed imminent. The Food and Agriculture Organization of the UN (FAO) defines it as, "all people, at all times, have physical and economic access to sufficient, safe and nutritious food that meets their dietary needs and food preferences for an active and healthy life." It loosely states that the four pillars of food security are: availability, access, utilization, and stability, which factors in the previous three aspects over time. However, this definition was coined over 50 years ago and the UAE's challenges are quite specific to those of arid climates.

Some of those include: harsh desert conditions that limit local agricultural production, fresh water scarcity, and extreme temperatures for most of the year, a high rate of food waste, rapid population growth, and the reliance on imported food. Since a vast majority of the UAE's food supply is currently imported, fluctuations in global food prices can impact affordability and accessibility.

As such, taking those nuances into consideration, food security is further defined within the context of *Pressure Cooker* as follows:

Availability: Addressed through local urban integration of the new greenhouse and its affordability and ability to insert itself within the existing built environment.

Access: Addressed through the various degrees of public and private space, as part of community members' lives.

Utilization: Addressed through the greenhouse's output and selected food categories that are experimented with throughout the project.

Stability: Addressed through the greenhouse's mutability, time, and season-based adaptation both as a physical space and as a measure of output.

**Wishful Thinking**

In response, *Pressure Cooker* builds on a three-pronged research approach — archival research, fieldwork, and design-build — as it investigates the relationship between architecture and the methods of food production in the UAE. Revealing intertwined global and local histories, the project started by looking into local archives that explore notions of food security and their overlap with architecture. This was closely followed by visiting existing food-growing infrastructures in the UAE, located in resource-rich landscapes that are often obscured, overlooked, or physically separated from urban centers. Local design solutions that were conceived under conditions of food scarcity, over the years, are delved into, ranging from the vernacular to the technologically sophisticated. Finally, during the design build phase, *Pressure Cooker* explored how reformulating the greenhouse model can respond to food security challenges in the UAE and worldwide, resulting in a possible future in which these forms can be adapted, refined, and integrated throughout our built and lived environments.

A kit-of-parts demonstrates the research project's outcome that not only responds to the UAE's hot arid climate but also corresponds to the food category they are intended for growing. In this context, the new greenhouse's architectural vocabulary is broken down into its basic architectural elements (roof, wall, floor, tools, and materials). These components are mixed and matched, resulting in multiple scenarios of input, output, and assembly. In addition, the exhibition examines a range of applications for the kit-of-parts, or greenhouse assemblies, that cater to multiple scales from domestic spaces to urban centers in the UAE. Ultimately, *Pressure Cooker* reimagines how food production, architectural form, and new conceptions of space can overlap, informing applications and solutions for arid climates (Fig. 02).

That being said, in a harsh desert climate, where do the locally produced blueberries *really* come from?

Fig.02 A family visiting the greenhouse, Saadiyat project, Abu Dhabi, 1974, by Dr. Merle Jensen, Courtesy of UAE National Library and Archives.

# Side Note

Azza Aboualam

*Women In Architecture, or WIA, is a global initiative with the mission to accelerate the pathway for women in architecture to amplify the impact of the discipline worldwide. While this phrase has no fixed meaning, its original intention was constructed to initiate a reframing of the field, in order to be more inclusive, signaling a shift in the perception of architecture. However, in reality, women have always contributed to the field, shaping architecture in ways that expanded and enhanced the entire discipline.*

While I started off this project with extreme optimism and immense excitement, given my past experience with local fieldwork, reality slowly hit me as time went by. When thinking about the built environment and architecture, power and dominance usually come to mind, which are often associated with masculinity. Architecture is a field known for its difficulty — studies show it is the second hardest major after medicine — as well as being traditionally and socio-culturally male-dominated. Being the first Emirati woman to curate the architecture exhibition for the National Pavilion United Arab Emirates (UAE), following five successful male architects, local farms were a sweet reprieve from the adversarial challenges, biases, and the constant stream of ageist comments that came with this project. The realities and consequences of this gendered experience made it extremely difficult not to reflect on them as part of my journey, with issues my predecessors were unlikely to face. In parallel, the quest for asserting feminine values in this architectural project, also came with its own set of challenges. There is a danger when "femininity" is essentialized, as if all women, everywhere, have the same eternal set of attributes that distinguish them from men. This clearly is not the case. The past decade has seen a resurgence in the term "women in architecture" coupled with the renewed debate around its use as well as challenges from feminist historians and theorists to recognize and legitimize diverse forms of architectural practices. I am both for and against the term "woman architect," as it implies gendering the role of architects in the field all the while further differentiating architectural work produced by women from their male counterparts. While this version of the National Pavilion UAE proudly presents an all-female local Arab research and design team, half of which are Emirati, I can safely say that we have carved our own path toward a future that values talent regardless of social constructs as we simultaneously and constantly grapple with the gender and age divide.

# Editor's Note

Azza Aboualam

Cooking and architecture have a lot in common. Both start with a set of ingredients that are combined to create a whole; one that is often greater than the sum of its parts. Bread in my kitchen, for example, is made by bringing together ingredients from a variety of sources: flour or processed whole wheat from the Mleiha farms in Sharjah; salt, a naturally occurring mineral shipped to the UAE from the Netherlands; and yeast, a fungus manufactured in France. And yet, bread is an infinitely flexible recipe with a wide spectrum of outcomes, from crusty Italian ciabatta to Middle Eastern flatbreads. Architecture isn't that different. Using a distinctive set of building materials, their combination often leads to a multitude of end results. With both food and architecture, the process of combination is deeply intertwined with its cultural meaning, combinatory logic, and is highly dependent on its context. This makes the sum of its disparate parts, whether flour or concrete, a unique outcome.

This architectural cookbook features recipes that range from the historical to the fictional to the technical, showcasing a multitude of outcomes for a curated selection of key ingredients, providing creative, flavorful, and accessible ways to reflect on food production. Cookbooks go far beyond offering recipes; they hold key information when it comes to notions of nutrition, culture, and history, while often providing entertaining reflections and commentaries. As such, contributors were encouraged to creatively incorporate these ingredients in a personal and unique approach, highlighting their versatility as well as their overlap with the built environment, ultimately reflecting on the UAE as the binding agent, or *Pressure Cooker*.

For this edition, contributors were invited to make a meal using a provided list of core ingredients. While purchasing, foraging, gathering, steaming, blanching, baking, grilling, plating, or consuming the final outcome, they were encouraged to focus on the architectural spaces that ushered them throughout the process and helped them arrive at a final product. Additionally, architecture here is not only limited to the disparate parts and their respective spatial attributes, but it also extends into the combinatory process of the ingredients, emphasizing a fresh take on their synthesis all the while reflecting on the sensorial joys that food brings to the table.

# Acknowledgments

Azza Aboualam

Comparable to the degree of care and diligence that is required by people in agriculture and food production at large, this project would not have been possible without the support, guidance, and contributions of many individuals and organizations.

I am deeply grateful to the Salama bint Hamdan Al Nahyan Foundation and the Ministry of Culture for their unwavering support and providing the resources and funding necessary to bring this research to light as well as the selection committee for their nomination.

A special thank you to the National Pavilion United Arab Emirates team: Laila Binbrek's guidance and leadership, Farah El-Rafei's exceptional support and unparalleled dedication, Dana Al Sadek's commitment and outreach and Rawan Al Ramahi's logistical assistance.

To my research team and collaborators: Dimitri Brand and James Coleman who entertained my musings on food in the UAE from our first conversation during the open call phase. The ultimate local team: Noor Hamdan (Senior Researcher and Design Build Coordinator) - without her, this project would not have seen the light the way it does today - Nourhan Rahhal, Alya Al Rushdi, and Sara AlMahmoud. Kit Elsworth and Saeran Vasanthakumar for their technical prowess in building the digital tool. A very special thank you to Nujud Alhussain: this publication would not have been possible without her golden archival finds. Thank you to Ola Allouz and Khalid Mezaina whose photographs, sketches, snacks, and humor kept the long drives alive.

To my peers and colleagues at Zayed University (ZU): Dean Janet Bellotto for her continual support, Oliver Castelino for technical assistance, and Asma and Alanood Bukhammas and Zena Adhami, whose friendship, unwavering encouragement and (extra) long daily conversations cannot be overlooked.

I would also like to thank H.E. Dr. Amna Al Dahak, Minister of Climate Change; Dr. Shamal Mohamed, AgriTech Director at Silal; Dr. Tarifa Al Zaabi and Dr. Henda Mahmoudi at International Center for Biosaline Agriculture; the Chancellor's Office and Mr. Bader AlTamimi at Al Foah Experimental Farm at United Arab Emirates University; Charlie Paton at Seawater Greenhouse; the teams at iyris and Pure Harvest; and the 300+ farmers, agricultural enthusiasts, and engineers who opened their doors to us and whose input and cooperation were integral to this research. Thank you to ZU Dubai for giving us space to build our contextual greenhouses and Sharjah Art Foundation/House of Wisdom/Sabaku for hosting us in the thick of the publication production phase.

Eiletz Ortigas Architects: Mateo Eiletz and Claudia Ortigas for bringing our kit-of-parts to life.

Möbius Design Studio: Hala Al-Ani, the project's lead, Riem Ibrahim, Hadeyeh Badri, and the whole team, for your patience, cooperation and continuous enthusiasm.

Kaph: Nour Salamé and her leadership as well as the rest of the team: Zeina Assaf, Ziad Chakaroun, and Mohammed Hamdan.

My family, friends, and mentors: Nada Taryam for cheering me on, Amal Taryam for social reprieves, Samar Halloum for coffee catch-ups, Julie Turgeon for the *unmatched* editing skills, Faysal Tabbarah whose inside jokes and immense help gave me hope and Kevin Mitchell whose mentorship over the past decade has been instrumental.

This project represents the culmination of collective effort, inspiration, and resilience, as it taught me about my own country in ways I could not have imagined. I am deeply thankful to all who have been part of it.

And finally, thank you, Mom, for helping me with my first-ever research paper on Galileo in the fourth grade (and asking me about those blueberries).

# *Journey Through a Meal*



Illustrations by Khalid Mezaina

*Chapter* **01**

# Where to Begin: *Historic Grounding*

Azza Aboualam

***Ingredients***

Dates
Eggs
Rice
Factory
Shack
Fence

---

*The Qur'an 106:1-4 (Translated by Dr. Mustafa Khattab).*

---

*Quraysh is the ruling tribe of Mecca at the time of the birth of the Prophet Muḥammad. Britannica, T. Editors of Encyclopedia "Quraysh."* ***Encyclopedia Britannica****, August 6, 2024. https://www.britannica.com/topic/Quraysh.*

---

*Tom Wilkinson, "Gardener's World,"* ***Architectural Review****, accessed December 22, 2024, https://www.architectural-review.com/essays/ecology/gardeners-world.*

---

*James C. Scott,* ***Against the Grain: A Deep History of the Earliest States*** *(New Haven, CT: Yale University Press, 2017), http://ebookcentral.proquest.com/lib/zu-ebooks/detail.action?docID=6424075.*

---

*National Geographic Society, "The Development of Agriculture,"* ***National Geographic Education Resource Library****, accessed January 27, 2025, https://education.nationalgeographic.org/resource/development-agriculture/.*

بسم الله الرحمن الرحيم
**لِإِيلافِ قُرَيْشٍ * إِيلافِهِمْ رِحْلَةَ الشِّتاءِ وَالصَّيْفِ * فَلْيَعْبُدُوا رَبَّ هذَا الْبَيْتِ * الَّذِي أَطْعَمَهُمْ مِنْ جُوعٍ وَآمَنَهُمْ مِنْ خَوْفٍ ***
صدق الله العظيم

At least for the favor of making Quraysh habitually secure – secure in their trading caravan to Yemen in the winter and Syria in the summer, let them worship the Lord of this Sacred House, who has fed them against hunger and made them secure against fear.

**Permanent Transience**

Food and security have always gone hand in hand: Quraysh have moved between the Levant in the north during summer and Yemen in the south during winter, equating daily provisions with safety. Traveling seasonally from place to place for long-distance trade, they acted as custodians of the places through which they were moving. Carefully managing the region's ecosystem with this seasonal relocation, they settled in oases along their routes, where methods of subsistence consisted of foraging practices. Despite recounted stories of food scarcity in the region, food, and its cultivation have been a prominent feature of the social and cultural landscape and its relationship to the region's inhabitants. Mainly due to the arid and harsh climate, traditional agricultural methods for food production which are dependent on fertile soil and freshwater, have been repeatedly deemed difficult.

But what about the relationship between food and the built environment? It is worth noting that the earliest evidence of sedentary life predates fully developed agricultural systems by millennia, when the act of cultivation began approximately 12,000 years ago. This transition, between nomadism and sedentism, was not a linear one, especially after the spread of agricultural practices. This period, also known as the Neolithic Revolution, was fundamental to the development of human societies, when the ability to live in a fixed place facilitated the construction of permanent housing. Traditional hunter-gatherer lifestyles slowly transitioned in favor of permanent settlements and a reliable food supply. Thanks to agriculture, crops and animals could be farmed to meet demand. Cities and civilizations grew and the global population expanded from some five million people ten thousand years ago to eight billion today. Those permanent human settlements inevitably encouraged a sense of privacy and possession that not only influenced transient patterns but also disrupted the pooling of food and agricultural resources at the scale of the village or tribe.

At the intersection of food and sufficiency, architecture emerges as a byproduct. As we look into the architecture of food production and examine the relationship between their form and purpose, a feedback loop takes shape, highlighting how the two influence each other throughout history. By continuously asserting their unique identity, these spaces remain deeply connected to the food production systems they engage with, shaping and being shaped in return. If the same argument applies, could we, then, examine the directly proportional relationship between food, its production, and the built environment in the United Arab Emirates (UAE)?

This essay explores the historical relevance of three distinct time periods: 1500–1871, 1872–1965, and 1965–1989. These periods highlight the relationship between food and the built environment in the UAE all the while aligning with pivotal changes in governing structures. The first period marks the arrival of the Portuguese, while the second traces back to British treaties, and the third positions itself at the time when HH Sheikh Zayed Bin Sultan Al Nahyan became ruler of Abu Dhabi, and later the UAE's first president. By examining these three distinct periods over the span of 500 years, this piece offers original research that uncovers the impact of food production and its trade on the local built environment, drawing unique, previously unexamined parallels that connect the two.

### ***Seasonal Maritime Discoveries 1500–1871***

### Fables and Harvest Cycles

This period represents a more rudimentary approach, marked by simplicity and resourcefulness born out of necessity. Both food production and building practices were modest, relying on locally available materials and techniques that prioritized functionality.

«إذا طلع سهيل، تلمس التمر في الليل»

In Arabic folklore, stories were recounted about the star Suhail (also called Canopus) to recall its significance. The star marks the beginning of autumn, indicating the weather's transition to cooler temperatures. It also signals the start of various activities, such as fishing and bird migration, or the end of others, such as the date harvest season. With the rise of the star, an intense period of heat combined with high humidity would prevail and

*"When Suhail rises, you can feel the ripeness of the dates at night."*

فادية هاني، «سهيل نجم الأساطير وملهم الأدباء والشعراء»، **صحيفة البيان**، 23 أغسطس 2024، https://www.albayan.ae/culture-art/culture/23-08-2024-1.4923092.

*Ibid.*

*Sultan Muhammad Al-Qasimi, **The Myth of Arab Piracy in The Gulf, second edition**, (Oxon: Routledge, 1988), 6.*

الدكتور سلطان بن محمد القاسمي، **وصف قلعة مسقط وقلاع أخرى على ساحل خليج عمان**، (الشارقة: منشورات القاسمي، 2009)، 21-22.

last until the autumn equinox in late September, which locals call "وعكة سهيل" or Suhail's distress. It is also referred to as "حرة الدبس" (molasses heat), as well as "حرة المساطيح," referring to the place where fresh dates "رطب" are left to dry "تمر". Following this period, the Earth's subsurface cools, making it the ideal time for harvesting palm dates of all kinds.

With the commencement of moist winds "هبايب سهيل," a reduction in high temperatures is palpable, marking the beginning of the agricultural season when various seeds are sown. By early October, seedlings are transferred to permanent soil, in addition to the relocation of saplings and trees. Simultaneously, fishermen would go to the seashore to feel the temperature of the sand beneath the surface. The dip in water temperature marks the start of their abundant season, indicating that Suhail is either about to appear or has already risen.

With the Gulf's calm waters, fishing became a main source of local sustenance. Oases were recorded in mountainous foothills, such as in Hafeet and Al Hajar, that benefited from groundwater for agriculture, despite limited output, such as in Al Ain and Masafi. Water-abundant locales, such as Ras Al Khaimah, were centers for food production at the time. Outputs included wheat, barley, dates, and other fruits and vegetables such as onions and sweet potatoes. Dibba and Kalba also contained a number of wells, with a notable growth of fig trees and melons as well as the raising of cows and goats. Simultaneously, Khor Fakkan had a substantial share of wells, where lemons, oranges, and watermelons were cultivated. Despite that, the widespread local diet was based on fish and dried dates, especially for coastal residents.

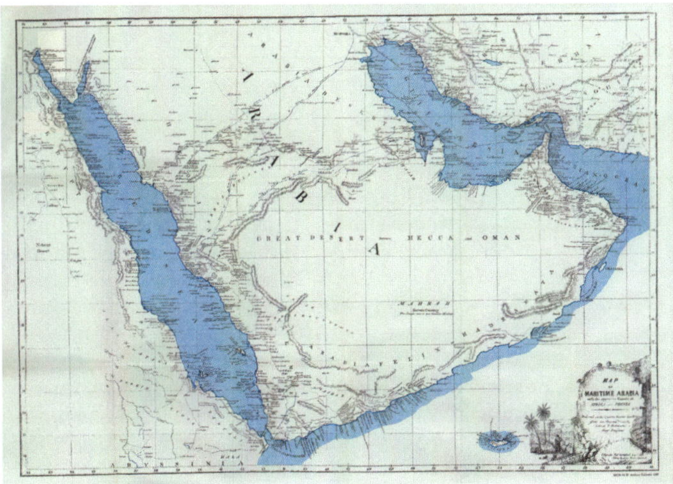


Fig. 01 Maritime Trade Route Map, insert in *Records of the Emirates 1820–1960,* edited by Penelope Tuson, vol. 10 (London: Archive Editions, 1990), Courtesy of UAE National Library and Archives.

## Trade Routes and Food Storage

Prior to the sixteenth century, transit trade was run by Arab and Indian merchants. Even though some of the traded items involved local produce, Arabs of the Gulf were less involved as consumers when compared to being traders – with the exception of coffee. Transported goods included coconuts, wheat, onions, garlic, saffron, and most importantly, the export of locally produced sugar. At the time, notable European states which were trading with the East included Venice and Genoa (Fig. 01).

When the European Renaissance ultimately led to the Portuguese to search for an alternative eastern route to India, Ibn Majid helped Vasco da Gama lead his troops. The Portuguese were able to set up their first colonial station in Goa, which then extended to other areas in the Gulf after taking over Hurmuz in 1514. Dominating trade in the Gulf, the Portuguese set up bases along the shores of the Trucial States.

The built environment mirrored the simplicity of food production, with architectural forms emerging from an intimate understanding of local climate and resources. While this time period is marked by trade routes and the constant movement of goods, the overlap of architecture and food production, here, is evident with the introduction of food storage, silos, and watchtowers to protect the landscape and accommodate for the constant flux of food products. This overlap is embodied by Dibba Fort, built by the Portuguese in the early seventeenth century, as well as the structures noted by the Dutch in the early nineteenth century.

Dibba Fort is a series of three structures constructed out of mud bricks. Containing a central water well and neighboring a small village of 300 people, mainly fishermen, it was wedged between palm tree plantations and the shoreline. The fort complex contained storage spaces and shacks to sell dates and fish, and to trade tobacco. Experimenting with growing fruit, the Portuguese built watchtowers to protect their orchards from being plucked or looted. It was noted that the first point of action for the Portuguese when arriving to the shores of the Gulf was to unload their foodstuffs (especially rice from India) and fill their forts with food. Similarly, upon their departure, and particularly in Dibba, the food storage was emptied

*Ibid.*

الخليج العربي في مواجهة التحديات، **محاضرات الموسمين الثقافيين السابع والثامن *1974 – 1975***، مؤسسة الوحدة للنشر و التوزيع الكويت، (تقديمـ الموسمين الثقافيين السابع والثامن *1974-1975*)، *17*.

الدكتور سلطان بن محمد القاسمي، **وصف قلعة مسقط وقلاع أخرى على ساحل خليج عمان**، (الشارقة : منشورات القاسمي، *2009*)، *67*.

الدكتور سلطان بن محمد القاسمي، **تاريخ اليعاربة في عمان *1623*مـ - *1747*مـ**، (الشارقة : منشورات القاسمي، *2022*)، *33*.

*Arnold T. Wilson, **The Persian Gulf: An Historical Sketch from the Earliest Times to the Beginning of the Twentieth Century** (London: Oxford University Press, 1928), 13.*

*Sultan Muhammad Al-Qasimi, **The Myth of Arab Piracy in The Gulf, second edition**, (Oxfordshire: Routledge, 1988), 5.*

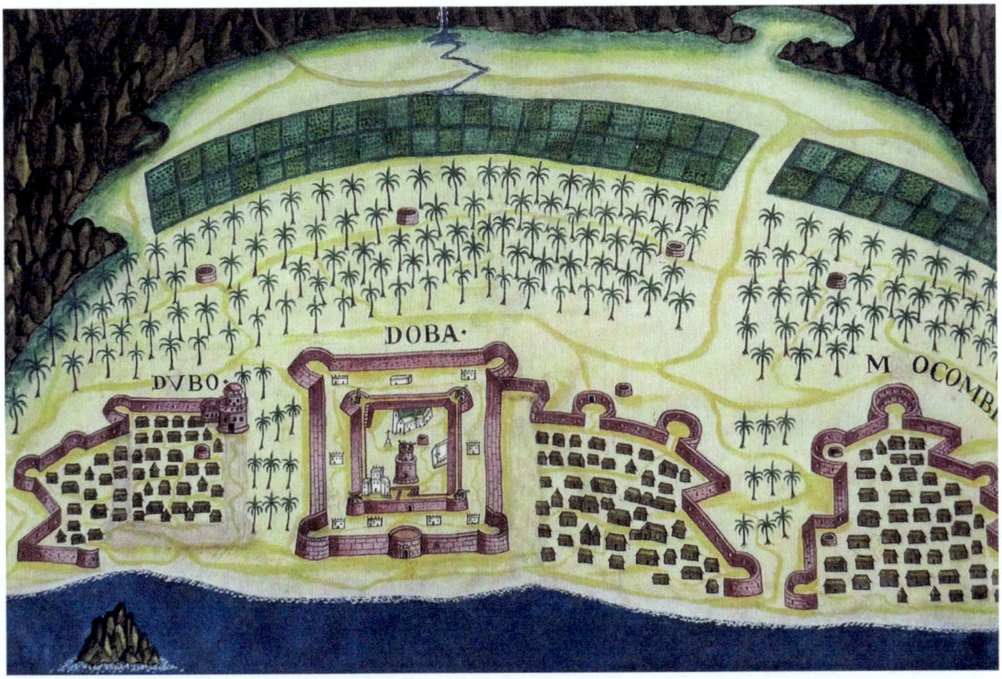


Fig.02 Dibba Fort in the seventeenth century, from
«وصف قلعة مسقط وقلاع أخرى على ساحل خليج عمان،»
Al Qasimi Publication, 2009, 65. Courtesy of Al Qasemi Publication.

first and brought onboard ships (Fig. 02). The Portuguese's arrival was closely followed by the British, the French, and the Dutch. Trade in the last quarter of the eighteenth century was mostly run by the English East India Company and lasted till 1813. A report on trade in the Gulf, written by Dutch admirals T.F. van Kniphausen and J. van der Hulst in 1756, reveals another instance of overlap between architecture and food trade mentioning: "There are three places on the coast, 'Ajir, Qatar, and Sharjah, each of which had only a few (structures), where from Basrah dates and rice were brought to sell to the Arabs of the desert or to pearl divers." Those shacks were prominent features along the shoreline. Built out of palm tree fronds or coral blocks, they were filled and emptied based on the pearl-diving season and cycles of maritime trade (Fig. 03).

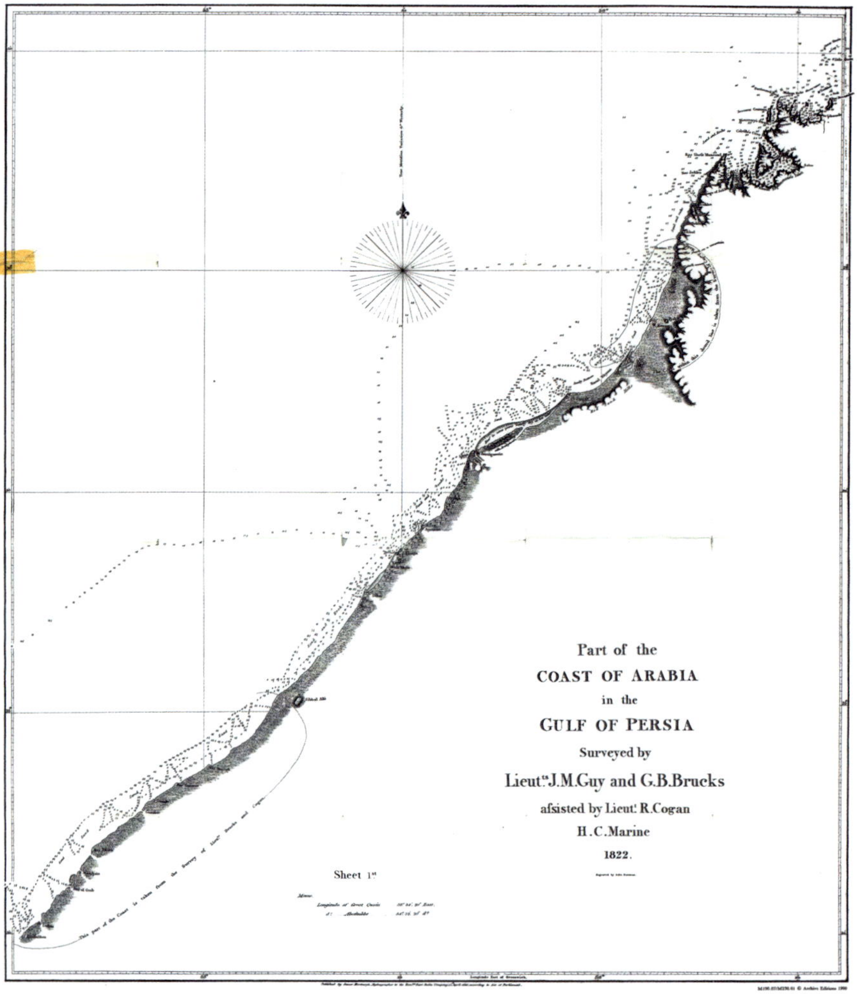


Fig. 03 Palm Tree Map, insert in *Records of the Emirates 1820–1960*, edited by Penelope Tuson, vol. 10 (London: Archive Editions, 1990), Courtesy of UAE National Library and Archives.

Penelope Tuson, ed., ***Records of the Emirates 1820–1960***, vol. 4, (London: Archive Editions, 1990), 127.

## (Mis)conceptions of Food Scarcity 1872–1965

### Tours and Correspondence

This period represents a notable growth in agricultural and food production practices, highlighted in the expansion of the built environment and increased funding by the British government. It also highlights the first instances of large-scale projects that reflect the expansion of the social fabric and, in tandem, the increased need for food supply and the built landscape.

Tours of the Gulf by Colonel Miles and Lord Curzon in 1873 and 1903, respectively, enabled the British to create a holistic study of the Arabian Peninsula from naval posts, bases, coaling stations, telegraph stations, and anchorages. Those descriptions of the Trucial States, from economic and historical factors to geographic and statistical documentation, offered a *subjective* insight into the state of the area at the time (Fig. 04).

CONFIDENTIAL

COI DENTIAL
(1285)

British Residency,
BAHRAIN.
March 9, 1960.

RECEIVED IN ARCHIVES 14 MAR 1960 BA 1282/13

Please refer to Arabian Department's letter BA 1282/4 of February 26 requesting a copy of the van Ollenbach report referred to in Jack Eyre's letter of January 22 to me.

2. I enclose a copy of the report but not of the Appendices, which are meaningless. Apendices A1 to A8 are lists (in Latin) of 81 crops; Appendix B1 is a paper (copied from a text-book) on the technique and interpretation of a single intradermal comparative tuberculin test, which Percy Durran says that Huntington must on no account attempt; Appendix B2 is a list of veterinary medicines; Appendix B3 gives details of equipment for a suggested poultry farm; and Appendix C1 gives a list of plant protection chemicals and where to obtain them.

(A.T. Lamb)

W.F. Marshall, Esq.,
Arabiah Department,
Foreign Office,
LONDON, S.W. 1.

CONFIDENTIAL

1. CROPS
General — Although the established crops on the Trials Station were seen to be doing reasonably well the actual number of crops being grown was small in comparison to other similar establishments in other parts of the world. In view of the fact that the Ras-Al-Khaima Station is the testing area for crops throughout the Trucial States it is suggested that the scope and variety of crops should be increased very appreciably.

(b) Vegetable — Due to the late arrival of seed vegetable crops were only just being planted out on the "trials station" and under the circumstances the growing season is likely to be seriously curtailed. As it has now been established that good quality vegetables can be produced in the area, work should be directed towards the introduction of disease resistant varieties and also to varieties that will increase the length of the season.

(c) Cereals — Unfortunately due to low rainfall in the Trucial States the area is not really suitable for the production of rain-grown cereal crops.

As a certain amount of wheat is grown in the area experimental work in connection with the introduction of "rust resistant" types should be carried out and seed should be distributed to the local farmers as local crops are very susceptible and yields are low.

Further trials should be undertaken with Tiwanese types of "short term" rice and efforts should be made to introduce millets and sorghums. (See Appendix A.1)

(d) Green Manure Cover Crops & Legumines — The soil in the Trucial States is low in fertility and deficient in Nitrogen content. An improvement in the physical and mechanical condition of the soil can be obtained by the introduction of green manure and cover crops which

/supply

Fig. 04 British Correspondence on Agriculture in the UAE in 1960, from *Records of the Emirates 1820–1960,* edited by Penelope Tuson, vol. 12, (London: Archive Editions, 1990), 510-11, Courtesy of UAE National Library and Archives.

> "The road after leaving the belt of palm groves and cultivation, (we turned) N.W. for an hour to a little patch of date groves and gardens irrigated by a felej and then turned west over a stony gradually rising plain covered with acacia jungle. (...) Rainfall (...) is rarely heavy; the water that is not absorbed by cultivation is sucked in by the porous soil. (...) No vestige of any edifice of architectural pretensions remains."

When visiting Al Ain, Colonel Miles noted that the "bostans" were great objects of interest. Local houses were made of mat and palm-leaf construction, where the settlements were scattered among the date groves. He mentions:

> "The verdant appearance of this oasis (...) soon makes (the eye of the traveler) oblivious of the drear and arid waste he has traversed to reach it, while the luxuriant vegetation, the sight and sound of running water, the almost entire absence of unproductive trees and plants convey an impression of prosperity."

Through his journey east, specifically to Budeya (a town in Fujairah), he notes a simple cattle barn and dairy shed that was built similar in design to the local houses in Al Ain. "It is very important to site the buildings so that the maximum use is made of natural shade." Other structures to note were the 200 warehouses in Sharjah along the creek, where wheat, rice, and dates were deposited. This marks an expansion from the shacks noted by the Dutch in the previous century.

## Cows in Transit

The early twentieth century saw the continuation of trade, including the purchase of dates from Iraq and their export to India, where traders imported spices, perfumes, and rice, notably from Burma. Flour came from Australia while coffee came from Brazil, mainly for local consumption.

Diets mainly consisted of dates, onions, bread, rice, and fish, either fresh or cured. Camels and goats were occasionally consumed, depending on socioeconomic status. Milk was used to create cream cheese using the juice of spurges, replacing rennet for its coagu-

---

*Ibid., 455-456.*

*Ibid., 461-462.*

*Ibid.*

*"Development of agriculture in Trucial States,"* ***Arabian Gulf Digital Archives****, accessed December 21, 2024, p.58 https://www.agda.ae/en/catalogue/tna/fo/371/126956/n/3.*

*Penelope Tuson, ed.,* ***Records of the Emirates 1820–1960****, vol. 9, (London: Archive Editions, 1990), 640.*

*Penelope Tuson, ed.,* ***Records of the Emirates 1820–1960****, vol. 12, (London: Archive Editions, 1990), 507.*

*Ibid., 552.*

*Ibid., 506-507.*

*Todd Reisz, "A Seed Sown in Digdaga For a Stomach In Dubai," in* ***On Foraging: Food Knowledge and Environmental Imaginaries in the UAE's Landscape****, ed. Dima Srouji, Faysal Tabbarah, and Meitha Almazrooei (Abu Dhabi: Warehouse421, 2020), 44.*

*Trucial State's development scheme reflected such emphasis. In the 1959/1960 fiscal year, agriculture amounted to 43,285 out of 97,414 English pounds, in addition to water survey and solid conservation amounting to 11,030 pounds. The latter was a part of a larger multi-prong plan that included the boring of new wells, led by Colonel Merrylees, the repairing of the falaj system, notably in Al Ain and Al Dhaid, as well as the building of dams for water conservation.*

lation. Red Sindhi cattle were imported in December 1957 to test their adaptation to the local context as well as to encourage local breeders. However, poultry breeding was deemed impossible at the time due to prevalent diseases and a lack of trained personnel.

**A Fishmeal Factory and an Agricultural School**

Closely following pearls, fishing was one of the most valuable resources in the Gulf. Toward the end of this time period, the architectural landscape started to change to include food processing facilities as well as an emphasis on knowledge production. Those projects included new factory proposals, an agricultural school, and a fortification of Dubai's port.

British correspondence between 1955 and 1960 shows evidence of plans to build a fishmeal factory in Dubai with an input of 60 tons of raw fish per day leading to an output that reaches 12 tons every 24 hours. Here, traditional fishing methods were to be incorporated along with developing new skills among local personnel. A number of fish were to be processed in the factory, which would be later supplemented by an ice factory, an ice store, and a canning plant. This architectural proposal was a new introduction to the built landscape, one that signifies the beginnings of large-scale food production.

Eventually, the fate of the fishing plant remained unclear and the British government turned its focus to investment on agriculture. Starting in September 1955, the Agricultural Development scheme aimed at expanding cultivation in the Trucial States that had been deemed "limited" to the production of dates, local tobacco, limes, and wheat (in certain areas), and four vegetables — tomatoes, onions, eggplants, and white radishes. This was attributed to the lack of knowledge, technique, and mechanical equipment. That year, efforts were made to cultivate a variety of crops such as melons, cereals, oil crops, fibers, and fodder. A small packing station was set up to distribute the produce to the local market and oil companies. Other projects included The Agricultural Trials Station, which was later known as Al Digdaga School, in 1955. Two years later, the Dubai branch of the Jashanmal store sold the first harvest from the trials. The emphasis on agricultural development and education led to building the school, with its *areesh* (palm frond) classrooms. With its existence, the link between agriculture and the act of building manifested once again.

> "1959/60 will in fact be the critical year for the agricultural scheme. We have now captured the interest of the Trucial States Rulers and people in improved methods of agriculture and more varied crops (a clear example is the increase in the number of students at the Agricultural School from 4 to 30) and an improvement in the agricultural potential of the area must, in the absence of oil revenues, contribute more than anything else to raising the standard of living of the people and to the creation of economic activity." (Fig. 05)

*Penelope Tuson, ed.,* ***Records of the Emirates 1820–1960****, vol. 11, (London: Archive Editions, 1990), 543.*

TRUCIAL STATES DEVELOPMENT BUDGET - PROPOSALS FOR 1959/1960

AGRICULTURE

| Item | Approved 1958/59 | Proposed 1959/60 | Remarks Sheet Serial No. |
|---|---|---|---|
| 1. Personnel | | | |
| (a) Salaries | | | |
| Supervisor | 900 | 1,250 | 1 |
| Overseer | 800 | 1,200 | 2 |
| Pest Control Officer | - | 360 | 3 |
| Clerk | 360 | 360 | |
| Engineer (Pumps etc.) | 362 | 400 | 4 |
| Mechanic/Tractor Driver | 317 | 317 | |
| Tractor Driver | - | 280 | 5 |
| Drivers:- | | | |
| Landrover | 227 | 250 | 6 |
| Landrover - Pest Control | - | 227 | 7 |
| Lorry | 280 | 280 | |
| Water-Bowser | - | 260 | 8 |
| Gardeners and Labourers | 2,200 | 3,000 | 9 |
| (b) Allowances | | | |
| Supervisor's Foreign Service Allowance | 750 | 1,110 | 10 |
| Travelling and Subsistence | - | 100 | 11 |
| TOTAL | | 9,394 | |

\- 2 -

| Item | Approved 1958/59 | Proposed 1959/60 | Remarks Sheet Serial No. |
|---|---|---|---|
| 2. Services | | | |
| (a) Transport | | | |
| Spares and Running Costs | 1,500 | 2,500 | 12 |
| Transport and Travelling Expenses | 596 | 806 | 13 |
| (b) Farm Operations | | | |
| Trials, seeds, trees | 2,200 | 3,000 | 14 |
| Fertilisers | 600 | 800 | 15 |
| Insecticides | - | 500 | 16 |
| (c) Animal Husbandry | | | |
| Veterinary equipment and medicines | 500 | 500 | |
| (d) Buildings | | | |
| Local Palm Frond buildings | 300 | 500 | 17 |
| Upkeep of buildings | 200 | 200 | |
| (e) Office Expenses | 150 | 200 | 18 |
| (f) Consultation | 600 | 600 | |
| (g) Agricultural Credits | 5,000 | 5,000 | |
| (h) Contingencies | - | 500 | 19 |
| TOTAL | | 15,106 | |

Fig. 05 Trucial State Budget Proposal For 1959/1960, from *Records of the Emirates 1820–1960*, edited by Penelope Tuson, vol. 11, (London: Archive Editions, 1990), 553-554, Courtesy of Dr. Sultan Al-Qasimi Centre.

Simultaneously, rice trade necessitated the construction of sufficient ports and dockyards for loading and unloading shipments. Due to the import of this commodity and Dubai's small number of inhabitants at the time, docks needed to be rebuilt and fortified in order to facilitate its trade, import, and re-export. In 1957, coinciding with the import of 10,000 tons of cement, the British sought to fortify the port in order to deter the creek from "silting up," and avoid what happened in Sharjah and Ras Al Khaimah. The port's development scheme included dredging the creek, then inserting concrete and steel channels. This led to not only the act of building the creek and its docks but also the expansion of Dubai's market, with additional food storage spaces. The act of fortification, here, reveals the intersection of economic necessity, protecting the flow of goods while architecturally expressing the city's expansion.

*Penelope Tuson, ed., **Records of the Emirates 1820–1960**, vol. 9, (London: Archive Editions, 1990), 639.*

*Todd Reisz, Showpiece City: **How Architecture Made Dubai**, (Stanford, California: Stanford University Press, 2020), 76-80.*

*"With the blessings of God and the determination of Zayed, no one can fail to recognize this great man's deep love for the land of agriculture."*

كفاح الكعبي و يسري يوسف، «غابات وسط الصحراء.. كيف؟»، **صحيفة الاتحاد**، 25 مايو 1985، 3.

«حديقة فاكهة لكل بيت» **صحيفة الاتحاد**، 2 فبراير 1985، 2.

### *Greening the Desert 1966–1989*

#### Food Security Was Always a Priority

This period represents a boom in food production and the emergence of food security concepts. Newly introduced food projects not only reshaped the agrarian landscape but also the domestic space and eventually the city, with a notable emphasis on trade expansion.

كان عطاء الله وكانت عزيمة زايد، وما من احد الا ويدرك مدى حب هذا الرجل العظيم لأرض الزراعة ■

> "We drove in that desert landscape, on the edge of the Empty Quarter, at 3pm... Our driver, Nader, swerves in order to avoid getting stuck in the dunes. The ochre landscape slowly changes to a green hue. Abdulmajed, the engineer, mentions that the greenery we saw was one of the forests that His Highness, the president, planned for to be grown in the middle of the desert... Efforts were not only focused on planting fruit and palm trees, but also experimenting with agriculture in greenhouses, especially in Ghiyathi." ●

Upon the unification of the Trucial States in 1971, the UAE as we know it today was formed, founded by Sheikh Zayed. *Aletihad Newspaper* recounts pivotal food security projects in the country, such as:

> "Every house in Delma Island was supplemented with a small fruit garden. Each garden can provide fruit for a whole family. This included six palm trees, two lemon trees, two tangerine trees, two orange trees, four grape vines, two guava trees, two berry bushes, two coconut palms with a total of 24 trees. This was in addition to free fertilizers and supervision by agricultural engineers. This project was expanded to include Delma's hospital, which would also be used as an extension of the island's agrarian landscape." ▙ (Figs. 06-12)

عائد البترول في خدمة الزراعة

هدفنا تحسين الظروف الاقتصادية والاجتماعية في القطاع الزراعي

قروض المزارعين ارتفعت الى ١٥ مليون درهم

تأخر وصول الجرارات لاسباب تتعلق بالدول المنتجة ونحن في الانتظار

Fig. 07 Oil revenue in service of agriculture, *Aletihad Newspaper*, June 13, 1976, Courtesy of UAE National Library and Archives.

الاكتفاء الذاتي والتصدير هدفان أساسيان لبرامج الزراعة والثروة السمكية في الدولة

محطات تجارب وبيوت زجاجية وزراعات محمية

Fig. 06 Self-sufficiency and export are key objectives of fisheries program in the country, *Aletihad Newspaper*, December 8, 1985, Courtesy of UAE National Library and Archives.

الصفحة الحادية عشرة

الاتحاد ملحق خاص لمناسبة عيد الجلوس

أغسطس ١٩٨٤م

# ...عد أوقات زايد يقضيها فى الصحراء لتفقد
## ...ال المواطنين ومتابعة تنفيذ المشروعات الحضارية والعمرانية

□ من الأشياء التي تسعد زايد رؤيته اللون الاخضر والاشجار اثناء جولاته الميدانية.

□ في قلب الصحراء انتشر اللون الاخضر والبيت المساكن الشعبية والعيادات الصحية.

• بقية ص ١٠ •

كفاح ونجاح

الصحراء بفضل توجيهات وجهود قائد مسيرة الخير والرخاء وخاصة ان القمح من المحاصيل التى لاتنمو الا فى المناطق الباردة والمعتدلة، فقرية «العوهة» تحفها التلال من جميع جهاتها تاركة فى وسطها سهلا واسعا منبسطا ولكن يتعرض لكثير من المشاكل لتاثره بظروف واحوال المناخ وأهمها زحف الرمال التى تتكرر كل عام بسبب تاثير هبوب العواصف الجنوبية الشديدة كما ان هذه المنطقة كمثيلاتها من المناطق الصحراوية تمتاز بمناخ حار جدا خلال فترة الصيف يصل الى ٤٥ درجة ومعتدل شتاء، صحيح ان منطقة العين عرفت زراعة القمح منذ فترة زمنية طويلة كمحصول رئيسى تتم زراعته وانتاجه واستهلاكه محليا وكانت عملية الزراعة تتم بالخبرة وبالطرق البدائية ولكن تطور زراعة القمح حديثا فى هذه المنطقة يرجع الفضل فيها الى صاحب السمو الشيخ زايد بن سلطان آل نهيان رئيس الدولة حيث زاد الانتاج خلال ٦ سنوات بنسبة ١٢٠٪ وتضاعفت بالمساحة المزروعة ٦ مرات، ويرى خبراء الزراعة ان مايحدث الآن على ارض منطقة العين فى مجال زراعة القمح يعتبر ثورة زراعية كاملة قادها وخطط لها زايد الخير ومازال يرعى خطواتها ويصدر توجيهاته السامية برعايتها.

### جنة خضراء

ولقد اول زايد اهتماما كبيرا ببناء المساكن الشعبية لمواطنى البادية، وحيث تبدو اليوم واجهة حضارية مشرقة امام العيان فى اعالى الجبال ووسط كثبان الرمال. بعد أن كانوا يعيشون فى بيوت تبنى من الاحجار والصخور والطين وسعف النخيل والخيام تهددها العواصف والاعاصير، فالمساكن الشعبية مزودة بكافة الخدمات والمرافق التى تهيئ جوا صحيا مناسبا لافراد الأسرة ويتم صيانتها وتطوير نماذجها وفقا لاحتياجات الأسر وظروف المناطق التى يعيشون فيها. ولقد اسهمت خطة بناء المساكن وسط الصحراء فى توطين البدو داخل قراهم وفى الحد من تدفق الهجرة الى المدن وتحقيق المجتمع العصرى الذى يوفر للمواطن مستوى لائقا من الحياة.

وبالطبع فان بناء هذه المساكن واستقرار البدو فيها تطلب توفير المرافق واجهزة الخدمات الأخرى لهم مثل العيادات الطبية والمدارس والمساجد والطرق وغيرها من المشروعات التى تعوضهم عما لاقوه من صعاب وماعانوه من شظف العيش قبل تدفق النفط والتى حولت الصحراء الى جنة خضراء مترامية الأطراف كنموذج واضح على النجاح والانجازات الضخمة التى تتحقق على هذه الأرض الطيبة فى ظل مسيرة الخير والرخاء التى يقودها صاحب السمو الشيخ زايد بن سلطان آل نهيان رئيس الدولة.

□ بلا وسطة يلتقي زايد بالمواطنين ليحل مشاكلهم ويلبي مطالبهم.

□ رئيس الدولة يتطلع باعجاب الى انتاج احدى مزارع غياثي من التمر والفواكه.

Fig. 08 Zayed spreads the green color in the heart of the desert, *Aletihad Newspape*

الصفحة العاشرة — الأنوار — ملحق خاص بمناسبة عيد الجلوس — الاثنين ٦ اغسطس ٨٤

من أجل توفير حياة أفضل لأبناء البادية

# زايد ينشر اللون الأخضر فى قلب الصحراء ويبنى المدارس والعيادات ومرافق الخدمات فى القرى والمحاضر والمناطق النائية

من اسعد اللحظات فى حياة زايد تلك التى يقضيها فى قلب الصحراء، فحبه لها يشغل حيزا كبيرا فى قلبه ووجدانه، وشغفه بالسير على رمالها والتجول بين وديانها وربوعها شغف لا حد له، ولا غرابة فى ذلك فهى مدرسته الأولى التى امضى فيها سنوات صباه وشبابه الاولى والتى تعلم من ظروف الحياة الصعبة فيها الصبر والصلابة فاكسبه ذلك عزيمة لا تلين وتجارب حياتية سخية وخصائص قيادية متفردة ومتميزة.

فبلا برنامج رسمى محدد، وبلا بروتوكولات او مراسم يخرج زايد من وقت لآخر الى الصحراء فى جولات ميدانية تستغرق عدة ايام يتفقد القرى والوديان والجزر والمحاضر ويحمل الى سكانها الخير والرخاء متمثلة فى مشاريع بالتنمية الحضارية والعمرانية التى يأمر سموه بتنفيذها من اجل توفير حياة كريمة لهم ولبناء غد مشرق سعيد لابنائهم من بعدهم.

## فلسفة الحكم

وبلا كلل او ملل تراه يتنقل من منطقة الى اخرى بهمة ونشاط يتابع عن كثب انتشار اللون الاخضر فى الصحراء ويرى انتاج المزارع من الفواكه والخضروات ويطمئن على توفير المياه اللازمة للزراعة. ويستمع الى التقارير اليومية لمراحل تنفيذ المساكن الشعبية والمدارس والمستشفيات ومرافق الخدمات الأخرى التى يحتاج اليها المواطنون ثم يجلس بينهم يستمع الى مشاكلهم ويأمر بحلها على الفور. ويداعب ابناءه من الشباب والأطفال ويحنو عليهم ويغرس فى قلوبهم الحب والايمان ويتطلع اليهم فى زهو وهو يرى فى عيونهم الغد المشرق المأمول ويسترجع معهم ذكريات الماضى وتاريخ وتراث جيل المعاناة من الآباء والأجداد. ولا يقف الأمر عند هذا الحد بل كثيرا ما يشارك المواطنين من ابناء البادية والمناطق النائية افراحهم واعيادهم ورقصاتهم وأهازيجهم الشعبية وذلك كله تعبيرا حقيقيا عن فلسفة الحكم التى يؤمن بها وينفذها منذ ان تولى قيادة هذا الوطن فى ٦ اغسطس عام ١٩٦٦ والتى تعتمد اساسا على سياسة الباب المفتوح واللقاء المباشر بين الحاكم وشعبه.

ويعبر سموه عن هذه الفلسفة فيقول. فى لقاءاتى مع المواطنين والمسئولين اتبع دائما سياسة الباب المفتوح والمصارحة التامة، وقد استمددت هذا من ابائنا واجدادنا. ان اللقاء بين القائد والشعب هو فى مفهومى لقاء بين الاب وابنائه وأى ابتعاد من القائد عن الشعب يبعد عنه الصورة الواقعية لاحتياجات شعبه وبذلك يحصل النفور والابتعاد من قبل الشعب تجاه القائد المغرور.

ويضيف سموه: ان سيدنا محمدا صلى الله عليه وسلم كان خير البشر وخير الرسل، وكان يلتقى بالناس ويتكلم معهم وكان اى فرد يستطيع ان يتوجه الى حيث يجلس صلى الله عليه وسلم ويسأله مايشاء. ونحن لسنا ملائكة، ولسنا بأنبياء فلماذا لانفتح للجميع الأبواب ونلتقى بالجميع؟

## القيادة مسئولية وواجب

وعندما نتمعن فى هذه الفلسفة ونحاول سبر اغوارها والتعرف على ابعادها واهدافها السامية نجد ان القيادة عند زايد رسالة ومبدأ ومسئولية وواجب وبذل وعطاء وتشييد وبناء وعمل دائب مستمر من اجل تحقيق كل امال وتطلعات الشعب فى حياة حرة كريمة والسهر على راحته ورعاية شئونه. فالحاكم فى رأيه يجب الا يكون بينه وبين ابناء شعبه اى حواجز مهما كانت الظروف وان يقف منهم موقف الأب من ابنائه يرعى شئونهم ويهتم بمشاكلهم ولا يميز بينهم. وان اى مسئول يتجاهل هذه العناصر والمبادئ لايكون صالحا لتولى مسئولية القيادة. فالقائد ليس سوى فرد من افراد الامة ويجب عليه ان يكون امينا على امته تماما كما هو امين على اسرته، وان يؤدى بأخلاص هذه الأمانة التى عهد بها الله اليه.

وهذا النهج الذى يتبعه زايد فى الحكم يستمد اصوله من مبادئ ديننا الاسلامى الحنيف الذى يعتبر الخليفة او الحاكم مسئولا مسئولية كاملة عن احوال رعيته يسهر على راحتهم ليل نهار ويسعى بينهم بلا كلل يستقصى اخبارهم ويلبى احتياجاتهم ومطالبهم. كما انه يعبر عن اصالته العربية وتمسكه بالعادات والتقاليد العريقة التى عرفها مجتمعنا العربى منذ الاف السنين. وعن اخلاصه لوطنه وتفانيه لخدمة مواطنيه تجسيدا لقولته المشهورة، ان العمل الذى نؤديه لوطننا فى هذه الدنيا هو خير مانذهب به الى الدار الآخرة..

ولا شك ان نشأة زايد البدوية جعلت تصرفاته تتسم بالبساطة فى كل شيء وبما عرف عن النفس البشرية وهى على سجيتها وطبيعتها، كما جعلته شغوفا بقضايا الناس وحريصا على التواجد المستمر فى دائرة مشاكلهم يعايشها ميدانيا ويستمع الى التقارير من مصادرها الأصلية وبلا وسطاء او لجان رسمية، فيقدم بذلك للعالم نموذجا فريدا فى الحكم وقيادة الشعوب فى عالمنا المعاصر.

## مراكز الاشعاع الحضارى

ان عشق زايد للصحراء جعله يكرس جهوده منذ بداية حكمه لتعميرها ونقل مراكز الاشعاع الحضارى اليها من اجل ان يعوض انسان البادية عن سنوات المعاناة التى عاشها قبل ظهور النفط، ففى نفس الوقت الذى دارت فيه عجلة البناء فى المدن لاقامة المساكن الحديثة والمدارس والمستشفيات والمصانع انطلقت ايضا قافلة التعمير الى الصحراء، لتحقيق هدف كبير من اهداف زايد السامية وهو توطين البدو داخل حدود آمنة وتأمين حاضرهم ومستقبلهم..

ولقد كان زايد يدرك منذ البداية ان الماء هو اثمن شيء فى الصحراء، وهذه الحقيقة رسخت فى ذهنه منذ ان كان حاكما لمدينة العين، فأمر بتركيز العمل على حفر الآبار وشق القنوات واقامة الافلاج، وبفضل توجيهاته ومتابعته المستمرة لمراحل العمل المختلفة على الطبيعة بدأ اللون الاخضر ينتشر فى الصحراء وأصبحنا نرى الاشجار والمزارع ومشروعات التشجير فى مناطق ليوا وغياثى والمرفا ومدينة زايد ومحاضر الظفرة الشرقية ومروان وقطوف

...ust 6, 1984, Courtesy of UAE National Library and Archives.

الاربعاء ١٢ ديسمبر ١٩٨٤ م — الاتحاد — الصفحة الخامسة

عملاً بتوجيهات زايد:

# شجرة البن.. تزدهر في العين

## نجاح زراعة الهيل والكركم والفلفل الأسود والزنجبيل

تولى بلادنا اهتماما خاصا وكبيرا بالزراعة لما لها من اهمية في حياتنا، فهي مهنة كثير من الآباء والأجداد في السابق.. اعتمدوا عليها اعتمادا يكاد يكون كليا في حياتهم ومعيشتهم.. وباعتبارها عنصرا اقتصاديا لايمكن اغفاله من عناصر اقتصادنا الوطني، ولما لها ايضا من اثر هام وطيب لراحة النفس البشرية اولا، وعلى تلطيف جو بلادنا الحار ثانيا.. ولكونها جانبا من جوانب الجمال والروعة يضيفه لونها الأخضر على مدننا وقرانا.

وانطلاقا من توجيهات صاحب السمو الشيخ زايد بن سلطان آل نهيان رئيس الدولة.. استطاعت الجهود المستمرة تقليص اللون الأصفر على رقعة بلادنا، وامتد اللون الأخضر يكسو وجه ارضنا بالتفاؤل، ومع كل عود اخضر ينبت على ارضنا.. ينبت معه امل جديد في التغلب على كل اللون الاصفر، وان تكسو صحراءنا وجبالنا الخضرة الدائمة.. ولتتحقق امنية صاحب السمو رئيس الدولة ان تكون بلادنا واحة خضراء.

ايضا.. وبناء على توجيهات صاحب السمو رئيس الدولة.. تعدت الجهود المخلصة عمليات الزراعة التقليدية وانطلقت توفر كل حديث من اجل توسيع الرقعة الزراعية كما وكيفا.. باختيار افضل الوسائل، وافضل البذور، وافضل الطرق، وتوفير الخبرات العربية والأجنبية لتساهم في تحقيق الهدف، كما تعدت هذه الجهود ايضا حدود الزراعة المحلية المعروفة وعملت على استنبات واستجلاب انواع جديدة.. وتجربة انواع أخرى كان متعارفا من قبل انها لاتصلح للزراعة في بلادنا.. والحمد لله.. نجحت معظم هذه التجارب.. وامكن في بلادنا زراعة القهوة والهيل والفلفل الاسود والكركم والزنجبيل والقرفة وانواع أخرى متعددة من الفواكه التي لم تكن تزرع ليس في منطقة الخليج فقط.. وانما في العالم العربي كله.. وبالتالي فإن نجاح هذه الزراعات يعتبر تجربة رائدة في المنطقة.. ويمكن أن يكون مفتاحا لدخول انواع جديدة من الاشجار والنباتات والفواكه الى دول الخليج العربي.

عن هذه التجارب الناجحة كان لنا هذا التحقيق الذي التقينا فيه مع محمد جوعان الخيلي الوكيل المساعد لادارة الغابات التي تتولى الاشراف على مزرعة التجارب بالعين التي نجحت فيها الزراعات الجديدة.

قال محمد جوعان: ان التجارب رغم انني اعتبرها انها مازالت في البداية.. إلا انه يمكن اعتبارها ناجحة.. فقد نبتت فعلا شجرة القهوة التي تم جلب بذورها من عدة مناطق في بنجلاديش واليمن والهند.. وبقليل من تهيئة الظروف المناخية.. اعطت الشجرة في العام الماضي انتاجا اوليا يبشر بالخير بإذن الله.. إلا ان هذا العام هطلت على العين امطار صيفية في وقت ازهار النبات.. مما ادى الى سقوط الزهور.. لكن الاشجار عموما ينتظر منها محصول وفير في العام الثالث من بداية الانتاج.. اي في العام القادم بإذن الله.

### افضل الانواع

ولايهمنا الزراعة والانتاج فقط.. وانما من خلال التجارب يهمنا اختيار افضل الانواع ايضا.. فكما ذكرت — والكلام لمحمد جوعان — زرعنا انواعا من اليمن والهند وبنجلاديش.. وستصل خلال ايام الف شتلة قهوة من العراق لتجربتها.. وباتصالات مع السفارة البرازيلية في البلاد سيتم بإذن الله جلب عدد آخر من الشتلات لزراعتها.. ومن خلال النتائج.. وبعد نجاح التجارب.. وعند النية لتوسيع الرقعة المزروعة من القهوة سيتم اختيار النوعية التي حققت اكثر نجاحا في ظل ظروف جو وتربة الامارات.

وهذا الكلام ينطبق ايضا على الفلفل الأسود والكركم والهيل.. وتركيزنا على القهوة لانها اكثر هذه الانواع قربا من قلوب المواطنين.. فهي جزء من التراث والعادات.. والمشروب الذي لايخلو منه اي بيت في الامارات.

المزرعة التي نجحت فيها هذه التجارب.. امر بانشائها صاحب السمو الشيخ زايد بن سلطان آل نهيان في ام غافة بالعين.. وامر سموه ان تكون حقلا خصبا للتجارب الزراعية لاستنبات النباتات التي كان متعارفا عليها من قبل انها لاتنجح زراعتها في جو الامارات.

كانت البداية في يناير ١٩٨١ وبعد ٤ شهور كانت المزرعة جاهزة تماما للزراعة.. ولتكون حقلا غنيا للتجارب الزراعية.

## أنواع جديدة من الفواكه تزرع في العالم العربي لأول مرة

● اشجار البن اصبحت اطول من قامة الرجل واعطت انتاجا يبشر بالخير

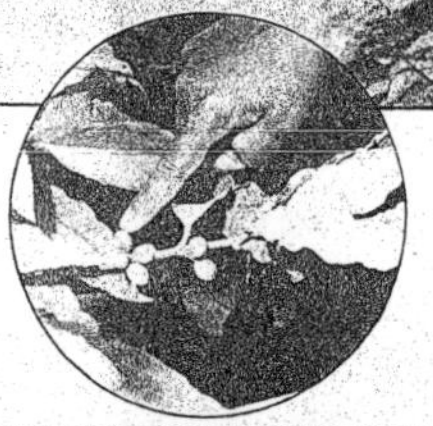

تحقيق:
حمدى نصر
تصوير: ربحى سعد

● انتاج الكركم سيتم حصاده كاملا بعد شهرين

● الزنجبيل.. اعطى انتاجا مشجعا لزيادة الرقعة المزروعة

● احدى اشجار الهيل ينتظر ان تثمر في العام القادم

● الفلفل الاسود زرع في عام ٨٢ ويثمر في العام القادم

### ٩٩٦ شجرة بن

محمد امير الاسلام.. مهندس.. قال: انه في قطاع واحد من المزرعة تم زراعة ٩٩٦ شجرة بن.. منها ٢٦٦ من اليمن و ٥٠٦ من بنجلاديش و ١١٥ من الهند، و ١٠٩ شجيرات من بذور تم جلبها من بنجلاديش وانباتها في الامارات.

ونجحت الزراعة واصبحت بعض شجرات البن حاليا اطول من قامة الرجل.. والعام الماضي اعطت مايقارب ٦ كيلوجرامات من البن وهو اول طرح لها، وعادة تعطي الشجرة انتاجها الطبيعي في العام الثالث من بداية الانتاج، اي ينتظر ان تنتج في العام القادم انتاجها المرجو.

محمد امير الاسلام قال: ان مايدعو التفاؤل انه لم يتم اتخاذ اجراءات معقدة لانجاح زراعة البن في الامارات.. وانما سمدت الارض وسمدت. والشجرة تروى مرتين اسبوعيا.. لكن الجديد هنا ان شجرة البن من طبيعتها انها تنمو في ظل شجرة اخرى.. في بنجلاديش واليمن والهند تنمو في ظل اشجار اكبر منها.. اي انها ليست تحت ضوء الشمس مباشرة.. وقد تغلبنا على هذه العقبة هنا بعمل مظلات من السلك الشبكي فقط.. وهي لاتحتاج الى برودة او اي اجراءات معقدة.. وكما قلت.. فقد نبتت الشجرة واعطت ثمرا وحاليا يتم زراعة اشجار كبيرة حتى يمكن مستقبلا زراعة اشجار البن تحتها.. ولنرى النتائج فيما بعد.. نفس الكلام ينطبق على باقي الانواع التي تمت زراعتها في المزرعة، مثل الفلفل الأسود.. فقد تم زراعة ٥٢ شجرة في مايو ١٩٨٢، ونأمل ان تعطي انتاجا في العام القادم.. وهي ايضا شجرة تحتاج الى ظل.. وتعتبر من النباتات المتسلقة، لذلك فهي تزرع بجوار او تحت اشجار كبيرة.

### الكركم والزنجبيل

المهندس محمد امير حسين / مهندس آخر بالمزرعة يقول: ان الكركم والزنجبيل نجحا تماما.. وبعد شهرين سيتم حصاد المحصول وتباشيره حاليا تبشر بالخير.

الكركم تم زراعة ٣٠٠ شجرة منه في شهر مارس الماضي.. وتم استيراد بذوره من بنجلاديش، والزنجبيل زرع منه ١٠٩ شجيرات في شهر فبراير الماضي ايضا.. وكلاهما يعطي محصولا تحت الارض مثل البطاطس والبطاطا.. وعن القرفة يقول المهندس امير حسين ان شجرتها نجحت ايضا.. فقد تم زراعة ١٢ شجرة نبتت جميعا.. ولحاء هذه الشجرة هو القرفة المتداولة.

كذلك تم زراعة ٣ انواع من الهيل من مليار وميسور (الهند) وبنجلاديش.. الزراعة تمت في اغسطس عام ١٩٨١ وكانت حوالي ٢٥٠ شجرة نبتت جميعا. وينتظر ان تعطي انتاجا في العام القادم

### انواع جديدة من الفواكه

اثناء زيارة صاحب السمو الشيخ زايد بن سلطان آل نهيان رئيس الدولة الى بنجلاديش.. شاهد سموه نوعا من الفواكه يسمى (جك فروت)، وابدى سموه اعجابه بها وامر بتجربة زراعتها في الامارات، وفعلا — والكلام للمهندس محمد امير الاسلام — تم زراعة ٩٥٠ شجرة نجحت جميعها في ظل ظروف عادية جدا.. وقد بلغت سعادتنا حدا كبيرا بنجاح زراعة هذه الفاكهة لانها اولا تلبية لرغبة صاحب السمو.. ولأن هذه الفاكهة لم تكن معروفة من قبل في العالم العربي، وهي تتميز بطعم حلو المذاق الى حد كبير.. والشجرة الواحدة منها تعطي ثمارا لاتقل عن مئة حبة للشجرة الواحدة.

ومن الفواكه.. يقول المهندس محمد امير الاسلام مهندس المزرعة أنه تم زراعة ٢٢ نوعا من الفواكه نجحت كلها.. فقد تم زراعة ١٥٠ شجرة ليمون بدون بذور، تتميز بأنها مثمرة طوال العام، كذلك تم زراعة ١٧٩ شجرة مانجو.. وقد تقول ان المانجو موجود في الامارات.. نعم.. ولكن مانجو الامارات يأتي على الثمار حر شهر مايو فتفسد، وهذه الاشجار الجديدة تنتج قبل شهر مايو.. وهي ثلاثة انواع ممتازة (النجلا — فزلي — جوبال فوج) وهناك نوع جديد من اشجار النخيل يعطي عصيرا سكريا ممتازا.. ونحن في بنجلاديش — والكلام للمهندس محمد امير الاسلام — نصنع منه السكر ونصدره للخارج، وقد تم زراعة ٨٩ شجرة في عام ١٩٨٢ ونجحت زراعتها فعلا

اما النبق.. فقد نجحت زراعته بشكل مشجع جدا، والشجرة التي تزرع تعطي ثمارا في العام التالي مباشرة.. وهو نبق تطعيم.. وتم في العام الماضي تطعيم ١٠٦٥ شجرة وهذا العام ٣٥٠٠ شجرة، وبصفة عامة تم زراعة ٢٢ نوعا من الفواكه تعتبر جديدة في الامارات نجحت جميعها بشكل مشجع نذكر منها: نبق، مانجو، سابوتا، اقلج، كاجو، تمر هندي، تفاح كاستر، ليمون كبير، ليمون بدون بذور، يوسف ماندلينا من بنجلاديش، يوسفي من لبنان، رمان، وود ابل، جام، ببايا، فيروبنا، كراندس، جوافة بدون بذور، اناناس، ابل بالم، بامبرابام.

ويقول المهندس محمد امير حسين انه نجحت ايضا زراعة الفول السوداني واليانسون والزعتر والحلبة والحبة السوداء والكمون والسمسم الاسود

واخيرا.. وبعد مشاهدتنا لمدى نجاح تجربة زراعة القهوة في الامارات.. وتبعا لكلام المهندس المسئول.. فإننا نتمنى ان نراها في كل امارة.. وطالما ان التجربة الرائدة التي جاءت بناء على توجيهات صاحب السمو الشيخ زايد بن سلطان آل نهيان رئيس الدولة قد آتت ثمارها بهذا الشكل المشجع.. ونتمنى ايضا ان نرى كل شبر من ارضنا وقد اكتسى بالخضرة الدائمة.

## أشجار نخيل تعطى شرابًا يصنع منه السكر وشجرة ليمون بدون بذور ومستمرة طوال العام

● محمد جوعان الخيلي / الوكيل المساعد لادارة الغابات

● مهندس محمد امير الاسلام ● مهندس محمد امير حسين

● شجرة القرفة لاتحتاج الى عناية متميزة ويمكن زراعتها في الامارات بنجاح

Fig. 09 Coffee tree in Al Ain and new types of fruits planted for the first time in the Arab world, *Aletihad Newspaper*, December 12, 1984, Courtesy of UAE National Library and Archives.

Fig. 10 Zayed oversees agricultural projects, *Aletihad Newspaper*, January 3, 1989, Courtesy of UAE National Library and Archives.

Fig. 11 Agricultural advancements in Al Ain is a reflection of Zayed's efforts, *Aletihad Newspaper*, October 26, 1985, Courtesy of UAE National Library and Archives.

Fig. 12 Ad for animal feed by Abu Dhabi Mills and Feed, *Aletihad Newspaper*, December 14, 1980, Courtesy of UAE National Library and Archives.

10

الاتحاد

طحنون «للاتحاد»:

نجاح زراعة القهوة والهيل والحمضيات .. وفواكه تزرع فى الامارات لاول مرة

٧٤ مليون درهم قيمة انتاج الخضراوات فى سنة .. وفائض الانتاج قيمته ٤٦ مليون درهم

11

12

### Poultry Boom and Cooking Appliances

With the introduction of electricity, the birth of the union, and the expansion of international trade markets, attitudes and daily habits of food consumption in the UAE experienced a noticeable shift starting in the late 1960s. The emergence of commercial food production, from dairy to poultry, diversified the daily Emirati diet. The year 1985 marked the starting point when the UAE became self-sufficient in the local production of eggs and poultry, and processing farms started to appear in Al Khawaneej, Al Dhaid, and Falaj Al Mualla. (Fig. 13) In addition, the Friesian cows that kickstarted Al Ain dairy farms started to shift the focus towards mass production, as opposed to localized outputs in past decades.

The Dubai Port reported an increase in imports of foodstuffs during 1984 in particular. Items included a variety of rice such as basmati, Chinese, and long-grain parboiled, in addition to sugar, tea, ghee, and vegetable oils. It wasn't only the importation of goods such as canned food and beverages that began to reshape dietary habits but also new household electrical devices as well (Figs. 14-18). This in turn changed the domestic space to follow more Western-based designs for kitchens such as the inclusion of cabinets for storage and utilities to connect to gas stoves and electrical appliances. The same year marks the establishment of food labs in order to test local food quality. This included Sharjah Municipality's lab which tested imported food products that came from Port Khalid.

Fruits and vegetables were imported and became available all year round, regardless of the season, transitioning from a luxury to a necessity. This was reflected by the increase in the number of farms which jumped 600%, between 1975 and 1985 leading to the production of more than 500,000 tons of fresh produce intended for local consumption. Daily meals started to include more meat and became less dependent on the fresh catch of the day. In the 1980s, crops in Fujairah, for example, expanded to include citrus fruits, bananas, guavas, and pomegranates, which started to be grown regularly on a large scale. Other notable crops at the time were zucchini, cauliflower, eggplant, watermelon, and cabbage.

«الإمارات تحقق الاكتفاء الذاتي من لحوم الدواجن و البيض،» **صحيفة الاتحاد**، *9* نوفمبر *1985*، *1*.

براهيم احمد، «*141768*مليون درهم واردات غذائية في *11* شهراً،» **صحيفة الاتحاد**، *14* مارس *1984*، *4*.

«*14* ألف مزرعة في الدولة تنتج أكثر من *500* ألف طن من الخضروات والفواكة،» **صحيفة الاتحاد**، ١٦ نوفمبر ١٩٨٥;
« تسليم *73* مواطنا مزارع جديدة في منطقتي العراد و أم غافة بالعين،» **صحيفة الاتحاد**، ٢٦ مارس *1984*، *2*.

Fig. 13 UAE achieves self-sufficiency in poultry, meat, and eggs, *Aletihad Newspaper*, November 9, 1985, Courtesy of UAE National Library and Archives.

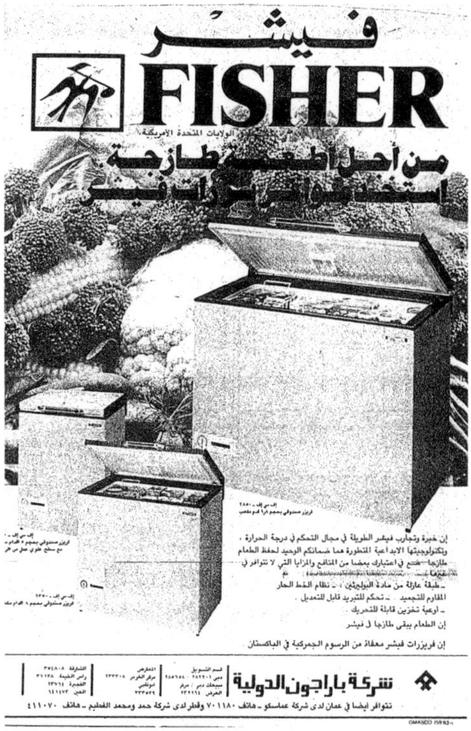


Fig. 14 Fisher fridge Ad, *Aletihad Newspaper*, February 4, 1984, Courtesy of UAE National Library and Archives.

Fig. 15 Ariston oven ad, *Aletihad Newspaper*, March 20, 1984, Courtesy of UAE National Library and Archives.

Fig. 16 Sharp fridge ad, *Aletihad Newspaper*, March 19, 1985, Courtesy of UAE National Library and Archives.

Trade also expanded with the exchange of expertise. Greenhouse models were imported and implemented by collaborating Emirati and Dutch companies, in addition to equipment from Germany and Italy. Those architectural forms were spread throughout the landscape, from Liwa to Al Dhaid. The material used for greenhouse construction at the time was mainly fiberglass, and cooling was dependent on an "automated system (Figs. 19-21)."

محمود النجار، «ازدياد الطلب على البيوت البلاستيكية يؤكد نجاح هذه التجربة في الإمارات،» **صحيفة الاتحاد**، *26* أكتوبر، *1985*، 3.

Fig. 17 Tang ad, *Aletihad Newspaper*, June 21, 1985, Courtesy of UAE National Library and Archives.

Fig. 18 Rainbow milk ad, *Aletihad Newspaper*, July 2, 1985, Courtesy of UAE National Library and Archives.

السبت ٢٥ مايو ١٩٨٥ م — الاتحاد — الصفحة الثالثة

الاتحاد في المنطقة الغربية — التشجير .. والغابات

# غابات وسط الصحراء .. كيف؟

## ٤١ مشروعًا تغطي ٣٠ ألف هكتار من الغابات

### مشاتل لإنتاج أشجار الغابات في غياثي

في تلك المنطقة الصحراوية القاحلة.. وعند اطراف الربع الخالي كانت الساعة تقترب من الثالثة ظهرا. ..درجة الحرارة تجعل الرمال تزداد لمعانا فتنعكس منها شرارات بيضاء.. لم يكن اي شيء يوحي بان هناك وجودا للحياة. فقط اثار طريق رملي غزير لاتعبره سوى سيارات «الجيب» الصحراوية.. سائقنا واسمه «نادر» يعد من الخبراء في مثل هذه المناطق ولكن رغم ذلك فقد وقع المحظور، فغرزت السيارة في الرمال.. ولكنه سرعان ماخرج من المأزق..

استمرت هذه المشاهد لمدة تزيد على النصف ساعة كان خلالها حديث المهندس عبد الماجد يعلو ويخفت.. ومر الوقت سريعا وسط هذا الهدوء الذي لايعكره سوى صوت هدير محرك سيارتنا..

وفجأة تحول اللون الداكن.. الى لون اخضر يبعث الامل والحياة.. نعم وسط هذه الصحراء المترامية الاطراف.. بدا اللون الاخضر في الظهور وقال المهندس عبد الماجد.. انها احدى الغابات التي امر صاحب السمو رئيس الدولة بزراعتها في وسط رمال هذه الصحراء.. لتتحول هذه المناطق الصحراوية القاحلة بين ليلة وضحاها.. خضراء

## في الحقيقة

## بين السطور

## تجربة مميزة لزراعة الخضر والفاكهة داخل وخارج البيوت الزجاجية

### زيادة المساحة المزروعة بالفراولة المستوردة من أوروبا بعد نجاح زراعتها في المنطقة الغربية

تحقيق كفاح الكعبي — يسري يوسف — تصوير محمود صوالحة

### ٤١ مشروعا و ٣٠ الف هكتار

### كيف تتم الزراعة والاشراف على اي مشروع

### تكلفة الشجرة الواحدة ١٢٠ درهما

### توزيع ٢٢٠ مزرعة للنخيل

### الابار كافية .. ولا يوجد مشكلة في المياه

### والنباتات الغابية تحتاج الى علاج

### غابات وسط الصحراء

### البيوت الزجاجية وتجربة متميزة



Fig. 19 Experiments in growing vegetables and fruits inside and out of greenhouses, *Aletihad Newspaper*, May 25, 1985, Courtesy of UAE National Library and Archives.

السبت ٢٦ اكتوبر ١٩٨٥م ملحق الزراعة بالعين الصفحة السابعة

لاول مرة فى الامارات

# زراعة الموز والفراولة فى البيوت المحمية

تلعب الشركات الزراعية فى العين دورا مهما وكبيرا فى عملية التطور الزراعى فى المدينة.. من خلال مساعدتها للمزارعين فى تطبيق الخطط الزراعية التى تضعها دائرة الزراعة والانتاج الحيوانى.. او من خلال توفير افضل ادوات الانتاج سواء أكانت بذورا ام مبيدات حشرية او ماكينات زراعية.

وشركة المواد الزراعية تعتبر احدى الشركات الرائدة فى هذا المجال بالعين.. فقد تأسست فى شهر يوليو عام ١٩٦٩ اى انها عاصرت بداية النهضة الزراعية فى المدينة.. وساهمت مع دائرة الزراعة والانتاج الحيوانى بجهد كبير فى المشوار الطويل الذى قطعته الزراعة فى العين.

المدير الاقليمى لشركة المواد الزراعية:

## ابتكرنا يوم الحقل ونظمنا ندوات ومحاضرات وشاركنا فى المعارض الزراعية سعيا وراء الافضل

● احد اكبر مشاريع البيوت المحمية التى تم تنفيذها من قبل شركة المواد الزراعية

## النهوض بالحركة الزراعية فى العين يتطلب ضرورة اشراف دائرة الزراعة على جميع الشركات الزراعية

Fig. 20 Farming of bananas and strawberries in greenhouses, *Aletihad Newspaper*, October 26, 1985, Courtesy of UAE National Library and Archives.

السبت ٢٦ اكتوبر ١٩٨٥م — ملحق الزراعة بالعين — الصفحة الثالثة

# ازدياد الطلب على البيوت البلاستيكية يؤكد نجاح هذه التجربة فى الامارات

على الرغم من ان نشاطها يمتد ليشمل تقديم البذور والاسمدة والمبيدات الحشرية والادوية والمعدات الزراعية للمزارعين.. الا ان شركة الاتحاد الزراعية رأت ان تساهم بقدر اوفر واكثر فعالية فى عمليات التطوير الزراعية الحديثة فى العين.. فاضافت نشاطا جديدا الى نشاطاتها وهو انشاء الوحدات الزراعية المبردة (الجرين هاوس).. والتى تمتاز بامكانية زراعتها طوال الاثنى عشر شهرا.. لتوفير الخضروات فى غير اوقاتها. كما اضافت وحدات التحلية لمعالجة مشاكل الملوحة بالمياه

هذا الكلام قاله المهندس زهير الحجاوى مدير الشركة.. وقال ان هذه البيوت اثبتت نجاحا كبيرا واعطت انتاجا مضاعفا فى غير اوقات الخضروات مما حقق ارباحا كبيرة للمزارعين.

• المهندس زهير الحجاوى مدير شركة الاتحاد الزراعية

## شركة الاتحاد الزراعية بالعين

تقدم للمزارع فى الامارات خلاصة تجاربها الناجحة فى انشاء البيوت البلاستيكية وتحلية المياه

**•• البيوت البلاستيكية:**

- وحدات بلاستيكية مغطاة بطبقة بلاستيكية مكفولة لمدة سنتين
- وحدات بلاستيكية مغطاة بالكامل بالواح الفيبر جلاس
- وحدات كبيرة تبدأ من مساحة الف متر مربع مغطاة بالواح الفيبر جلاس

**•• وحدات تحلية المياه:**

- وحدات تحلية مياه المانية وايطالية تقوم بخفض ملوحة المياه من ١٠ آلاف جزء فى المليون الى ١٥٠ - ٢٠٠ جزء فى المليون
- وحدات ٣٠٠٠ جالون.. وحدات ٥ آلاف جالون يوميا
- وحدات من ٢٠ الى ٣٠ الف جالون يوميا

مياه خالية من الاملاح.. مياه خالية من المواد العضوية مياه خالية من الغرويات.. مياه خالية من الجراثيم

وتقوم الشركة بتوفير الحراثات الصغيرة والبذور والاسمدة والمبيدات الحشرية والادوات البيطرية والمعدات والمواد الزراعية من كبريات الشركات العالمية:

شركة باسف BASF — nunhems zaden — شركة BCS BIASION Farmer Equipment

شركة سيرفس بلس Servic-plus — CELAMERCK CM سابرول — شركة Dalsem

## شركة الاتحاد الزراعية بالعين

ت: ٦٤٢٩٧٣ ص. ب ١٦٠٢٢ تلكس: ٣٤٠٩٦ أجريكو أى ام - العين شارع الشيخ خليفة

• وحدة تحلية المياه

• نجاح كبير للزراعة فى البيوت المحمية او الجرين هاوس

Fig. 21 Increased demand for greenhouses confirms success of the experiment in the UAE, *Aletihad Newspaper*, October 26, 1985, Courtesy of UAE National Library and Archives.

السبت ١٠ اغسطس ١٩٨٥ م — الاتحاد — الصفحة الثالثة

معالى وزير الزراعة والثروة السمكية لـ"الاتحاد":

# ٤ محاور للحركة الخضراء

- تحقيق الأمن الغذائى .. وتوفير الطعام لكل فرد
- تشجيع الصيادين .. والحفاظ على الثروة السمكية
- الاستغلال الأمثل للمياه .. والبحث عن مصادر جديدة
- الاهتمام بالبحث العلمى .. والتدريب لتنمية القطاع الزراعى

□□ معجزة خضراء فوق ارض الامارات حققها زايد بن سلطان آل نهيان، وانصافا للتاريخ سواء على صعيد منطقة الخليج او على صعيد الوطن العربي كله، فلم يحدث من قبل ان استطاع حاكم ان يحدث تحولا حضاريا في مجال الزراعة مثلما شهدت هذه الارض الطيبة.

ان القطاع الزراعي في الدولة حظي بعناية خاصة من صاحب السمو رئيس الدولة واخوانه اعضاء المجلس الاعلى للاتحاد حكام الامارات، وذلك ادراكا لاهمية الزراعة في توفير الامن الغذائي لابناء هذا البلد...

معالى سعيد الرقباني

لقاء اجراه: محمد عبد الكريم

بين السطور — محمود يوسف

في الحقيقة

الأربعاء ٦ نوفمبر ١٩٨٥ م — تحقيق العدد — الصفحة الحادية عشرة — الاتحاد

بعد مبادرة صاحب السمو الشيخ صقر القاسمى بتشجيع التعليم الفنى:

# دور كبير للدولة فى تدعيم وتطوير التعليم الزراعى

## دعوة للاهتمام بمشاكل الخريجين الزراعيين وتوفير فرص للبعثات الخارجية لهم

صاحب السمو الشيخ صقر بن محمد القاسمي عضو المجلس الاعلى حاكم راس الخيمة اصدر توجيهاته بصرف مكافآت شهرية لطلاب المدرسة الثانوية الزراعية ايمانا منه باهمية التعليم الزراعي ودعما لمسيرته حيث امر سموه برصد حوافز تشجيعية للطلاب كخطوة اولى تتبعها خطوات اخرى لدعم هذا اللون من التعليم وقد تم تحديد المكافآت الشهرية بحيث تتراوح ما بين ٣٠٠ الى ٤٠٠ درهم شهريا وسيتم صرف هذه المكافآت على دفعتين الدفعة الاولى في النصف الاول من العام الدراسي والدفعة الثانية في النصف الثاني منه وذلك تشجيعا لهذا النوع من التعليم في البلاد.

تحقيق: حمدية سامي — تصوير ذو الفقار علي

● محمد المري.

● عبد الرحمن حسن احمد سالم.

● المبنى الجديد.

● طالب يعمل بالتراكتور.

● الطلبة اثناء الدراسة.

● الطلبة اثناء وجودهم في المختبر.

امارة ابوظبي — دائرة بلدية ابوظبي — اعلان وظيفة

## Legislation, Farms, and Feeding the Masses

This period marks a clear shift in focus toward food security and local food production. In addition to domestic spaces responding to new dietary staples, the urban fabric included permanent agricultural schools, food testing labs, and canning factories.

The Ministry of Agriculture and Fishing was initiated with the intention for it to become the second largest source of income for the country, after oil (Fig. 22). The budget in 1975 for the farming and fishing sector amounted to 4.8% of the government development projects that year, including a large-scale wheat production experiment near Al Ain. In addition to surveying and planning out specific crops that each local farm would grow that year, funding included aid for farmers, subsidized electricity bills, new fertilizers, seeds, drip irrigation, and the digging of wells. This illustrated a clear trajectory in investing in farmers, all the while enhancing their skills and knowledge. For example, in 1981, Al Digdaga School moved to its new location in a typical building that followed the Khatib & Alami school typology. Here, agricultural engineers started to experiment with new fruits and vegetables, such as grapes, mangoes, figs, and pomegranates, in addition to expanding its technical explorations to include 215 greenhouses in its new location in 1986. (Fig. 23) Other national projects included experimenting with crops that are more suitable for the desert such as wild corn, a sweet corn substitute, which could be later used for oil and sugar extraction.

The opening of United Arab Emirates University (UAEU) and its agricultural college in 1980 bolstered efforts to achieve food security by expanding local farming techniques and improving the fishing economy. The annex included a small single-story building with a few classrooms to support experimentation and agricultural innovation.

محمود النجار، «خطوات هامة لدعمـ و تطوير القطاع الزراعي في الدولة،» **صحيفة الاتحاد**، *17 أبريل 1976*، 4.

سليمان الماحي، «تجارب جديدة لزراعة أصناف الفواكه بمشروع الدقداقة،» **صحيفة الاتحاد**، *17 يناير 1981*، 2.

محمود النجار، «الزراعة.. وتنمية الامارات الشمالية،» **صحيفة الاتحاد**، *30 مايو 1975*، 3.

Fig. 22 Minister of Agriculture and Fisheries introduces Four Axes of the Green Movement, *Aletihad Newspaper*, October 8, 1985, Courtesy of UAE National Library and Archives.

Fig. 23 Significant role in supporting and developing agricultural education, *Aletihad Newspaper*, November 6, 1985, Courtesy of UAE National Library and Archives.

Also in 1980, after multiple complaints by local fishermen in regards to unpredictable weather conditions, a weather station was built in response to their needs in both Port Khalid and Sharjah Airport. This led to the expansion of both sites, significantly, and the introduction of a daily weather report, in the local dialect, aired in the early hours of the morning before they went out to sea.

Larger agricultural projects included Mazyad Farm in Al Ain which produced a number of crops such as tomatoes, eggplants, zucchini, jute mallow (*molokhiya*), cucumbers, watermelons, and a variety of citrus trees. With irrigation that mainly depended on the Mazyad *falaj* (pl. *aflaj*, irrigation system), its output of crops and food products were sold in local markets for a lower cost when compared to imported products. And even though the quality needed improvement, it was noted that it wouldn't be long before local farms accounted for food security and Emiratis would be able to eat locally. Other records show a development proposal by a private French company that presented 15 hectares of land for cultivation, whose output was to include fruits, vegetables, pulses, grains, fodder, and 500 chickens. The plan also listed an electric station and staff housing as additional amenities to be included on site.

New fruit, vegetable, meat, and fish markets, specifically in Abu Dhabi, were part of the infrastructure as well. This included supermarkets and bakeries as they were starting to emerge in Emirati cities on a larger scale (Figs. 24-26). Simultaneously, plans for canning factories were put forth as a proposal to tackle the notion of food waste from local farms and encourage local production, especially adapting to the UAE's climate and its seasonally limited vegetable output. The first of its kind began its operation in Al Ain in January 1986. Outputs included tomato paste, frozen vegetables, pickled foods, and ketchup. Water dams and desalination plants also emerged in order to support local agricultural endeavors.

---

فتحي رزق، «مع الامواج و الرياح في غياب؟ نشرة جوية خاصة بهم،» **صحيفة الاتحاد**، *9* ديسمبر *1980*، *3*.

---

«كانت مزرعة مزيد و كان غيرها من المزارع المنتشرة في العين،» **صحيفة الاتحاد**، *8* يناير *1970*، *2*.

---

«زايد يزور المركز التجريبي الزراعي بالعين الذي تقيمه شركة البترول الفرنسية وتقدمه "هدية" لأبوظبي،» **صحيفة الاتحاد**، *23* مارس *1972*، *6*.

---

«أول مصنع لتعبئة الخضروات،» **صحيفة الاتحاد**، *16* يوليو *1984*، *3*.

---

حمدي نصر، «المساحات الزراعية في العين تضاعفت مرتين خلال *4* سنوات،» **صحيفة الاتحاد**، *12* أغسطس *1985*، *3*.

Additionally, date production also notably expanded. In 1985, for example, 58,000 tons of dates were produced in the UAE and the total number of palm trees reached 2,800,000. With this expansion, the built environment responded to accommodate this change. The introduction of chain-link fences was subsidized by the Ministry of Agriculture to local farmers, marking the urban boundary between farms and public space. Wells were dug and aflaj were maintained with concrete fortification and shallow walls to demarcate their streams. Storage and drying spaces also emerged as a byproduct. As opposed to drying racks scattered near agricultural land, which still continues in localized farms, large industrial and production practices required built spaces, such as greenhouses, for date processing and factories for syrup extraction. Processing plants emerged to transform dates into fertilizer and fodder.

Fig. 24 Spinneys ad, *Aletihad Newspaper*, August 1, 1984, Courtesy of UAE National Library and Archives.

Fig. 25 Local produce in Souq Al Jubail in Sharjah, *Aletihad Newspaper*, July 3, 1984, Courtesy of UAE National Library and Archives.

Fig. 26 Al Ain Dairy Farm ad, *Aletihad Newspaper*, November 9, 1985, Courtesy of UAE National Library and Archives.

إيهاب الخضرجي، «الخضروات المستوردة تملأ الأسواق»
**صحيفة الاتحاد**، *14 يناير 1984*، 3.

## What's Next?

Local farmers in Kalba posed questions in an interview with *Aletihad Newspaper* in 1984: Can local produce be shipped to the rest of the UAE instead of being concentrated in the Eastern Region with its limited supply and demand? Would it gain traction in local supermarkets? And could it, potentially, overtake imported crops that regularly enter the country through Dubai's ports?

In 2025, at a time when locally produced blueberries are in many of our kitchens, it is safe to say that the UAE has definitely invested in producing as many food products as possible within its borders.

While by no means comprehensive, this examination of the UAE's food landscape through time highlights unique spaces and building activities that have emerged along the way. Ranging from rudimentary practices to more grand responses, attitudes toward food consumption and its production created a clear imprint on the built environment. Those instances are amplified today with the expansion of projects from technologically advanced vertical farming to large-scale wheat, dairy, and poultry projects in the UAE. The cultivation, production, and trade of food does not only shape the daily lives of a place's inhabitants but also its physical attributes.

Ultimately, the overlap of these two realms invites us to rethink our relationship with the environment and our surroundings, as they boil down to what sits on our dining table, chills in the fridge, or cooks in the oven. Consumption habits have drastically changed in the past 500 years. This reminds us that the local production of food is not just a change in the color of the landscape but embodies a deep ethos of care, creativity, and history. And it will only expand from here on (Fig. 27).

Fig. 27 Locally grown vegetables, *Aletihad Newspaper*, April 25, 1984, Courtesy of UAE National Library and Archives.

# Growing Papayas in the Desert:

## *An Agricultural Engineer Recounts a Transnational History of Greenhouses in the UAE, 1970s–1990s*

Huma Gupta

*This anecdote was shared not only by my father and his colleagues, but also appears in other scholarship featuring interviews with municipal workers who similarly testified to Sheikh Zayed's deep commitment to afforestation. See Natalie Koch, "AgTech in Arabia: 'Spectacular Forgetting' and the Technopolitics of Greening the Desert,"* ***Journal of Political Ecology*** *26, no. 1 (2019): 89.*

***Ingredients***

Customization
Automation
Exchange
Aflaj
Trusses

Fig.01 The author and her father in front of the Agricultural Research Center in Dibba Al-Fujairah, Courtesy of Narinder Gupta's Personal Collection, April 8, 1987.

**Introduction**

Abu Dhabi spans over 60,000 square kilometers, comprising desert, salt flats, coastal islands, and two oases Liwa and Al Ain, where I was born in the late 1980s. As the daughter of an agricultural engineer, Narinder Gupta (b. 1957), I spent parts of my childhood traveling across this expanse to visit farms and greenhouse projects from Liwa to Dibba and back. For a time, we also lived near the Agriculture Research Center in Dibba Al-Fujairah set against the backdrop of the Musandam Mountains. (Fig. 01) When I got a little older, I sometimes traveled to remote worksites in off-road vehicles with my father and his colleagues. Sitting in the backseat, I would overhear them sharing stories from the horticultural lore of the late HH Sheikh Zayed bin Sultan Al Nahyan, founding President of the United Arab Emirates (UAE) and former Ruler of Abu Dhabi (1918-2004). A famous anecdote I heard repeatedly was how Sheikh Zayed responded when a group of workers ripped out a *ghaf* tree (*Prosopis cineraria*) grove because it was obstructing a road project. He admonished the workers, instructing them to never remove ghaf trees. Instead, they were told to build the road around existing ghaf regardless of monetary cost because these drought-tolerant trees were invaluable in an arid landscape. Sheikh Zayed's legacy of "greening the desert" (his eco-cosmology or "Zayedisms" as coined by Pernilla Ouis ) was also highlighted in this directive: "Plant more palm trees and still more palm trees. The desert is before you. Confront the yellow invasion with the green invasion." In fact, Gupta recalls that companies were incentivized to plant and maintain ghaf trees at a rate of 120 dirhams per tree during this period.

As my family's presence in the Emirates was predicated on Sheikh Zayed's avid participation in the international "green revolution," his horticultural lore loomed large in my childhood. Realizing his vision required a steady influx of experts who could implement the newest agricultural technologies (AgTech). These technologies carried the promise of self-sufficiency for UAE's food production that could offset costly imports and foreign dependence on essential produce. Considering Gupta was educated during India's own "green revolution" at the Punjab Agricultural University (PAU) in Ludhiana, he shared Sheikh Zayed's optimistic vision and belief in the scientific potential of AgTech. Thus, Gupta spent much of the 1980s and 1990s applying technologies like drip irrigation and automated greenhouses in the UAE to continue the mid-century developmental project of establishing a controlled, engineered version of desert agriculture.

The techno-politics of this "green revolution" was deeply linked to architectural design — especially in how it structured agricultural landscapes, energy regimes, and labor systems. To sustain this new technocratic ideal, both migrant workers and natural resources would need to be commodified. The "green revolution" in the UAE was therefore not only a technical transformation of agriculture, but also a systemic reorganization of how food was produced and distributed *and by whom*. Yet histories of the UAE's greenhouse production have traditionally focused on North American or European experts, firms, and institutions. Through a combination of oral history, existing literature, personal photographs, and archives, this article offers more textured insights into this transnational history and other circuits of knowledge transfer between North America, South Asia, and the Arabian Gulf. It also shifts the focus from the history of imported prefabricated greenhouse designs to the messy realities and novel aspects of their implementation.

*Pernilla Ouis, "'Greening the Emirates': The Modern Construction of Nature in the United Arab Emirates,"* ***Cultural Geographies 9****, no. 3 (2002): 338.*

*Habeeb Salloum, "Abu Dhabi Has Been Converted from Desert Land to a Land of Gardens,"* ***Washington Report on Middle East Affairs,*** *December 1995, Available: https://www.wrmea.org/1995-december/abu-dhabi-has-been-converted-from-desert-land-to-a-land-of-gardens.html.*

*Timothy Power and Peter Sheehan, "The Origin and Development of the Oasis Landscape of Al-Ain (UAE), "****Proceedings of the Seminar for Arabia Studies 42,*** *Papers from the forty-fifth meeting of the Seminar for Arabian Studies held at the British Museum, London, 28 to 30 July 2011 (2012), 291-307.*

*Dale R. Lightfoot, "The Origin and Diffusion of Qanats in Arabia: New Evidence from the Northern and Southern Peninsula,"* ***The Geographical Journal 166****, no. 3 (2000): 215-226.*

*Alamira Reem Bani Hashim,* ***Planning Abu Dhabi: An Urban History****, (London: Routledge), 2019, 89.*

*Zayed: A Tour in the Land of Virtue",* ***Aletihad Newspaper****, June 12, 1975.*

*"Al Aflaj, traditional irrigation network system in the UAE, oral traditions, knowledge and skills of construction, maintenance and equitable water distribution," UNESCO: Intangible Cultural Heritage, 15.COM 8.b.10, 2020, https://ich.unesco.org/en/RL/al-aflaj-traditional-irrigation-network-system-in-the-uae-oral-traditions-knowledge-and-skills-of-construction-maintenance-and-equitable-water-distribution-01577.*

*Ibid.*

زايد وجولة في أرض الخير

● العين ــ عيسى خليل :

منذ ان وصل صاحب السمو الشيخ زايد بن سلطان ال نهيان رئيس الدولة الى مدينة العين منذ عدة ايام .. وسموه يستقبل كل يوم مئات من مواطني المدينة .. وعشرات من المسئولين في الدولة .. يستمع اليهم .. ويشير عليهم .. ويحل مشاكلهم ..

ومع زحمة اعماله ، وعظم مسئولياته .. وكثرة زواره، لم ينس سموه ان يطمئن على الامكانيات الضرورية للنهوض بالزراعة في المدينة ، واهمها توافر المياه اللازمة . فخرج امس يرافقه سمو الشيخ طحنون بجولة في المناطق الزراعية بالعين ، حيث تفقد المزروعات ومنسوب المياه في الابار وحالة الافلاج والمناطق المستصلحة والتي يمكن استصلاحها .

وفي نهاية جولته امر سموه بتوفير جميع الامكانيات العلمية الحديثة لحفر مجموعات جديدة من الابار وزيادة معدلات استخراج المياه من باطن الارض حتى تكسو الخضرة اكبر مساحة ممكنة من سطح هذه الارض الطيبة الخيرة والمعطاء لكل شيء .. ولكل انسان .

تصوير :
عبد الله خميس

Fig.02 "Zayed: A Tour in the Land of Virtue," *Aletihad Newspaper*, June 12, 1975, Courtesy of UAE National Library and Archives.

## From Aflaj to AgTech

Before the introduction of agricultural technology such as greenhouses and drip irrigation, farming in the UAE, particularly in Al Ain Oasis, relied on sustainable irrigation practices adapted to an arid environment dating back over 3,000 years. The primary technique used was the *falaj* (pl. *aflaj*) irrigation system, an ancient and ingenious water management method that expanded the spread of arable land through channeled underground water using gravitational force to a communal basin for crops in a manner that maximized efficiency while minimizing evaporation. In 1946, when Sheikh Zayed was appointed the *wali* (governor) of the Eastern Region, which included Al Ain, he initiated projects to repair the old aflaj system and dig additional wells to improve agricultural production (Fig. 02). He also worked toward re-instituting a traditional model of timed water distribution that would more equitably disburse the resource to all farmers. The aflaj, however, would be deemed insufficient in the second half of the twentieth century as some farmers wanted to extend the cultivation season and expand production beyond areas with abundant water sources.

Despite losing its centrality to agricultural production, the aflaj system was inscribed into the UNESCO list of Intangible Heritage in 2020. In order to emphasize the social relations upholding this infrastructure, the inscription included "related oral traditions, knowledge and skills of construction, maintenance and equitable water distribution." In an effort to represent the archaeo-botanical heritage of Al Ain, an oasis garden was also set up to showcase the tripartite system of cultivation traditionally used in oases. The first tier featured ground-level crops that can thrive in arid environments with little water, such as aloe and henna. The second layer include mid-level fruit-bearing trees, such as pomegranate, olive, fig, and lemon trees that required more consistent access to water. Finally, the third layer constituted tall trees like date palms that provided shade to the plants and trees growing below. To highlight the role of the oasis as a node in trade routes from the Indian Ocean to the Mediterranean, the oasis garden also included the neem tree from India, the frankincense tree from Oman, and the moringa tree from Africa. The co-mingling of native and transplanted trees was intended to communicate the symbiotic relationship between species that can thrive together in arid environments.

While the aflaj system continued through the 1940s and 1950s, "scientific" cultivation methods were being trialed by the British on a limited basis in Digdaga, Ras al Khaimah, in the mid-1950s through the 1960s to promote commercial agriculture and dairy farms. However, once Sheikh Zayed assumed control of Abu Dhabi in 1966, his commitment to promoting agriculture was renewed by shifting the focus toward replicating experiments taking place in North America. In 1969, he invited Carl N. Hodges, the director of the University of Arizona's Environmental Research Lab, following the apparent success of his agricultural experiment in the coastal desert lands of Puerto Penasco, Mexico. The experiment involved growing vegetables using desalinated seawater in controlled environment greenhouses that were inflated using diesel generators. Other recruited technical experts included the founder of the Controlled Environment Agriculture Center (CEAC) at the University of Arizona and Hodge's colleague, Merle Jensen, who arrived in Abu Dhabi in 1970 to participate in the Saadiyat Greenhouse Experiment.

Greenhouse experiments were just one example of the transition from older agricultural practices to the eventual, widespread use of AgTech. Gupta recalled another example where his team was asked to lay a 7-kilometer cement-concrete water pipeline (~30 cm diameter) to facilitate water transmission

*Sangeetha Swaroop, "Al Ain Oasis: World Heritage Site takes a refreshing step back in time,"* ***GulfNews.com****, 29 September 2019, Available: https://gulf-news.com/travel/al-ain-oasis-world-heritage-site-takes-a-refreshing-step-back-in-time-1.2304600.*

*Todd Reisz, "A Seed Sown in Digdaga, For a Stomach in Dubai,"* ***On Foraging: Food Knowledge and Environmental Imaginaries in the UAE's Landscape****, Eds. Dima Srouji, Faysal Tabbarah, and Meitha Almazrooei, (Beirut: Kaph Books), 2023, 40-47.*

*Koch, 672.*

*Dr. Alamira Reem Al Hashimi, "The Saadiyat Experiment: A Conversation with Dr. Merle Jensen,"* ***On Foraging****, 110-117.*

for a forestry project around one of Sheikh Zayed's residences near the Dubai-Abu Dhabi Road. Similar to his oversight over the aflaj repair process, Sheikh Zayed frequently visited the pipeline project. These site visits also had a secondary effect of animating a sense of pride and purpose in the project team who saw themselves as serving a national developmental ideal. These anecdotes do not present AgTech as something that was imposed on Abu Dhabi by outside experts, rather, it foregrounds Sheikh Zayed as a persistent figure who, conversely, often defied foreign experts who argued that the emirate's arid landscape could not support afforestation and large-scale agriculture.

The seasonally dependent, biodiverse, and communally managed productive landscape of the Al Ain Oasis could now be abstracted, simulated, and multiplied. Through the design of greenhouse farms, the integration of drip irrigation, and the use of controlled-environment agriculture, labor, capital, and ecological practices would be reorganized in new ways to reflect a broader vision of technocratic governance that combined modernity, technological sovereignty, and national identity. These technologies were packaged not only as environmental solutions, but also as part of a larger government project to assert the UAE's global technological leadership and its self-sufficiency in food production on a global scale.

**Fig. 03 Gupta's colleagues inside Boys' Hostel at Punjab Agricultural University** in Ludhiana (left to right: Bansal, Goyal, and Ilahabadi), Courtesy of Narinder Gupta's Personal Collection, c. 1976-1977.

*PAU's campus was designed by Aditya Prakash who was part of the first generation of modernist architects in India. Prior to working on PAU, he had worked with Jane Drew, Maxwell Fry, and Le Corbusier for the Chandigarh Capital Project in the 1950s. After visiting OSU's agricultural campus in the late 1990s, Gupta surmised that even the architectural design of the buildings, specifically the layout of offices and labs felt reminiscent of his alma mater.*

*US technical assistance to establish Indian agricultural universities was facilitated through the Agricultural Education and Research Project and the Agricultural University Development Project from the 1950s to 1970s. Kathleen M. Propp, "The Establishment of Agricultural Universities in India: A Case Study of the Role of USAID-U.S. University Technical Assistance," University of Illinois College of Agriculture Special Publication, 1968.*

*Phoebe Springstubb, "A Landscape 'Difficult to Describe,': The Model Village and the Capital City,"* ***Architectural Theory Review 26****, no. 3 (2022): 486-518.*

*Ibid.*

*From Gupta's class of 1979 cohort of 25 engineers, four ended up working abroad. And beyond his cohort, he knew many others who had migrated to work in the US, Canada, Australia, New Zealand, and various Gulf states.*

Fig. 04 Gupta using a tilling machine at a farm in Los Baños, Philippines, Courtesy of Narinder Gupta's Personal Collection, March 1980.

Fig. 05 Gupta in a US-funded training program at the International Rice Research Institute in Los Baños, Philippines, Courtesy of Narinder Gupta's Personal Collection, March 1980.

## Transnational Circuits of Knowledge Transfer from the Atlantic to the Indian Ocean

Circuits of knowledge transfer of agricultural technologies from the US to India to the UAE can be illustrated by Gupta's trajectory during the second half of the twentieth century. He graduated with a degree in agricultural engineering from his alma mater Punjab Agricultural University (PAU) in 1979. It was one of the central academic institutions and nodes of producing technical expertise to support India's "green revolution." PAU was formally inaugurated in 1963 by the first Prime Minister of India Jawaharlal Nehru, whose developmental vision was reflected in large-scale infrastructure projects, such as feeding a growing nation through the Bhakhra-Nangal Dam projects. Other projects included housing a fragmented nation within newly planned modernist cities like Chandigarh which could absorb those displaced during the cataclysmic events of the 1947 partition between India and Pakistan. Gupta's own family was among the over 14 million people uprooted. They were forced to leave their ancestral village in Punjab overnight as it was incorporated into Pakistan. Gupta's father found a job as a schoolteacher near Amritsar in a small village, which had been home to a large Muslim community before partition.

PAU was established through a technical assistance project that recreated the US land grant university model in India for the purpose of establishing agricultural universities. In order to help create a globalized agricultural education system, Ohio State University (OSU) partnered with PAU to adapt its curriculum and run a faculty exchange program. The curriculum emphasized practical training and research in agricultural mechanization, soil and water conservation, food processing, and structures such as grain silos and greenhouses. Gupta studied under figures like Vice Chancellor M.S. Randhawa and Dean of Agricultural Engineering B.S. Pathak. Randhawa, for example, was instrumental in growing the university and supporting agricultural mechanization efforts promoted by USAID and OSU. After independence, Randhawa had initially focused on developing model villages, followed by his tenure as chairman of Chandigarh's Landscape Committee in the 1950s where he focused on botanizing the asphalt landscape of the modernist regional capital. For Randhawa, mid-century Indian cities like Chandigarh with rapidly growing populations called for the expansion of agricultural productivity in rural areas through the complementary projects of modernizing villages like Gupta's *and* establishing agricultural universities like PAU.

While these initiatives served a national developmental ideal, the university also fostered a generation of international engineers. PAU graduates would sometimes go on to train or work outside India in burgeoning agricultural industries like the Arabian Gulf. (Fig. 03) In 1980, for example, Gupta was recruited to participate in a US-funded training program at the International Rice Research Institute in Los Baños, Philippines (Fig. 04). He and his fellow participants from China, India, Indonesia, Sri Lanka, and Vietnam were trained on using rice tilling, sowing, and threshing machines (Fig. 05). The selection of country participants reflected the US government's post-Second World War era strategy that used technical assistance as a mode of soft power during the

Fig. 06 Al-Darmaki Greenhouse Project (5000 sq. m.) on Al Ain-Dubai Road to grow cucumbers and tomatoes with Gupta's brother, Courtesy of Narinder Gupta's Personal Collection, July 20, 1986.

Cold War. One of the technologies on display was a multi-crop thresher designed to be used for both rice and wheat. However, Gupta explained that despite claims of the thresher's superior technology, he had to modify the thresher's design as it did not work as effectively in the wheat fields of Punjab. For Gupta, the opportunity to work in the UAE was therefore a natural extension of this moment of global exchange. His technical training, which was cultivated in India's rapidly changing agricultural landscape, equipped him with an adaptive mindset toward the possibilities of designing greenhouse technologies in an arid environment.

**Growing Papayas in the Greenhouse**

In 1988, Sheikh Zayed's son HH Sheikh Khalifa bin Zayed Al Nahyan, commissioned a peculiar greenhouse modification in his residential compound in Al Ain. The goal was to adapt an existing design of a Van der Hoeven-manufactured A-frame greenhouse spanning 432 square meters. It was initially intended for vegetables like tomatoes and cucumbers, but Sheikh Khalifa wanted to adapt the structure to grow towering papaya trees. These tropical trees, typically reaching a height of three to four meters, required a significant redesign to accommodate their stature and thermal needs. At the time, greenhouse technology in the UAE was heavily reliant on prefabricated imports from foreign distributors of agricultural technology like Dutch Agro (Fig. 06). However, this particular commission demanded further customization — a task entrusted to Al-Darmaki & Partners, an Emirati agricultural enterprise founded by a local farmer which had installed the original greenhouse.

The Al-Darmaki team of around 25 workers, led by Gupta who was the company's technical manager at the time, transformed the greenhouse as per the client's directive. Steel columns and trusses were extended from 3 meters to reach a height of 4.5 meters, fiberglass coverings were added, and automatic temperature-controlled Dutch oil-fired heaters were installed in the center to maintain nighttime warmth (Fig. 07). As these changes were made, engineers and workers had to rework the technical drawings on-site with Dutch Agro, adapting the plans to fit the unique constraints of the environment. The undertaking also relied on a diverse workforce of laborers and technicians, hailing from India, Syria, Pakistan, and Bangladesh. For example, (Fig. 08) features some Al-Darmaki team members such as Manjeet (Hoshiarpur, Punjab) who worked on the structural installation of greenhouses, Alex (Mumbai, Maharashtra) who took care of electrical work, and Amer (Syria) who worked as the project foreman.

However, transitioning toward food sovereignty also demanded shifting from an over-reliance on costly, imported greenhouse kits and components from Europe. In order to mitigate costs, Gupta and his colleagues at Al-Darmaki collaborated with local fabricators in a Syrian-owned workshop to develop less expensive, intermediate greenhouse models that combined imported components, such as Italian fans (Euro-Emme) and Swedish cooling pads (Celdek), with steel sourced from the local construction market. The steel would then be cut, formed into columns and trusses, and galvanized locally. While the original greenhouse designs called for the use of c-section purlins, the team substituted them with o-section purlins that were locally available. In the meantime, fiberglass was sourced directly from the United Kingdom, cutting out middlemen. Another strategy was reducing freight costs by importing unassembled fans. Where 29 assembled fans could be loaded into a 20-foot container, 120 unassembled fans could be shipped in the same amount of space. And workers were incentivized to more efficiently assemble fans for a bonus of 15 dirhams per fan. Therefore, this was a pragmatic negotiation between imported designs and locally available materials, between the ambitions of patrons and the practicalities of construction.

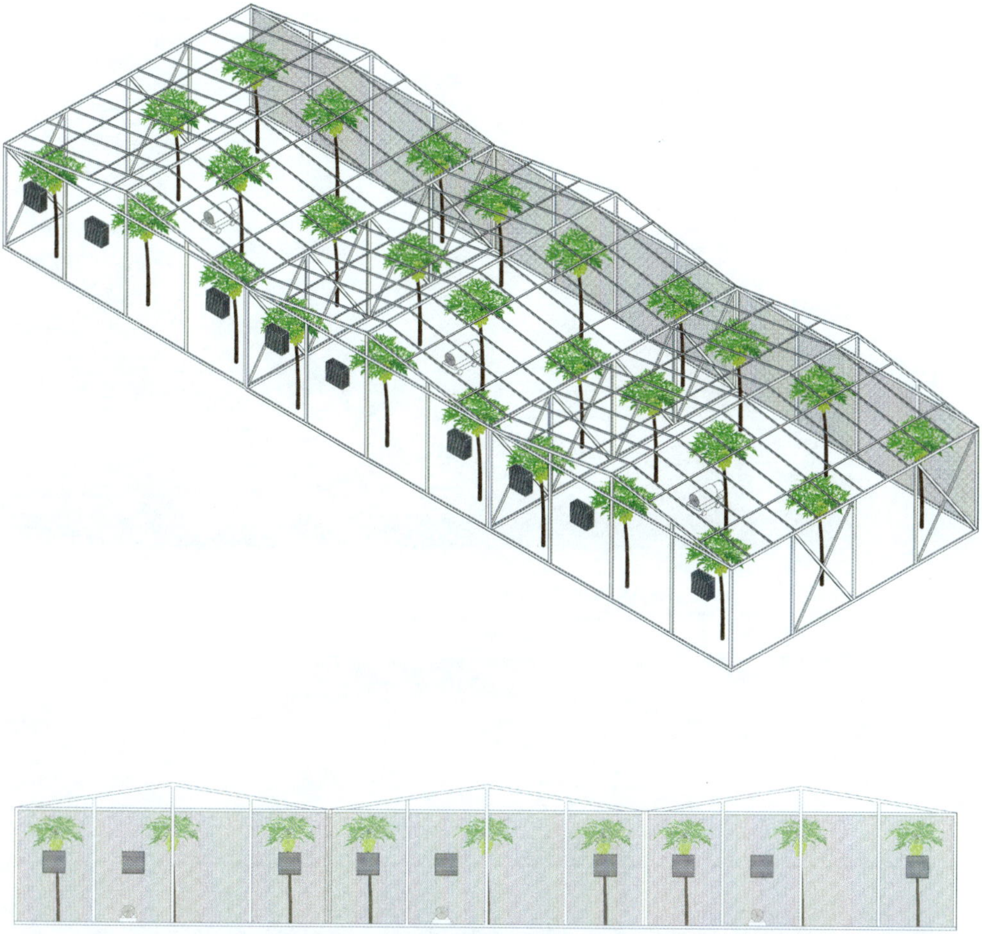

Fig. 07 Front elevation and isometric drawing of a greenhouse redesigned for Sheikh Khalifa bin Zayed al Nahyan to grow papaya trees. Drawing by Nooralhuda Al Qayem, January 10, 2025.

Fig. 08 Al-Darmaki team members working on a greenhouse project (left to right: Manjeet, Alex, and Amer), Courtesy of Narinder Gupta's Personal Collection, April 29, 1986.

Fig. 09 Gupta with his colleague at an exhibition booth showcasing water filtration and desalinization technologies for the Arab Water Programme by the Norddeutsche Seekabelwerke company based in Nordenham, West Germany, Courtesy of Narinder Gupta's Personal Collection, c. 1983.

## Conclusion

In the UAE's evolving agricultural landscape, farmers, ranging from affluent landowners to smaller-scale cultivators, emerged as key patrons of greenhouse technology. Farmers utilized greenhouses to increase yields and extend growing seasons. These structures allowed for year-round cultivation of high-demand crops such as tomatoes, cucumbers, and peppers. For affluent individuals like the late Sheikh Khalifa, greenhouses were more than tools for food production; they were symbols of modernity, innovation, and self-reliance. In projects like the papaya greenhouse in Al Ain, patrons invested not only in cutting-edge technology but also in customization, tailoring designs to specific crops and personal preferences. Here, growing tropical papayas in the desert was as much about achieving agricultural novelty as it was about showcasing the UAE's potential for ecological transformation. It also marked a technological shift that prompted Sheikh Zayed to move away from his earlier investment in repairing the aflaj. While cultivation in the oases during the 1940s supported a tripartite system, the papaya greenhouse offered an alternative approach. For one, the tall papaya trees in the greenhouse were no longer seen as having a dual purpose of bearing fruit and providing shade for smaller plant species. This shift in vision followed the international "Green Revolution," which was characterized by the introduction of new technologies such as high-yielding seeds, chemical fertilizers, and mechanized irrigation that eschewed traditional agricultural practices.

The process of constructing greenhouses in the UAE was not, however, a straightforward technology transfer of pre-engineered designs. Rather, it was a dynamic and often "messy" process marked by adjustments, innovations, and improvisations. Undertaken by laborers, engineers, and patrons on site, the adaptions to the desert's context simultaneously defied and complied with the intentions of the greenhouse's original design. Simultaneously, the process was highly collaborative, involving skilled workers from multiple regions, each contributing their expertise to make local substitutions and adaptations. Moreover, in the processes of education, training, and onsite experience, engineers, laborers, and patrons were interpellated as subjects of an uneven and variegated international "green revolution" (Fig. 09). Yet, the labor force that built and maintained this infrastructure remains underrepresented within these histories. Not unlike the relationships, oral traditions, knowledge, and skills of construction necessary to maintain the aflaj system, the human infrastructure underlying the installation and maintenance of prefabricated greenhouses calls for its inclusion in the architectural history of controlled environment agriculture and the related ecological ramifications of the "green revolution."

*This article would not have been possible without the brilliant research support of Nooralhuda Al Qayem, master's student in the Aga Khan Program for Islamic Architecture at MIT.*

---

*Louis Althusser, "Ideology and Ideological State Apparatuses" in* ***Lenin and Philosophy and Other Essays****, Ed. Louis Althusser, (New York: Monthly Review Press), 1971.*

# From Land to Hearth: *Diet in the Arabian Desert*

Sarah Saad Alajmi

*Also called* ***Terfezia boudieri.***

### *Ingredients*

| | |
|---|---|
| أقط | ʾigṭ |
| بيت الشعر | bayt al-shaʿr |
| عرفج | ʿarfaj |
| فقع | Fagaʿa |
| تمر | Dates |
| موقد النار | Fire pit |

I recall how the desert looked in the spring when I was a child in the 2000s: wildflowers and green shrubs adorned the landscape. Looking for cracks in the sand was a favorite pastime of mine and my siblings. As I poked around with my small shovel, I searched for vibrant plants, looking for indicators of a prize that was buried underground. "I found one!" shouted my brother in the distance. I ran with my small shovel and empty plastic bag to see the prize: a mid-sized desert truffle, or *faga'a*, covered in dirt.

Before the discovery of oil, the Arabian Desert was, and still is, filled with edible plants and truffles that were incorporated into the diet of the Badu, the tribespeople of the Arabian Peninsula. The Badu's diet was mainly comprised of dates, camel's milk, meat, rice, and coffee, in addition to desert plants and truffles. Coffee was an essential component to the Badu community. Around fire pits, it was prepared for family members and guests alike, signifying a shared activity, revolving around a form of sustenance. In the Badu's homes, they congregated around these spaces of food and beverage, exchanging stories and reciting poems. Between truffles and coffee, the Badu's landscape of nourishment emerged, manifesting spatially in the desert.

This essay explores food systems that existed in the Arabian Desert before modernization, where markets and trade routes played a significant role in the Badu's diet. Specifically, it will retrace the unique spatial landscape vital to the Badu's hearth and existence. This will be explored on three scales: individually, between the Badu and the land; communally and socially, with food and coffee; and finally, regionally, with the Badu engaging with villages, towns, and ports.

**Buried Prizes in the Sand**

كل قاع له نبته

*Every land has its plants*

The relationship between the Badu and the desert was an ancient one, where knowledge of the desert and its soil was passed down through generations. This was evident in the Badu's repertoire and heightened senses to endure the desert's harsh conditions. The land — with its colors, attributes, and plants — was read, understood, and utilized.

The Badu moved across the Arabian Desert for water and pasturelands for their herds (Fig. 01). While their movements might have been construed as arbitrary, the Badu were intentional in where they resided and in the vicinity of what resources. Within the vast desert, they forged spatial pockets that not only facilitated their connection with the desert environment but also with their tribe and other tribes. Simultaneously, they maintained a reciprocal relationship with the nearby markets in towns and villages. Proximity to shrubs and plants was important for the Badu's survival wherever they chose to reside. Just as the desert fauna played a significant role in the Badu's lives and diet, the desert flora was integral and found its way into the Badu's hearth.

Leaves, fruits, roots, and underground truffles, were plucked, dug, and foraged to be eaten. The Badu knew the edible plants; what was safe to be consumed and what to use for alternative purposes.

Following autumn's rainfall during what is known as *alwasm* season, the desert becomes a viable ground for the growth of edible fungi and small-prized delicacies, such as the desert truffle. It is only in the spring that desert truffles begin to appear, growing near a plant known as *ragrūg* (also called *Helianthemum lippi*). ◢ There are a number of types of desert truffles based on size, color, and taste, such as *al-zubīdī*, *al-khalāṣ*, and *al-hubīrī*. ▞

During the nomadic days in the desert, once the truffle was found and foraged, it would be cooked with plain rice or occasionally with meat, while some would be dried and stored. ▚ In her book *Forty Years in Kuwait* (1971), the botanist Violet Dickson described her journey through the region of Dibdibba — a desert that stretches from the western region of Kuwait to the northeastern region of Saudi Arabia — and documented her findings on desert truffles (Fig. 02). The trip took place in the spring of 1968, after

Fig.01 Camels grazing in the Arabian Desert. Source: Middle East Centre Archive, St Antony's College, Oxford. GB165-0364 Violet Dickson Collection Alb 8 no 18, 1968.

◢ *Violet Dickson, **The Wild Flowers of Kuwait and Bahrain** (George Allen & Unwin, 1955), 49.*

▞ *James P. Mandaville, **Bedouin Ethnobotany: Plant Concepts and Uses in a Desert Pastoral World** (University of Arizona Press, 2011), 125.*

▚ *"(al- fag'a).. nabāt fiṭrī tajūd behe al-ṣaḥrā' ba'ad mawsim al-amṭār wa-yazkhur bil-'adīd min al-'anāṣer al-ghidhā'eyah," **Kuwait News Agency (KUNA)**, February 4, 2023, https://www.kuna.net.kw/articledetails.aspx?id=3079853.*

◓ *Dickson reported that a kilogram of desert truffles was valued at 6 KD in February 1968. See Violet Dickson, **Forty Years in Kuwait** (George Allen & Unwin, 1971), 307.*

◓ *Ibid., 308.*

◉ *Mandaville, **Bedouin Ethnobotany**, 125.*

◖ *Dickson, **The Wild Flowers of Kuwait and Bahrain**, 86.*

┫ *Mandaville, **Bedouin Ethnobotany**, 108.*

┫ *Ibid., 111.*

◣ *Based on one of my interlocutors' experience with the ḥambaṣīṣ.*

♣♣♣ *Dickson, **The Wild Flowers of Kuwait and Bahrain**, 81.*

Dickson heard about the sale of truffles in the market. Alongside her three companions, they were able to collect 150 kg of truffles, some of which were boiled for dinner (Fig. 03). Dickson observed how the desert of Dibdibba in the spring was occupied by the Badu in their homes.

Whispers and tales of places to forage for truffles rendered the desert a place for expeditions to hunt, an exciting endeavor. An expansive knowledge of the desert and its soil was essential in the hunt, where locating known plants and measuring soil moisture aided in such a pursuit. The Badu understood the conditions that allowed for the truffles to grow, and they possessed a spatial awareness of the desert ecology, enabling them to navigate thoroughly. Some of the Badu kept the truffle locations secret in order to revisit them every spring.

Another common edible plant in the Arabian Desert is called *rubaḥlah* (also known as *Scorzonera papposa*). This perennial plant has pink flowers and leaves with wavy edges. According to Dickson, its roots produce an edible brown tuber that was described to have a similar taste to Brazil nuts. Commonly found on rocky grounds making them hard to dig out, the Badu found the rootstock of rubaḥlah to be delicious, as observed by James P. Mandaville in his book about plants in the Arabian Desert.

Described as a plant that lays and stretches out on the ground of sandy terrains, the *ḥambaṣīṣ* (also called *ḥamṣīṣ*, *ḥanbaṣīṣ*, or *Rumex pictus*) is an annual herb known for its edible leaves which are reported to have a bitter taste, and it is decorated with small red and green flowers. Another edible plant in the Arabian Desert is the *ḥammīḍ* (called *Rumex vesicarius L.*), an annual herb with edible leaves. Unlike the ḥambaṣīṣ, the ḥammīḍ grows upward with its thin flowers and extended leaves that taste sour. Other edible plants in the Arabian Desert include *ʿatter* (called *Glossonema varians* [Stocks]) and *murār* (called *Launaea arabica* [Boiss.] Cass.).

*Ibid.*

*Mandaville, **Bedouin Ethnobotany**, 112.*

*Dickson, **The Wild Flowers of Kuwait and Bahrain**, 44, 59.*

Ibid., 80.

Donald Powell Cole, ***Nomads of the Nomads: The Āl Murrah Bedouin of the Empty Quarter*** *(Harlan Davidson, Inc., 1975), 63.*

## Fire Pits, Coffee Pots, and Guests

جيب الحطب وشب النار

*Bring the brushwood and light the fire pit*

The Badu built nomadic structures in the Arabian Desert, which reflected their lifestyle and social relations. The tent, known as *bayt al-shaʿr* (house of hair), mainly consisted of woven textiles, wooden poles, and ropes (Fig. 04). Within the bayt al-shaʿr, spaces for female and male members of the family were delineated. Spaces for male guests dominated the eastern part of the house, while female members occupied the western part. The area for the kitchen was typically integrated into the female quarters or placed in a separate room toward the western end. The female and male spaces were separated with textile walls, and each of these spaces had a fire pit, or a hearth.

Young girls were usually tasked with the responsibility of collecting brushwood, fuel for the fire pits. They would spend hours searching for shrublets

Fig.02 Three desert truffles, known as al-zubīdī. Source: Middle East Centre Archive, St Antony's College, Oxford. GB165-0364 Violet Dickson Collection Alb 8 no 30, 1968.

Fig.03 A man pointing at a bulged crack in the sand, an indication of a truffle underneath. Source: Middle East Centre Archive, St Antony's College, Oxford. GB165-0364 Violet Dickson Collection Alb 8 no 29, 1968.

known as *ʿarfaj* (called *Rhanterium epapposum*). Tied and placed over their heads, Badu girls would walk home with the reaps. A well-known feature of the Arabian Desert, the *ʿarfaj* is a perennial shrublet that sheds its leaves in the summer and grows small yellow flowers. The brushwood of *ʿarfaj* was sold in markets, especially in Kuwait. ▙ On a more domestic scale, brushwood, once found, would be placed in piles and stored for future use. When it comes to the bayt al-shaʿr typology, two fire pits were lit within the perimeter — one for women and the other for men. Each of these fire pits were used differently and represented a different aspect of the Badu's social system. The women's fire pit was used to prepare meals for the household, and when needed, a bigger and communal meal for both their household and neighboring members of the clan. ◢ The Badu's diet mainly included ingredients that were accessible to them in the desert, ones that could be either foraged, made, or sourced from markets. For instance, when rice was not available, the Badu had other meals to sustain themselves throughout the day, containing fresh milk from goats and camels, and dates. After the milking process, fresh milk in waterskins would be rocked by Badu women to produce butter and *laban* (fermented milk). From these dairy products, they made *ʾigṭ* (dried milk) and *samen* (ghee). ʾIgṭ was made by Badu women by drying milk and shaping it with their palms to make small chunks to be consumed on their own or mixed with other plants. Those chunks were placed on the roof of bayt al-shaʿr to be dried in the sun.

*See H. R. P. Dickson,* ***The Arab of the Desert: A Glimpse into Badawin Life in Kuwait and Sau'di Arabia*** *(George Allen & Unwin, 1967), 59.*

*Ibid., 402.*

*As reported by my interlocutors.*

*Dickson, The Arab of the Desert, 198.*

*Saad Abdullah Sowayan,* ***Al-Ṣaḥrāʾ al-ʿArabiyah: Thaqāfatuhā wa-Shiʿruhā ʿabra al-ʿUṣūr: Qirāʾah Anthrūbūlūjiyah*** *(al-Shabakah al-ʿArabiyah lil-Abḥāth wa-al-Nashr, 2010), 238.*

*Ibid.*

Fig.04 A photograph of a group of women and children with a bayt al-shaʿr behind them and another one further in the background. In the left bottom corner, a waterskin can be seen. Source: Middle East Centre Archive, St Antony's College, Oxford. GB165-0085 Harold Dickson Collection Alb 2 no 185, undated.

Fig.05 Men preparing coffee while their homes were being built. A man is seen grinding coffee in this photograph. Source: Middle East Centre Archive, St Antony's College, Oxford. GB165-0364 Violet Dickson Collection Alb 8 no 8, 1968.

The other fire pit was placed within the male area of bayt al-shaʿr, which was mainly used to prepare coffee. Coffee making, here, was a male dominated practice in the Badu's lives: a ritual that manifested spatially in bayt al-shaʿr. This fire pit was an integral component of Badu men's social life, where they prepared coffee to be indulged by male family members or to be served to guests. Women were not allowed to interfere with this practice in the men's area; men ground coffee beans, started their fires with brushwood and *jallah* (dung), and poured water from waterskins into coffee pots (Fig.05). Around these fire pits were all the necessary items to prepare coffee for male household members or male guests, if something was needed, it would be fetched for the patriarch. During social gatherings, the patriarch of the household would typically sit in front of the fire pit to prepare coffee for his guests, with his son or an assistant by his side. Cardamom and cloves were used to flavor the coffee. After the coffee was served, the Badu exchanged stories and recited poetry. The fire pits created a space for social interactions in the Arabian Desert.

Fig. 06 A woman standing with a pot in hand and three homes appear behind her. Source: Middle East Centre Archive, St Antony's College, Oxford. GB165-0364 Violet Dickson Collection Alb 6 no 28, 1964.

---

*Mohamad Abdulhadi Jamal, **Aswāq Alkuwait Alqadīmah** (Center for Research and Studies on Kuwait, 2004), 29.*

---

*Tea was not as popular as coffee to the Badu. See Jamal, **Aswāq Alkuwait Alqadīmah**, 152.*

---

*Ibid., 155.*

---

*Based on information from my interlocutors, some Badu women prepared their own coffee in their fire pits.*

---

*Sowayan, Al-Ṣaḥrā' al-'Arabiyah, 155.*

## Food Systems and Trade

شريناه من السوق

*We got it from the marketplace*

In the early twentieth century, the Arabian Peninsula was a thriving network of markets, towns, farms, oases, nomadic settlements, and trade routes. There was a direct relationship between urban centers and the desert. The Badu relied on marketplaces to obtain food and necessary objects, and in return, urbanites relied on the Badu's products. Some of those prominent markets were in Kuwait, which supplied the Badu with essential ingredients and items to ensure their survival. In these marketplaces, the Badu sold their products and bought what they could not find in the desert. Before oil was discovered, Kuwait was known for its booming markets that connected merchants from the port, which was strategically positioned on the northern end of the Arabian Gulf, with the Badu residing in the desert. Food, spices, coffee, and other products were imported to Kuwait from India, Iran, Iraq, East Africa, and other Gulf ports, such as Dubai, Manama, Muharraq, and Muscat. Considered as a locus of gathering, those markets brought together the different lifestyles between sedentism and nomadism. In Kuwait, two markets were frequented by the Badu and their camels: Almanakh Square and Safat Square. The name of Almanakh Square is derived from the Arabic verb *nawwakh* which means to rest camels. Characterized by shops overlooking the square, Almanakh Square was also close to other desirable markets. Here, the Badu found wheat, barley, rice, spices, cardamom, sugar, coffee, and tea. After the 1920s, the Badu favored Safat Square for its spaciousness and shops. The Badu would buy a considerably large supply of dates to sustain themselves in the desert, transporting them to their homes via camels.

## Desert to Hearth

Always strategic, the Badu located their bayt al-shaʿr in proximity to water and pasturelands. Following traditional food systems, they foraged for seasonal edible plants and the prized desert truffle used in the Badu's diet. Bayt al-shaʿr represented a micro-unit that reflected the larger social and economic dynamics of the Badu's culture. Life in bayt al-shaʿr revolved around the hearth, which was an architectural element characterized by dominant social attributes, and it witnessed communal cooking, exchanges of historical events, and poetry, as well as the reception of guests. It also materialized the gendered spaces in the Arabian Desert, where food and beverages were divided: coffee making for men and preparation of food and beverages for women (Fig. 06). The women's fire pit was not only used to prepare food and drinks, but it was also used to indicate a social event — a signal inviting neighbors or close tribes to attend. Ultimately, the relationship between the Badu and their hearths extended beyond the boundaries of their homes, one that actively engaged with the surrounding context and the desert ecology.

# *Ingredients as Heroes*



Illustrations by Khalid Mezaina

*Chapter* **02**

# Fieldwork Findings

Azza Aboualam

***Ingredients***

Liwa

Hatta

Masafi

Al Ain

Al Zubair

Fig. 01 Sketch of route by British consul of Zanzibar and the Gulf region, from *Records of the Emirates 1820–1960,* edited by Penelope Tuson, vol. 10, (London: Archive Editions, 1990), Courtesy of UAE National Library and Archives.

Penelope Tuson, ed., **Records of the Emirates 1820–1960**, vol. 4, (London: Archive Editions, 1990), 547-548.

**Merriam-Webster.com Dictionary**, s.v. "fieldwork," accessed December 20, 2024, https://www.merriam-webster.com/dictionary/fieldwork.

Abir Ahmar, "'UAE oil power farms the desert in quest for food security'," in **Reuters**, February 16, 2023.

## Maps, Routes, and Sketches

> "So much for my sketch. I should like to say a word now about the existing map, the one compiled by Colonel Ross and reprinted by the Intelligence Branch in May 1901. Unless and until we eventually have a protectorate here there is little likelihood, under present conditions, of any regular trigonometrical or other survey being undertaken. Meanwhile, this map is all we have to go upon (...) I fear the latter will be of little value (...) but as some of the ground covered was new and the existing map has proved wrong in several particulars, the results are perhaps worth sending (...) None of the inland places visited have ever been accurately laid down, the general "lie" of it may of course prove a good deal out (...), I have every reason to hope that they will prove reasonably accurate. I used my compass whenever I could and made rough diagrams in my field-book of all noticeable features as I went along." (Fig. 01)

Written by Major-General Sir Percy Zachariah Cox, who was the British consul and Political Agent in Muscat at the turn of the twentieth century, this excerpt describes the route taken during his tour between Abu Dhabi, Muscat, and Buraimi. Even though this correspondence dates back to June 29, 1903, the parallels between it with its rudimentarily drawn map and the journeys taken for our fieldwork, in 2024 and 2025, were uncanny.

Merriam-Webster's dictionary defines fieldwork as work done in the field in order to gain knowledge through firsthand observation. This also includes the gathering of anthropological or sociological data through the interviewing and observation of subjects in the field. Fieldwork has always been an instrumental tool to further understand the built environment. Additionally, in a qualitative methodology like this one, the researcher's experience in the subjects and topics being studied is relevant as they play such a direct and intimate role in both data collection and analysis. Where and how does fieldwork happen? How does this apply to architecture and food production in the United Arab Emirates (UAE)? And how is it different from other forms of knowledge and cultural production?

Coinciding with extensive media coverage on food cultivation in the arid desert, the UAE has become one of the biggest success stories with its self-reliance in food production. Articles and news reports illustrating farming methods mostly pertain to specific architectural elements such as greenhouses, freshwater fish tanks, and climate-controlled cow sheds, with a mix of local expertise and technologically advanced mega projects. However, despite those references, very little is outlined on where these sites are located or who to contact, let alone how to access them or figure out how they actually function.

This text challenges the narrative that has been promoted by a majority of archival material and the local community: barely anything grows in the desert, especially in the summer. Fresh water is too scarce, the soil is inadequately saline, and the weather is extremely hot for most of the year. Palm dates might be the only exception, despite their reliance on a water-intensive irrigation system.

I have to admit, I was guilty of believing that narrative until I embarked on this journey. With starting points of British records that documented food production outputs at the turn of the twentieth century, and overlaid with geographical information and oral history, fieldwork was used to prove, support, or negate preconceived notions. By tracing back political and economic correspondence that paints the picture of scarcity or, in some cases, abundance, the thesis lays out a taxonomy of food growing projects, built by local ingenuity.

## Interpretations, Preconceived Notions, and Research Methodologies

What other disciplines term as primary or original research, architecture defines it as basic research. This includes the investigation of building typology, practice, or construction methods, forming the foundation of architectural inquiry. Applied architectural research, a process akin to secondary research in the sciences, involves utilizing insights from basic research and other previously conducted sources to address practical challenges, with a focus on evaluating their effectiveness. Both methods incorporate time-proven, documentation-driven approaches to basic research, such as the scientific method. In the May 1948 issue of *Yale Scientific Magazine*, Vincent Scully initially asked: "Is the Scientific Method Applicable to Architectural Design?" While the answer thirty-six hundred words later was "no," I argue that by customizing the support of research in, for, and through architecture. Whether it is to construct new models or to dismount previous assumptions, the answer can be "yes." We are repeatedly told, in academic contexts, that proper research is text driven, due to it being a universal language that can be produced and reproduced without the original researcher. However, in a context similar to the UAE's, one seeking written texts on a rapidly developing and continuously changing landscape faces a (few) conundrum(s).

Although a young country formed only 53 years ago, the UAE faces a lack of historical documentation since its founding and prior to it. What we have at our disposal does not paint the full picture. Evidence shows that the UAE, or the Trucial States as they were known beforehand, hosted human settlements for multiple millennia, with the earliest dating back to the Neolithic Age in Sharjah.

---

*Vincent Scully, "Architecture as a Science: Is the Scientific Method Applicable to Architectural Design?"* ***Yale Scientific Magazine****, May 22, 1948, 4.*

---

*National Library and Archives of the UAE, "The Civilization of the United Arab Emirates," accessed December 24, 2024, https://www.nla.ae/en/our-history/historical-periods/the-civilization-of-the-united-arab-emirates/.*

---

الخليج العربي في مواجهة التحديات، **محاضرات الموسمين الثقافيين السابع والثامن 1974 – 1975**، مؤسسة الوحدة للنشر و التوزيع الكويت، (تقديم الموسمين الثقافيين السابع والثامن 1974-1975)، 9.

---

*Salma Samar Damluji,* ***The Architecture of the United Arab Emirates****. (Garnet Publishing, 2006), 1.*

---

*Sultan Muhammad Al-Qasimi,* ***The Myth of Arab Piracy in The Gulf****, second edition, (Oxon: Routledge, 1988), xiii.*

---

*Ibid.*

---

*Paul Kapp, "Historic Preservation Design: Using Ethnographic-based Fieldwork to Introduce Theory and History in the Architecture Studio,"* ***Future Anterior: Journal of Historic Preservation, History, Theory, and Criticism*** *17, no. 2 (2020): 17, https://doi.org/10.5749/futuante.17.2.0017.*

With its location as an important node of trade routes, characterized by strategic ports along the silk route, the UAE is characterized by a transient culture: one that has always been adaptable to change. ■ Inhabitants were accustomed not only to trade being temporal and fluctuating, but also to the region's unique (albeit harsh) climatic conditions and local ecological system. Additionally, the specificity of the Gulf landscape has undergone an unprecedented form of development since the late 1960s. Bordering on the desert's expanse, the implementation of large urban and infrastructural projects has altered not only the built environment, but also the natural one. ●

Although the aforementioned instances in UAE history are significant and noteworthy, the scarcity of documentation regarding daily life during the turn of the century is evident, necessitating reliance on Western documented correspondence as a primary source. However, this dependence on solely Western perspectives to interpret my home country presents a challenging dissonance. One could argue that such representations served colonial purposes, reshaping how we study the Gulf's landscape at large. Even when the correspondence is perceived as an objective reference, a lot of the recorded information was conceived as rumors worded as facts, in addition to omitting or sidelining important details. ● As such, utilizing it as a benchmark should be used with caution (and taken with a grain of salt). ● And while this research was constrained by the lack of documentation and depth on historical accounts, it also aims at tackling a research gap in documenting current day practices from an Emirati lens. Here enters fieldwork: aiming at not only documenting but comprehending the built environment's tangible and intangible aspects. ■

## North, South, East, (and West)

"Do you know someone who owns a farm, *preferably with a greenhouse*?"

With this common opening question, the fieldwork began by overlaying maps on maps, day by day, and route by route. With the aid of satellite imaging and contacting local farmers through social media accounts and word of mouth, sketches of routes and pins of green patches materialized and were our main guide during the long arduous journeys in the UAE's heat. While the overlaying of maps was deemed more helpful in some emirates in comparison to others, the most illuminating findings were those that we stumbled upon. Despite having a clear trajectory when heading to specific agricultural belts, locations known for their farming capabilities, such as Sha'am in Ras Al Khaimah and Al Dhaid in Sharjah, were the most surprising. The chosen examples, out of 153 sites, are treated as paradigmatic ways of understanding the varying scales of food production in the UAE. Not only do those act as primary sources, but they also provide sites of investigation, where local knowledge is examined, documented, and preserved. (Fig. 02)

شو تزرعون هني

*"What do you grow here?"*

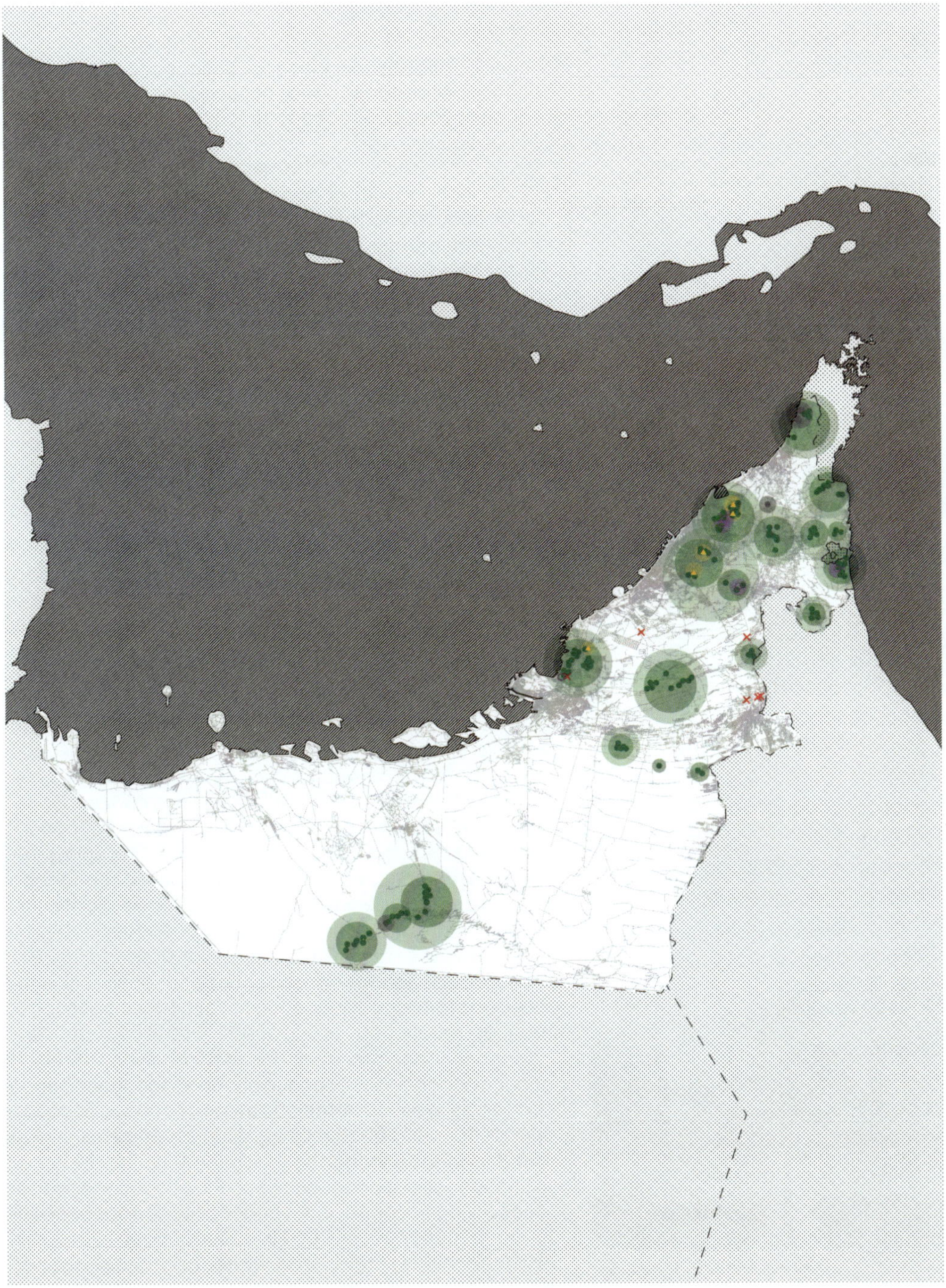

Fig. 02 Map of visited sites in the UAE. Map by Nujud Alhussain.

*Indian almond fruit trees, also known locally as Looz are a summer delicacy in the UAE.*

*"Development of agriculture in Trucial States,"* ***The National Archives****, accessed December 21, 2024, 58, https://www.agda.ae/en/catalogue/tna/fo/371/126956/n/3*

## Foraging in Shimal

"The purpose of my visit was to report and advise on agricultural progress and development at Ras al Khaima in the Trucial Oman and to discuss agricultural matters with Mr. A. W. van Ollenbach, the Director of Agriculture in Bahrain and consultant on agriculture in the Trucial Oman. Since my first visit (...) in 1955 more boreholes have been sunk, a station for agricultural trials and demonstrations has been started by Captain Huntington and many of the cultivators have noticeably improved their standards of cultivation. (...) Excellent crops of well grown tomatoes, cabbages, lettuce, onions and other vegetables were being grown, as well as flourishing plots of lucerne ("jet") for fodder."

J.C. Eyre, 1957.

**كنا نسبح في أحواض من الاسمنت وين الماء يستخدمونه لسقاية النخل و فوقنا يظلل علينا شجر اللوز، نقطف منه و ناكل. و كنا نتريا وحدة من سكان الجبال تيبلنا الحليب و اليقط.** (Fig. 03)

My mother always reminisces about her summers in Shimal, Ras Al Khaimah as a young girl. She used to always say: "We used to swim in shallow pools made with concrete walls. They were used as sources for the aflaj, in the shade of looz and palm trees. We would wait for the milk and fermented cheese from the locals to come down from the mountain." I was in search of this romantic dreamy state of foraging for fresh fruit in Ras Al Khaimah's abundant landscapes. Even though there were notable palm tree plantations in the vicinity of Sha'am, Ghalilah, and Al Rams, what we found was the most surprising. A lot of the farms that were clearly green on aerial images were dry with desiccating trees, while others were being encroached upon by newly built houses. A few of the conducted interviews informed us of the same answer: a lot of the groundwater has dried up over time and maintaining the farms was no longer financially viable. Some respondents mentioned moving to other emirates for work opportunities, leaving their farmland behind. Mohamed, a Sha'am farm owner, works in Abu Dhabi every other week. "The summer is always harsh. Come back on February 3rd," he said. "That is when we plant the seeds for watermelon and wheat in the mountains." (Fig. 04)

Fig. 03 Falaj system in Ras Al Khaimah. Photo by author.

Fig. 04 Ras Al Khaimah field visit. Map by Nujud Alhussain. Illustrations by Khalid Mezaina.

## Corn in Liwa

> "Liwa is the most remarkable of all the tracts. It consists of mainly white undulating sand dunes, altogether, without vegetation; but it contains over a score of small depressions. (...) At the bottom of each depression there is fertile soil, supporting the cultivation of a village. (...) These low-lying oases contain plantations of date palms. (...) The water level in Liwah and in the wells is of fairly good quality." (Fig. 05)
>
> J.G. Lorimer, 1908.

Liwa's agricultural belt, or *crescent*, sits on an ancient site of river convergence that once flowed from the Arabian Peninsula toward the Gulf. With its particular ecological makeup from small to medium-sized sand particles, which are silt-free, it has the ability to absorb and trap rainwater, resulting in the abundance of groundwater in the area. While the palm tree plantations, nestled in relatively high sand dunes, were visually the most stunning of all sites visited across the UAE, the fields of corn and passionfruit are also worth noting. Spotted from the main highway, gleaming polycarbonate arches caught my eye. The pin on Google maps described the location as a "Passion Fruit Farm," but, there were none left for the season. The groundskeeper, who was too busy with the zucchini and pumpkin flowers during that particular afternoon, did not fully comprehend why we were there, nor why we were curious about farming techniques in the desert. He mentions that tending to this farm is his everyday routine, while pointing to the corn bushes. Corn plants are known to attract beneficial insects like ladybugs and lacewings, which help control pests such as aphids that are detrimental to the plant. This natural pest control can benefit other neighboring crops, like the zucchini, creating a healthier ecosystem. Sweet corn, in particular, needs consistent moisture, especially during the growing season (Fig. 06). "We use groundwater here, which is relatively sweet, making sure the crop receives about 1 to 1.5 inches of water per week," he clarifies. The farm's owner gives him regular instructions as to when to add mulch around the base of the plants to retain soil moisture and suppress weeds as well as which fertilizer to experiment with for the season. "Corn is ready for harvest when the silk turns brown. They're not ripe yet, but come back in two weeks and we can give you some." (Fig. 07).

---

*Penelope Tuson, ed.,* ***Records of the Emirates*** *1820–1960, vol. 4, (London: Archive Editions, 1990), 248.*

---

لولوة المنصوري، «الحكاية الايكولوجية للمياة الاحفورية: من أين ينبع الماء في واحتي ليوا والعين؟،» **تراث: واحات الإمارات جواهر وسط الصحراء،** عدد 225، يوليو 2018، 45.

---

*Ibid.*

Fig. 07 Liwa field visit. Map by Nujud Alhussain. Illustrations by Khalid Mezaina.

Fig. 05 Palm tree plantations in Liwa. Photo by Ola Allouz.

Fig. 06 Corn fields in Liwa. Photo by author.

Fig. 08 Green mesh greenhouse in Hatta.
Photo by author.

Fig. 09 Sprinklers, banana trees, and grape vines in Hatta. Photo by Ola Allouz.

## Figs, Bananas and Grapes in Hatta

> "The village of Hajarain, 50 miles south-east of Dibai Town, (also known as) Hatta (...) consists of 45 date huts (...) among them 5 camels, 60 donkeys, 45 cattle and 200 sheep and goats. (...) Date trees number about 4,000 but yield is scanty, the only other cultivation is lucerne." (Fig. 08)
>
> J.G. Lorimer, 1908.

After spotting the green shade net peeking from behind a fence of a residential villa that overlooks a roundabout, I swerve the car and make it in time for the sharp right turn in order to take a closer look. While this destination was not a pin on the map, we stumbled upon it on the way to the last site of the day. After we were allowed to enter, the groundskeeper, who was busy at work during his late afternoon shift, was happy to let us into the makeshift "greenhouse" structure. The post-and-lintel form was made out of steel pipes, 2×4 lumber and thick twine. Green shade net covered the low 2.5-m-high enclosure. As we walked in, we were greeted with the smell of fig bushes sprouting from the earth. The groundskeeper immediately turned on the misters to express his pride and prowess in the design of the vernacular agricultural system (Fig. 09). He mentions that, in the summer, misters are turned on for 5 minutes every hour before 11 am and after 4 pm, while the hottest hours of the day require them to be on for 7 minutes every 30 minutes. The green shade net is replaced every six months to ensure its efficacy. He picks a cluster of grapes to share with us. "The saltier the irrigation water, the sweeter the grape," he adds (Fig. 10).

*Tuson, **Records of the Emirates**, 220-221.*

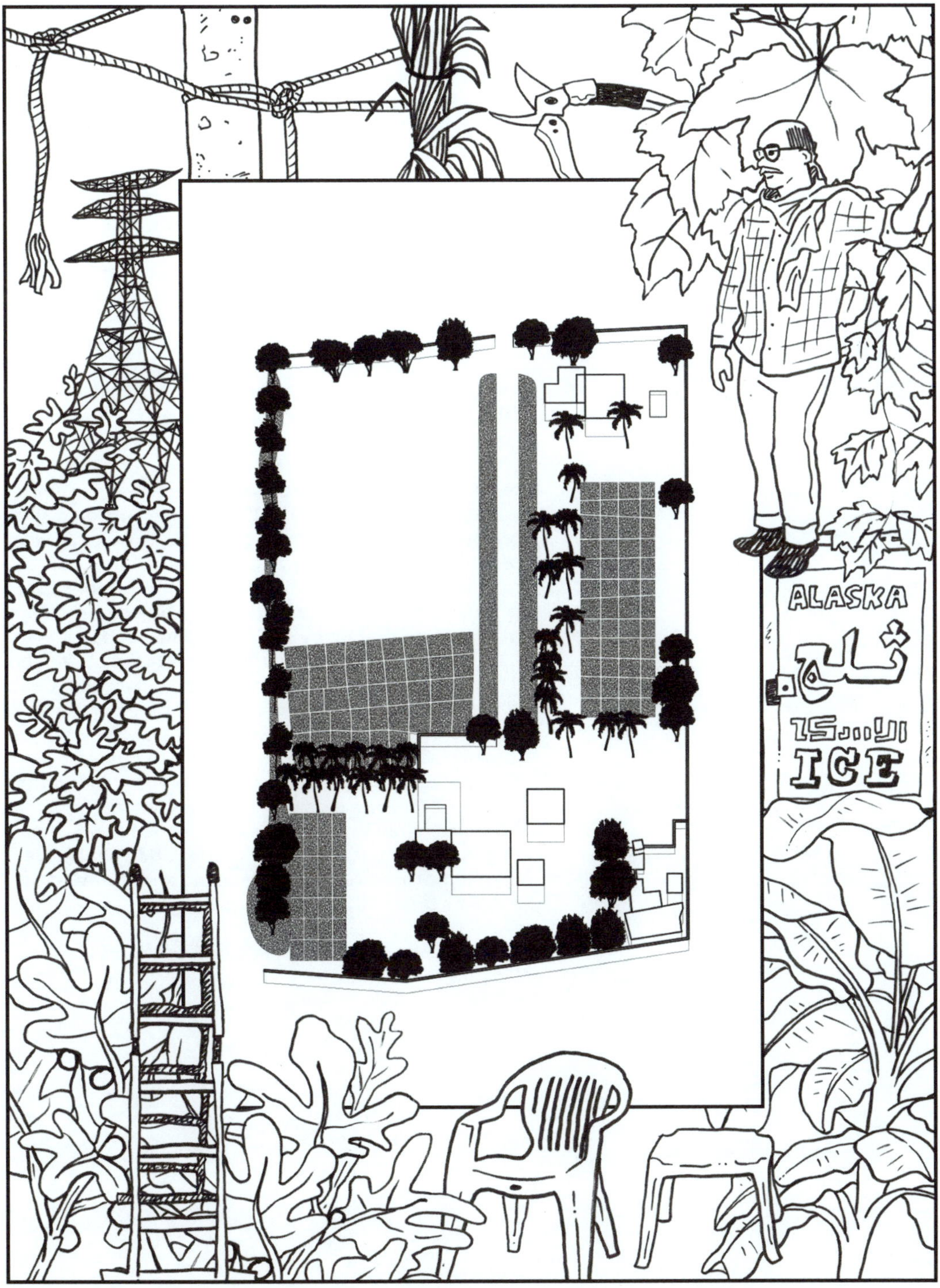


Fig. 10 Hatta field visit. Map by Nujud Alhussain. Illustrations by Khalid Mezaina.

## Fodder in Masafi

> The areas under cultivation in relation to the water available (in Fujeirah) is small and it appeared to me that less water could be used on the land without reducing yields. Some local cultivators are seriously over-irrigating. Simple trials on one or two crops such as tomatoes and onions should be made next winter season to find out if the amount of water required can be reduced." (Fig. 11)
>
> J.C. Eyre, 1957

Obaid, who inherited his love for farming from his late father, commutes every weekend from Abu Dhabi, where he works and lives, to Masafi to check on his farm. He mentions that this land was barren for a while, after his father's death. The farm sits on a small hill among rugged terrain at the foothills of Al Hajar Mountains. Despite growing molokhiya, mint, gourds, mangoes, bananas, palm trees, and chili peppers, he is most proud of his aquatic fern and semi-enclosed greenhouse that he built himself (Fig. 12). He shows us his fertilizer, also known as Azolla, which is used in Asian rice plantations. It also is acquired as fodder, since it is a great source of protein for the chickens and goats on the farm. After a year of researching on the internet, Obaid was able to import it to Fujairah. Another structure to note was a makeshift greenhouse to dry dates, which is used as an alternative fodder. "The greenhouse didn't work as planned and instead of giving up on it, I found a TikTok video that gave instructions as to how to reuse it to dry dates," he explains (Figs. 13, 14).

I came home with three kilos of fresh produce from Obaid's farm that day.

---

*"Development of agriculture in Trucial States."*

Fig. 14 Masafi field visit. Map by Nujud Alhussain. Illustrations by Khalid Mezaina.

Fig. 11 Falaj and rudimentary greenhouse in Masafi. Photo by author.

Fig. 12 Fodder greenhouse in Masafi. Photo by author.

Fig. 13 Date drying greenhouse in Masafi. Photo by author.

Fig. 15 Al Ain greenhouse. Photo by author.

Fig. 16 Barrier arm to agricultural areas in Abu Dhabi. Photo by author.

Fig. 17 Cucumber greenhouse in Al Ain. Photo by author.

## Cucumbers in Al Ain

> The vegetables grown (near Al Ain) are sweet potatoes, radishes, cucumbers, onions, and pumpkins (...), showing the quality of the soil which is fertile but thin. But more care and attention are bestowed on the fruits than on anything else and they consequently arrive at considerable excellence. All the best kinds of dates are cultivated; Fard, Khalas, etc. (...) The other fruits are peaches, mangoes, custard apples, limes, sweet limes, oranges, mulberries, pomegranates, melons, guavas, figs. Agriculture is in rather a mediocre state as regards cereals and vegetables, the principal object of culture being of course the date. They are not dependent on the annual rainfall which is small but are able to irrigate with certainty by means of their valuable aqueducts or felejs drawn from the hill range as well as from wells, water being abundant and at no great depth. (...) The water in this canal was quite warm to the touch, but I forget what they told me about the source." (Fig. 15)
>
> Colonel S.B. Miles, 1885

The expectations that were set for Al Ain were fields, upon fields, of palm trees. Known for its agricultural history and where the late HH Sheikh Zayed bin Sultan Al Nahyan, was born, his efforts cannot go unrecognized when it comes to its agricultural development. However, the endless cucumber greenhouses that we found cannot go unnoticed. From the estimated 26 greenhouses we visited in Al Hiyar, Al Ajban, Nahil, and Sweihan, towns in Al Ain, Abu Dhabi, over half were only cucumber producers. Designated farming districts in Abu Dhabi are often gated with an automated barrier arm, water is provided by the municipality, especially in regions that have scarce ground water (Fig. 16). One of the farms in particular, owned by a widower after her husband passed away from cancer, was proud of the seven tons of cucumbers her greenhouses produced in a season (Fig. 17). She mentioned how the UAE's laws, especially those issued by the late Sheikh Zayed, with regards to providing farmland for widowers have affected her passion for farming. "Even though the cucumbers don't provide a lot of profit, seeing that all of the revenue from their sale is spent on fertilizers, I am still proud of this greenhouse," she said (Fig. 18).

---

*Tuson*, ***Records of the Emirates***, *475.*

Fig. 18 Al Ain field visit. Map by Nujud Alhussain. Illustrations by Khalid Mezaina.

## Lettuce and Kale in Al Zubair

> "The date plantations in Sharjah include about 3,600 trees and the livestock of the place are some 500 camels, 550 donkeys, 130 cattle, 2,200 sheep and goats." ◢ (Fig. 19)
>
> J.G. Lorimer, 1908.

The closest sites visited in proximity to urban centers were in Al Zubair in Sharjah. Located at the border of Ajman and Umm Al Quwain, the abundance of groundwater seems to be helping with the thriving of local farms in the area. Particularly notable were the greenhouses built to facilitate the growth of lettuce and kale, even in the summer's harsh heat. Mohamed Rashed, the agricultural engineer behind the greenhouse's design, elaborated on the irrigation systems and the structure's mutability to be able to help mitigate high temperatures. The greenhouse is not only taller than usual, but also accommodates rising hot air to keep the lettuce's environment cool. In addition, he uses cold water beds to make sure that the plants' roots are comfortable (Fig. 20). Those systems, coupled with strong fans, evaporative cooling pads, and a retractable reflective shading material, alleviate the need for the use of air conditioning. Unlike lettuce, where the roots are not salvageable after their harvest, kale provides a longer cycle of harvest. Mohamed trims the leaves every few months, while the stems remain. "Look," he points, "those are one year old for example. As they continue to grow and offer new leaves, we continue to harvest and supply the local market with our produce." (Figs. 21, 22).

---

◢

*Tuson, **Records of the Emirates**, 239.*

Fig. 22 Al Zubair field visit. Map by Nujud Alhussain. Illustrations by Khalid Mezaina.

Fig. 19 Al Zubair greenhouses. Photo by Ola Allouz.

## Conclusion

Architectural documentation plays a vital role in preserving the memory of this intangible and tangible heritage. By foregrounding examples of fieldwork in sites of food production in the UAE, both historic and contemporary, a conversation is instigated. While this methodology has a stronger hold in other fields such as anthropology, geography, and other field-based practices, in this context, it creates a new method of knowledge production. It juxtaposes the past with the present in hopes that it will preserve knowledge for the future, in a rapidly changing landscape like the UAE's. Perpetuating the continuity of a "sense of place" was the ultimate goal in shedding light on underdocumented practices in contemporary food production. This sampling of projects offers an overview of the UAE in a moment in time.

Fig. 20 Lettuce greenhouse in Al Zubair. Photo by Ola Allouz.

Fig. 21 Kale in Al Zubair. Photo by Ola Allouz.

# Through the Companion's Eyes:
## *A Fictional and Probably More Accurate Retelling of Zwemer's Journeys*

Faysal Tabbarah

***Ingredients***

Kuphar
Lemon
Shrimp
Gravy
Coffee
Pomegranate

My third journey from the island of Bahrein to Abu Thabi began on Tuesday, May 14, 1901. I had not been in the Euphrates Valley since 1893, and despite having learned a lot since leaving my people, my land, and my river, I am always listening to the absent songs and conferences of the red-cheeked bulbuls of the river, but that's for later.

I was told by Ali, my bespectacled Bahreini friend who works as a surveyor and a guide across the island, that when the first quarter moon is in the skies, I can walk eastward across the coast until I can no longer see the land behind us and still have our heads above water. In Bahrein, the thick palm groves, seemingly everywhere on the island, reach up to the water's edge. From there, their fallen kin stand tall along the coastline in the form of fish weirs, or a *hadhra*, as the locals call it here. A hadhra is an ancient fishing contraption made by sticking fallen palm trees into the shallow coast and connecting them with palm-fiber rope, making transparent rooms in the water where men and women, armed with palm woven baskets, venture daily in search of grouper, mackerel, and shrimp. The captured fish and shrimp are then boiled, salted, and dried for a few days before they are stored. The locals call this *ihla*.

It is no surprise then, that Bahrein does not have any piers. We use a smaller boat to reach the larger wooden *bateel* that takes us to Abu Thabi. Both vessels are made from imported Indian timber, but I was told by Ismail, the bateel's *kubait*, that almost everything else on the boats, except for the pulley-blocks that come from Bombay, is made on the island. The kubait, well past his youth, appeared to be a coarse man on the outside, with his scarred body, cracked hands, and a permanent furrow running vertically between his eyes, but when he spoke, he did so softly and richly. His boat was rather small when compared to other vessels in these waters, around 15 meters in length with no interior cabins, but this was still far larger than the vessels back home. The only item that provided shade was a narrow sailcloth. During winters, the kubait transports travelers across the coast of Arabia, from Kuweit in the north to Ras-el-Kheima in the south, and sometimes up till Sohar on the Indian Ocean if the trip happens earlier in the year. In the summers, he spends about three to four months diving in search of precious pearls. The season was almost upon us, and this might have been the kubait's last trip before the start of the *Ghous Al-Kabir*, the pearl diving season. My companion and I were going to make our way back to Bahrein from Sohar on a different boat.

The journey between Bahrein and Abu Thabi takes between three to ten days, depending on the weather conditions. On this particular journey, which took seven days, the guest of honor was a gift from the ruler of Bahrein to the ruler of Abu Thabi: a magnificent honey-colored Arabian horse with a particularly high tail carriage, black silky hair, and an almost regal demeanor, being calm throughout the entire trip. The horse took the entirety of the midship, while the second gift, an Arabian saluki, also honey-colored, was tied to the forecastle. As for the rest of us, thirteen men including myself and the Reverend, who was my traveling companion, we settled on the poop deck.

As the days went by, the kubait would sing about the pearl coast, painting a picture of long months at sea, of days with multiple dives, armed only with nose clips, weighted ropes, and woven baskets. I saw the effects of the pearl economy firsthand on this third journey, as we stopped briefly at Dalma Island, which is about five hours sailing from mainland Abu Thabi. As the ghous approached, one could sense that the island had only recently woken up from its winter slumber. Seasonal workers had flocked onto the island to set up sleeping quarters, temporary lodgings, and a market center. I also saw fishermen prepare for their expeditions by examining their nets and mending them where needed.

Our food on the journey was primarily *ihla*, which we savored with droplets from a handful of freshly squeezed lemons we had on board.

I was born on the southwestern bank of the Euphrates, in Qashla, a town of 15,000 people that seems to shapeshift every once in a while. I have recently heard that some resident tribes have decided to abandon its Ottoman name, a rather simple one meaning military barracks, telling passersby that they have arrived in Al Bukamal. This rebirth might be warranted. For fear of flooding, the old mud-brick town was abandoned a few years ago and moved less than a couple of kilometers upstream, rebuilt this time with stone.

I came to this life moments before the Euphrates sparkled in the early morning sun, which would have signaled impending floods in the days before irrigation. I was born on the mud floors of my grandfather's simple mud-brick house, a few steps from the river, into a family who have been farmers for as far back as our stories go back in time, stories shared by families along the Euphrates as far north as its source. Despite my familial disposition for farming, which I could not escape, I had an equal disposition for traveling and acquiring languages, which I picked up from the many reverends who passed through Qashla. To this day, I think of myself as a farmer-wanderer: a contradiction I am acutely and constantly reminded of. Around 8,000 years ago, our people stopped wandering the Mesopotamian plains and settled on the banks of the Euphrates and the Tigris, while I wandered southward in search of their dissolving traces and disappearing farms.

By becoming the preferred companion for Europeans and others wanting to visit Doro-Europos, I improved my fluency in foreign languages such as English, French, and German. There were two kinds of travelers who knock on my door. The first half were dressed in their European garb, so ill-fitting with the landscape they thought they wanted to discover. The other half wore our garb, which their bodies wore so ill-fittingly, making their movements tired. What they all shared was an obsession with the "Pompeii of the Desert." I didn't know much about Pompeii, but Doro-Europos was an ancient Hellenistic, Parthian, and Roman frontier city that thrived for about 600 years before |it was finally destroyed in the third century CE by the Sassanians.

I used to take them north along the Euphrates aboard a *kuphar*, a circular boat made with palm reeds and waterproofed by bitumen, just like the boats that had been built by the Babylonians. Bitumen, I heard, was also used in the construction of the Hanging Gardens, which I yearned to see.

Thus, it was in 1893 that I traveled once and for all outside of my small familiar world, arriving in Baghdad aboard a kuphar, this time the journey took me much further north along the Euphrates than I had ever been before. It was supposed to be a short trip to the ruins of the gardens of Babylon, via the Al Hillah and its gardens in the water. As many know, the planting and harvesting of land first began in Mesopotamia. My journey took place long before an American man named James Henry Breasted announced to the world that agriculture developed around 10,000 years ago in what he oddly called the Fertile Crescent, an area of the world roughly bound by the stretches between the Euphrates and the Tigris. Despite the passing millennia since the rise and fall of Babylon and its gardens, our way of life has not been dramatically transformed, and I was compelled to set foot in my people's spiritual birthplace, to see where wild emmer wheat and two-row hulled barley were domesticated. Harvests like lentils, chickpeas, peas, vetches, and acorns — typically made into soups inside chimneyed-clay ovens — were stored while sheep provided abundant milk, meat, and wool. Needless to say, date palm orchards expanded rapidly, from which our life, in its fullest sense, was born.

It was then that I began working as a translator of people and documents for the British Residency of Turkish Arabia, a two-story stone building on the eastern banks of the Tigris, set amongst many palm trees. I used to spend as much of my working day as possible on the building's roof, from which you can see kuphars, sailboats, and barges come passing in both directions, with minarets poking through thick palm groves across the other side of the bank.

My first three journeys from Bahrein to Abu Thabi were taken with an American man named Samuel Marinus Zwemer, who introduced himself simply as the Reverend to English speakers. In fact, I have never heard him say his own name, which I have only seen written. He seemed as uncomfortable with his actual name as he was with our garb, which he insisted on wearing on our journeys. As for Arabs who did not speak English, he asked me to introduce him as *Al Rafiq*, or the kind friend.

These journeys were taken aboard kubait Ismail's wooden bateel. Our first trip to the sandy beaches of Abu Thabi, a place I had not been to before meeting the Reverend, was in May of 1900, while the second one was taken the following February, a few months before the third one. My fourth and final journey would come much later, during the Great War. Then, I spent a few good months in a stone house a few steps from the *Qasr*. Word has spread that the Reverend had settled in Cairo during that period and was publishing missionary literature for the Nile Mission Press.

The Reverend was a tall and fervent man more comfortable speaking than listening. To this day, I am not sure he registered much when we spoke. Despite his decade under our sun, his skin remained pale. He rarely smiled, looking just as he always appeared in his photographs. I found that he was rather fond of having these photographs taken, which he only took in his Western clothes, made from Italian wool for the winter and Indian linens for the summer. His hair was always cut short: crisply parted to his right. His eyes were long, running parallel to his constantly furrowed brows, wrestling in lines paler than his overall skin. He was a man with a great appetite, appreciating food on his journeys more than anything else. He was clearly surprised at the aromas, tastes, and colors of the delicious food we had on our travels along the entirety of the Arabian coast and even in the desert.

Before embarking on our first trip, the Reverend called on the British representative in Bahrein, a man named John Calcott Gaskin, who was always comically in his service shorts, the British solution to the weather, something I had seen as far north as Baghdad, and as far south as Sohar. Sitting in Gaskin's office and sipping an uninfused black tea, the Reverend told him that he prefers to travel as light as possible as he was weary of how the Arabs would treat strangers, especially Christian strangers. Did he not know I'm not Christian? Did he not know that Christians already lived in Arabia? Did he not know the Portuguese were here before him? Gaskin, a man I found as ignorant as he was confident, nodded in agreement.

In another meeting before our second journey in 1901, Gaskin, who was in the habit of sharing his accomplishments quite boastfully, told the Reverend that asphalt deposits were found at Jabal Al Dukhan in Bahrein, and that he was keen to secure the rights to extraction before the German company Wonckhaus & Co. claimed it. By asphalt, Gaskin meant bitumen, the same material from our kuphars, reservoirs, and the Hanging Gardens. Before our second trip in February 1902, Gaskin was a little less boastful as he informed the Reverend that Wonckhaus & Co. had indeed approached the ruler of Bahrein for exclusive rights to the extraction of said asphalt deposits. Suddenly, I remembered the kubait. The same Wonckhaus & Co. had set up offices engaging in the pearl trade in Bahrein and elsewhere along the coast to ensure their profits were maximized from an industry that was worth almost £260,000 at the time of our journeys. Gaskin had noted that Herr Robert Wonckhaus himself took extreme interest in mother-of-pearl.

During my last trip to Abu Thabi, I was told that Gaskin was working in Iraq and was imprisoned by the Ottomans either in Iraq or Aleppo for some time when the Great War broke out because he sunk the Baghdad Residency's ammunition in the nearest river to prevent it falling into Ottoman or German control. Ironically for Gaskin, who only referred to me as his "Mesopotamian Friend" after the Reverend introduced me as his "Mesopotamian companion" when I first met him.

The Reverend did travel light, except for a few books including a Bible, which he had both in English and Arabic, writings by Niebuhr, and another called Sir John Malcolm. He did not seem to admire their work, as he was always delighted by observing erroneous facts from their reporting. Once, during a moonlit trek toward Al Batinah, I had suggested that Niebuhr was last in Arabia over 120 years ago, and most probably never set foot on this coast. The Reverend's response suggested that this amount of time means too little for change in this region. I tried to tell him about Al-Maqdisi's accounts of the mountains and the coast, which I have read thoroughly in a library in Baghdad. I described the sounds of the middling waters within the mountains that Al-Maqdisi had so vividly described, but he remained uninterested.

We arrived on the island of Abu Thabi and called on its ruler so that we could deliver the gifts in our possession, the magnificent horse and the saluki. As expected, the ruler hosted us in one of his houses that is made out of coral, which is a particular tradition amongst this pleasant coastal region. The stones are bound by lime plaster and roofed by local mangroves or timber that is usually imported from India. The ruler caught a glimpse of my interest, and told me that the coral is imported from nearby reefs, but sometimes as far away as the Horn of Africa. It was clear why this was a treasured material, as the house kept cool and dry in the hot, humid climate.

The ruler promptly asked for a feast to be served in our honor, which was of a number of rice dishes steeped in a very light and mild gravy, with the rice forming a bed for the large pieces of tender lamb. Atop all of this, the hosts also garnished the dishes with nuts, dates, and dried grapes. The dishes were placed on mats made from palm reeds, surrounded with rose water, dates, and bread. On inquiring about the cooking method, I was told by a young man that the lamb is slow cooked for quite some time in an underground clay oven, which I suspect is what gives it its distinctly smoky flavor. The young kids laughed at my companion's forced seating posture, as it was obvious that he neither knew how to eat while seated on the floor, nor use his hands to eat. Our host promptly asked for a spoon to be fetched. Despite over a decade in our world, and his insistence on wearing Arab garb on our journeys, the Reverend had not learned much of our lives. From the corner of my eye, I could see a young man roast fresh green coffee pods on an open fire, which was served right after we finished our meal.

The following day, we made our way eastward toward El Maktaa, the point where our newly acquired camels would carry us across the water. We had to wait for a few days for the tide to subside, and once we received the signal from the round watchtower, built on a small man-made island between the island and the mainland, we mounted our camels and crossed through. The water was as high as our camel's necks, but this did not unsettle our trusted carriers. Despite their steadfast attitude, I heard the Reverend frantically whispering what I could only believe to be desperate prayers. From there, we rode further north along the coast, toward Sharka, passing by Debai, a prosperous town with a buzzing central market, filled with all manners of imported goods such as German-made ironware and English-made cakes. Despite it being out of season, I asked for pistachios but did not find any.

The Reverend was keen on continuing further north to arrive in Ras-el-Kheima, but I had other hopes. In Sharka, a local merchant selling all manner of Eastern silk told me about this year's uncharacteristically late autumn rains, which he confirmed was a blessing that came after repeated *salawat al-istisqa'*, an Islamic prayer for rain. Whenever I hear Arabs talking of autumn rains, I am immediately transported to the Temple of Baal in the Palmyran plains, where I have had some of the most delicious *kimme* on my journeys. It was thus that I convinced my companion to put the coastal path behind our backs and head into the interior, toward Bereimi and Al Ain, which was about a two-day camel ride.

The road between Sharka and Bereimi was notorious for its scarcity when it comes to people, food, and water, but it was filled with the salty tamarisk bush, which our camels devoured with the same excitement that we ate our sweet, meaty dates. I told the Reverend not to fret, food will be found. Along the desert road, there was a small hamlet called Al Faqa'a, where you can find *faqa'a*, which is what they call kimme. I took this as a good omen.

Kimme is an edible fungus that grows in the desert and lives entirely beneath the earth. I have found it as far north as the edges of the Syrian Desert, and have heard reports, when stationed in Baghdad, about how they could be found in Kewait and as far south as Najd. It is said that if rain is accompanied by thunder in the autumn, kimme will be found in the spring. I learned to find kimme during my travels across the desert from Qashla to Palmyra by searching for a low shrub that is filled with yellow roses, as kimme only appears next to this beautiful plant. Fortunately, the news I heard in Sharka had been true, and the desert was full.

To take off the dirt and sand of the kimme completely, I soak them in water for about thirty minutes. Afterward, I drain them while gently massaging them to ensure their surface is smooth. If there are any existing fissures in the kimme, I cut them along those lines to ensure that no sand is still lodged within. In any case, I don't prefer cooking them whole, as that takes a little bit more time. There are many ways to cook them, but given our situation, I opted for the simplest version, which is cutting and boiling them for around seven minutes, and then seasoning them with salt. They must remain a little firm, as over boiling them would soften their body too much, making for an unpleasant experience. What started off looking like potatoes ended up tasting far more brilliantly than any potatoes ever can, kimme has the distinctive quality of being sweet when cooked, but retaining some of its subtle nuttiness.

In Baghdad, a local cook used to selectively and exclusively acquire kimme from tribal women trekking from the steppe. He would prepare them with Egyptian imported short grain rice along with a mixture of aromatic spices including cinnamon and nutmeg, adding in local lamb.

After Bereimi, we rested in Al Ain, a town known for its seven oases, before heading northward to find a pass through the mountains. On our approach toward Ez-Zahira, the western edge of the mountains, Al Hajar rose like a fortress, an impenetrable mountain range of entangled striking reds, yellows, and browns. Through this fortress, we crossed into Wadi Hatta, and after a brief rest in Masfut, a village along the wadi, we rode east during a brightly lit white night, with the white moon reflected endlessly in the running waters of the wadi. As the winds swept through the tight mountain passes, the mountains sang in the night, sometimes quietly and as sweetly as if putting a child to sleep, and at other times with the fervor of a passionate preacher. In the morning, we chanced on a startled young girl wearing a bright green dress embroidered with gold-colored thread. She explained to me that she became separated from her people when she went looking for a lost camel. I gave her a handful of dates and some water, and despite the Reverend's protestations over our limited time, she rode with us until we found her search party. Throughout our journey in the mountains, we passed by stone-built villages centered around a mosque where water is also centrally managed. We saw terraced farms with barley, wheat, and sesame grown under the shade of mango trees, themselves coddled from above by palm trees. Outside of these farms, *ghaf* trees are also abundant, growing wildly on the foothills and along small streams.

After a twelve-hour journey through the wadis, the ocean could be heard, welcoming us with its own magnificent song. We followed a small stream toward the tune, and after a few maneuvers with our camels, we suddenly came upon a lush green landscape and a bright clear sky, orchards of palm, mulberry, and fig trees so thick we could only hear the ocean, less than two kilometers away. This is what Burckhardt might have felt when he chanced upon a long-lost treasure.

While the Reverend was taking a nap under an acacia tree in Kalba, I went for a walk in the fields that sat on the mountain's western foothills along Al Batinah. There, I met a young farmer named Rashid who was busy inspecting pomegranate trees. As we talked, he understood that I was also a farmer and somehow this brought us closer together. He asked me how deep our irrigation wells were dug back home and I explained to him that the systems along the Euphrates were very different, and relied more on the seasonal floods, and less so on deep wells.

Rashid told me that growing food within the mountains relied on groundwater reserves, which he believes are replenished by rainwater, and two types of *aflaj* to collect and deliver water to the fields and orchards. A *falaj* is a system of constructed channels, sometimes above ground and sometimes subterranean. The first type, what he called the *falaj ghayli*, refers to an open-air channel that allows surface water to flow from a wadi or spring. While the second type, what he called the *falaj da'udi*, collects water from a subterranean source such as an aquifer and includes subterranean channels that eventually emerge above ground.

Rashid explained to me that the falaj is more than just water. It is about building a community, which is why water first appears above ground in the *shari'a* or "a common place" in the village square, close to a mosque, and is stored in a cistern, where equal access is allowed for all. Once in the irrigation zone, the falaj branches out to individual farms. The community agrees to measure how much water each farm receives either using the movement of the sun or by a mechanical system, something as simple as a bowl with a hole in the bottom collecting water over a specific period of time.

At the end of our chat, Rashid insisted I pick anything, and as much as I needed, from the field, and I opted for a ripening pomegranate. The Reverend always asked for things he wanted, but now Rashid was asking me what I needed.

By chance, I recently found and read the Reverend's 20-year-old report on our trips in an American magazine called *The Geographical Journal*. I was the Mesopotamian companion he briefly wrote about, as though I was a ghost.

At first, I felt compelled to correct everything in his record, but when I began to write, I forgot his misrepresentations. The scraggy acacia tree he mentions in his report provided more than just shade on a hot day. It was a generous refuge under which he slept comfortably for many, many hours, to the sounds of its leaves rustling with the breeze. When he was napping under the tree, recorded in the photograph he published, I learned about agriculture in the mountains from Rashid.

It seems that he did not really *see*, *hear*, or even *taste* the landscapes we passed through. Meanwhile, I heard the bulbul of the Euphrates in every sound.

# Joining Together:

## *Architecture, Agriculture, and the Conceptualization of Craft*

Kevin Mitchell

***Ingredients***

Discernment
Deliberation
Proportionality
Joining
Mixing
Combining

• *Adolf Loos, **Neue Freie Presse**, Vienna, 1910, https://thecharnelhouse.org/2014/03/17/someone-is-buried-here-adolf-loos-on-architecture-and-death/ (accessed November 18, 2024).*

• *Ibid.*

• *Ibid.*

*Architecture* and *agriculture* — joining the two terms is not unreasonable given their obvious connections: raising livestock requires structures for storage and protection, while raising crops can utilize greenhouses and indoor hydroponic farms. Adolf Loos, the early twentieth-century architect who provoked peers by joining the terms *ornament* and *crime*, questioned the value of the work of his profession with claims that the farmer building his house may demonstrate greater sensitivity to the context than the architect designing a villa. To make his point, Loos invites us to imagine a mountain lake where:

> (...) the sky is blue, the water green and everywhere is profound tranquility. The clouds and mountains are mirrored in the lake, the houses, farms, and chapels as well. They do not look as if they were fashioned by man, it is as if they came straight from God's workshop, like the mountains and trees, the clouds and the blue sky. And everything exudes an air of beauty and peace...

Among the houses, farms, and chapels stands a villa created by an architect –"Whether a good or bad architect, I don't know. All I know is that the tranquillity, peace and beauty have vanished."

Loos proceeds to answer the fundamental question:

> (...) why is it that the architect, no matter whether good or bad, desecrates the lake? Like almost all city dwellers, the architect lacks culture. He lacks the sure touch of the farmer, who does possess culture.

In this context, "culture" is characterized by particular relationships between people and places that develop slowly over time rather than a concern for current trends and fascination with the fashionable. Loos makes a distinction between the architect's creation with the process of constructing the farmer's house, which relies on craft traditions and locally available materials. In contrast to the villa, the farmer's house and the cultivated landscape have not been formed for the purpose of presenting a pleasing visual appearance; nevertheless, the application of the practical knowledge and expertise of the farmer and builders, as well as their mastery of materials, contributes significantly to the tranquillity, peace, and beauty of the area surrounding the mountain lake. The gilding and gold that was, for example, present in the work of those associated with the movement known as the Vienna Secession — which Loos was briefly associated with and subsequently opposed — was conspicuously absent in the buildings surrounding the mountain lake. There is no pursuit of beauty for the sake of beauty, or innovation for the sake of innovation; nevertheless, both beauty and innovation exist as a result of the sustained focus on the application of continually refined knowledge and a concern for craft in both building and agriculture.

Fig.01 Double-leaf frontispiece from *Rasā'il Ikhwān al-Ṣafā'*. Baghdad, c. 1287. Suleymaniye Library MSS Esad Efendi 3636, fols. 3b-4a.

The role of craft in building is well established and Loos bases his critique of his contemporaries on the devaluation of craft traditions; however, agriculture is not often considered to be a craft. An exception is the exceptional *Rasā'il Ikhwān al-Ṣafā'* (Epistles of the Brethren of Purity), a treatise believed to have been written around the tenth century CE that addresses mathematics, epistemology, and metaphysical cosmology (Fig. 01). In an essay/photo series titled *Privileging the Pragmatic*, I considered how the ideas expressed in the treatise could inform thinking about the organization of small farms in the United Arab Emirates (UAE) and, as discussed below, the *Rasā'il* can also provide a means for conceptualizing the relationship between architecture and agriculture.

*Kevin Mitchell, "Privileging the Pragmatic" In: F. Tabbarah and M. Almazrooei (eds)* ***In Plain Sight: Scenes from Aridly Abundant Landscapes*** *(Abu Dhabi: National Pavilion UAE La Biennale di Venezia/Kaph Books, 2023), 300–317.*

*Godefroid de Callataÿ "The Classification of Knowledge in the Rasā'il" In: N. El-Bizri (ed)* ***Epistles of the Brethren of Purity. The Ikhwān al-Ṣafā' and their Rasā'il. An Introduction,*** *(Oxford: Oxford University Press, 2008), 58.*

Fig.02 Illustration from the *Kitab al-Diryaq* (Book of Antidotes), by Pseudo-Gallen (vellum).

Godefroid de Callataÿ describes the *Rasā'il* as, "(...) agnostic and philosophical encyclopedia which was written in Arabic in the classical age of Islam and whose nature, contents and purposes have no equivalent of any kind either inside or outside the Muslim world." Epistle 8, titled "On the Practical Crafts," establishes a conceptual framework that is hierarchical and based on whether or not the crafts "constitute a primary objective," defined as serving basic human needs. Some crafts are defined as the first order of priority, whereas others are "complementary and supplementary." Those considered to be primary and of the first order are agriculture (land-ploughing and planting), tailoring (made possible through weaving), and building: agriculture provides sustenance, clothing provides protection for the body, and buildings provide shelter.

Land-ploughing and planting, while classified as first-order priorities, are necessary but not sufficient for sustenance. Complementary and supplementary crafts were required to prepare the land and plant, harvest, process, and make crops ready for human consumption. In a region impacted by water scarcity, measures to control and maximize the use of water were vital (Fig. 02). Altering the topography to direct water, as well as ploughing, planting, and harvesting, would have required tools made possible by the supplementary crafts of carpentry and blacksmithing. After harvesting, some crops would require milling and grinding, which would also be dependent on tools produced through supplementary crafts. Prior to consumption, many crops would require cooking or baking, which the *Rasā'il* characterizes as complementary crafts. Tailoring is necessary to protect humans "created with a thin skin," and making clothes is dependent on the supplementary and complementary crafts of spinning, sewing, bleaching, stitching, and embroidering. Building, required for providing shelter and accommodating human activity, is supplemented by carpentry and blacksmithing.

The *Rasā'il* offers a mode of thinking about the relationship between architecture and agriculture that is more nuanced and substantive than I posited at the beginning of the essay. Just as Loos sought to contest the preconceptions that promote a status differentiation between architect and farmer, the conceptual framework presented in the *Rasā'il* challenges the hierarchical distinction between architecture and craft by establishing both building and agriculture as first-order crafts that serve basic human needs. Chapter 11, titled "That Every Craft is in Need of Thought and Intellection," also challenges the assumption that craft can be reduced to the replication of a learned practice, maintaining that engaging in craft depends on exercising intellect, discernment, deliberation, and ideation.

*Epistles of the Brethren of Purity. On Composition and the Arts*. Edited and translated by G. de Callataÿ and N. El-Bizri, (Oxford: Oxford University Press, 2018), 152.

The design and construction of buildings, agricultural production, and food preparation rely on making, considering the implications of possible options, and the capacity to form ideas. Architecture, agriculture, and cooking require combining constituent parts to create an integrated whole: joining together elements such as the floor, walls, and, roof to form a building; conjoining seeds, soil, fertilizer, and water to produce crops; and mixing ingredients to prepare food.

However, simply combining, mixing, and joining elements together does not ensure good buildings, nutritious crops, or appetizing food: intellect, discernment, deliberation, and ideation are necessary to determine the respective quantities of the constituent parts and the means of bringing disparate components together to create a cohesive whole that is greater than the sum of its parts.

Fig.03 “Preparation for a Feast,” Folio from a Divan of Jami.

Relying on ideas developed by Nicomachus of Gerasa and Euclid, Epistle 6 addresses the role that ratios and proportions play in craft by providing a quantifiable system for joining together, combining, and mixing disparate elements: "(...) of every crafted object that is made out of entities that are opposite in natures contrary with each other in powers, and different in shapes, what is most judicious and masterful is that whose parts and harmonized components are composed according to the finest proportion." (Fig. 03) Epistle 6 specifically considers the way in which the smell and taste of food depends on the proportional relationship between ingredients:

Ibid., 64.

> Other examples of this are cooking ingredients, which are of different tastes, smells, colours, and magnitudes, since when their amounts were proportionally cooked together, the food will have a delectable smell, a delicious taste, and would be made with finesse, whereas when they are not proportional what results is the opposite. It is for this reason that when it has been mentioned in the book of medicine and in the books of the (culinary) art that when prepared recipes are proportionally composed, and set according to a proportion, they are proper, while if this is not the case, then they get corrupted and are improper.

Ibid., 61.

The passage quoted above explicitly addresses the quantifiable elements that can be measured (amounts and proportions) and the qualitative aspects that can be experienced (tastes and smells). While qualitative aspects are often immeasurable, they result from, and are dependent upon, measurable amounts and proportions. The passage also implicitly acknowledges that a vital aspect of craft is the determination of limits and proportionality. Craft requires knowledge of when to limit and how to combine.

Fig.04 Grooming a horse, *Kitab al-bayṭara*, 1210, Topkapi Museum.

The houses, farms, and chapels surrounding the mountain lake that Loos asks us to imagine are physical entities that can be precisely described in units of measurement such as meters and hectares. Yet, as described above, neither amounts alone nor the mere combining, mixing, and joining together of houses, farms, and chapels are necessarily sufficient for achieving a sense of "tranquillity, peace and beauty." Transcending the quantitative, establishing limits, and achieving the qualities desired in buildings, landscapes, and food, requires — in the words of the *Rasā'il* — exercising intellect, discernment, deliberation, and ideation in ways that consider the properties and particularities of the constituent parts, establish proportionality, and combine components into a "harmonious" whole.

Reflecting on the conceptual framework of craft articulated in the *Rasā'il* provides a basis for thinking about the relationship between architecture, agriculture, and cooking as crafts that serve basic human needs. In addition to addressing practical applications, the text considers ethical questions that are relevant for thinking through the environmental impacts of architecture, agriculture, and the production, processing, and consumption of food.

Throughout the treatise, the emphasis on categorization is counterbalanced by a recognition of interdependency. This is evident despite the reliance on the Aristotelian method of hierarchical classification. In the *Rasā'il*, the hierarchy ascends from minerals to plants, animals, and finally human beings, who are argued to be superior and thus maintain a position of earthly dominance. However, the text maintains that superiority demands adherence to ethical standards and must be accompanied by an acceptance of responsibility. Perhaps the most explicit instance of this can be found in a fable that tells the story of animals that have taken a group of humans to court to contest their subjugation (Fig. 04). Throughout the trial, the humans' claims to the possession of distinct forms of virtue are negated by counterarguments made by the animals and, while the position of superiority of human beings remains unchanged, the ethical responsibility for limiting suffering is established.

Ethical and practical responsibility for proportionality and the establishment of limits is relevant when thinking through ways to mitigate the impact that architecture, agriculture, and the production, processing, and consumption of food has on animals, the environment, and humankind today and in the future. Often discussions related to sustainability focus on maintaining current levels of consumption rather than fundamentally questioning whether the amounts and proportions that we are accustomed to are sustainable. While the *Rasā'il* offers no direct prescriptions for greater sustainability, conceptualizing architecture, agriculture, and cooking as craft accentuates the continued importance of thought and intellection in establishing limits and accepting responsibility for what, and how, we build, plant, harvest, cook, and consume.

# *Cooking Techniques*

Course 1: *Cut, Slice, and Dice*

**Imported vs Contextual**
*by* Azza Aboualam

Course 2: *Simmering & Stewing*

**It's Not the Heat, it's the Humidity: Designing for Crop Growth and Human Comfort in Desert Greenhouses**
*by* Dimitri Brand and Kit Elsworth

Course 3: *Conceal & Reveal*

**Living Machines**
*by* HOME-OFFICE (Daniel Jacobs and Brittany Utting)

Illustrations by Khalid Mezaina

*Chapter* **03**

# Imported vs Contextual

Azza Aboualam

Jules Janick and Harry Paris, "History of Controlled Environment Horticulture: Ancient Origins," **Hort-Science** 57 (2022): 236–238, https://doi.org/10.21273/HORTSCI16169-21, 236.

Ibid.

Ibid.

Jules Janick and Harry Paris, "History of Controlled..." 236.

Keunhye Lee, "The Floor: A Reinterpretation of the Korean Home, Focusing on the Ondol," **Space and Culture** 26, no. 4 (2023): 505–21, https://doi-org.zulib.idm.oclc.org/10.1177/1206331220976486.

***Ingredients***

Form
Context
Assembly
Kit-of-Parts
Cucumber

## Greenhouse Definitions

When doctors instructed Emperor Tiberius to consume a fruit from the cucurbits family daily, he was presented with a dilemma. How could he grow these gourds, like melon and cucumber, year-round on his home island of Capri? Tiberius then ordered the construction of a *specularia*: a wooden frame structure covered with transparent stone, a form of gypsum, known to the Romans as *lapis specularia*.

"(He) had raised beds made in frames upon wheels, by means of which the Cucumis were moved and exposed to the full heat of the sun; while, in winter, they were withdrawn, and placed under the protection of frames glazed with mirror-stone." (Fig. 01)

According to Pliny the Elder, the Roman author, there was never a day in which Tiberius, who ruled from 14 to 37 CE, was not supplied with cucumbers. And with that, a clear instance of the overlap between architecture and food production took shape: the greenhouse. This architectural typology's main objective is to shield plants from the elements, whether excess heat or cold, prolonging the growing season. Although these structures are most commonly referred to as greenhouses, other terms such as conservatory, glasshouse, and hothouse are also often used interchangeably. Greenhouses, both productive and laborious, luxurious and decadent, are clear typologies that embody major transformations in our understanding of agriculture, food production, and food security. Eclipsing their initial conception as luxurious spaces for the elite while highlighting the trade and imperialism of the Western world, greenhouses have become an essential part of food security agendas, including in arid environments such as the United Arab Emirates (UAE). Resisting demise and having undergone centuries of development and innovation, greenhouse designs have advanced in formal expression and utilization from the original *specularia*, while spanning the globe with their technology, materials, and the crops grown within them.

## Heating and Extravagance

While the first greenhouse can be traced back to ancient Rome, other parts of the globe show evidence of the development of the form and its inner workings of climate control, especially with heat generation in cooler temperatures. In Korea in the 1450s, the royal physician of the Joseon dynasty documented the use of protected cultivation with the technology of a traditional underfloor heating system, *ondol*, to grow tangerine trees and ripen their fruit. Built into traditional Korean construction, the ondol, also called *gudeul*, is a traditional Korean floor heating system that is installed in an interior space, where hot gas and smoke produced by the fireplace pass under the floor to generate heat. (Fig. 02)

In the seventeenth and eighteenth centuries, *orangeries* emerged in France to protect fruit trees from cold temperatures in the winter. Made out of wood and stone, their large south-facing glass windows maximized sunlight exposure. Though these buildings were initially conceived as merely functional,

*Britannica, T. Editors of Encyclopaedia. "Palace of Versailles." **Encyclopedia Britannica**, October 28, 2024. https://www.britannica.com/topic/Palace-of-Versailles.*

*The Cultural Significance of Greenhouses: A Complicated Identity," **ArchDaily**, June 10, 2023, accessed July 6, 2024, https://www.archdaily.com/996895/the-story-of-greenhouses-a-complicated-identity.*

*Ibid,.*

*The Almería province in southeastern Spain contains the largest concentration of greenhouse horticulture in its semi-arid coastal plain. This agricultural experiment that started in the 1960s covers approximately 30,000 hectares and produces 70% of Spain's export of fresh produce.*

*Marian A. Nessim et al., "The Rise and Evolution of Wind Tower Designs in Egypt and the Middle East," **Sustainability** 15, no. 14 (2023): 10881, https://doi.org/10.3390/su151410881.*

*Merle H. Jensen, **Zayed: The Saadiyat Miracle**, (Abu Dhabi: National Archives, 2021), 17.*

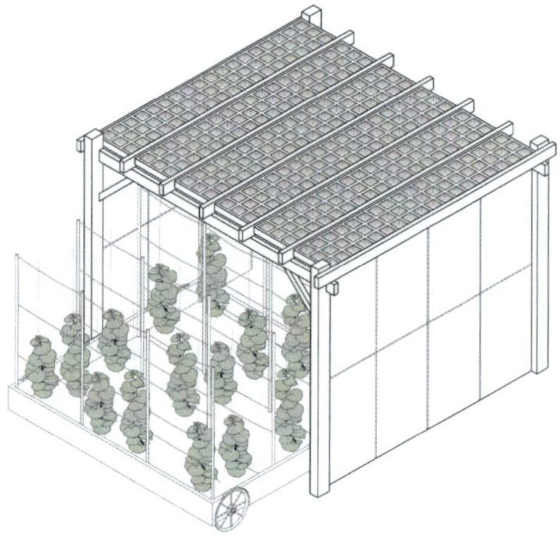

Fig. 01 Roman specularia. Drawn by Sara AlMahmoud.

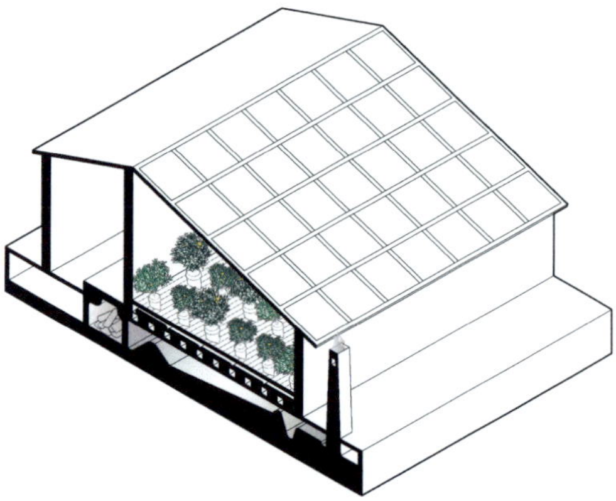

Fig. 02 Korean ondol floor. Drawn by Sara AlMahmoud.

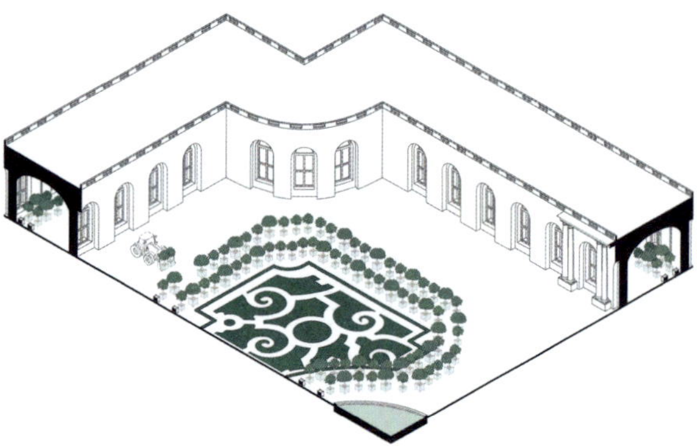

Fig. 03 Versailles' Orangery. Drawn by Sara AlMahmoud.

they slowly grew in extravagance, achieving maximum opulence in their physical and formal expression. The Orangery at Louis XIV's Versailles, for example, was approximately 150 meters long, 13 meters high, and warmed over 1,000 orange trees. (Fig. 03) With the improvement of glassmaking in the nineteenth century, the conservatory was materialized. This contributed to an outgrowth of global trade, imperialism, and innovation. Conservatories embodied a leap in the conjoining of architecture and agriculture by evidently extending the growing season. Large conservatories with wrought iron glasshouses embodied advances in structural design during the eighteenth and nineteenth centuries, which eventually had a significant impact on greenhouse designs developed during the twentieth century. The largely transparent, wide-span structures we know today were born as a result. The large public greenhouses of the Western world were fairly standardized with their general arrangement of an open plan that facilitated the free movement and rearrangement of plant collections. The provision of various zones came at a later stage where the interior spaces were further divided to accommodate plants that would dictate distinct temperature needs.

**Warm Weather Requirements**

While greenhouses were first developed to maximize heat levels and sun exposure, food production in hot arid climates presented an alternative predicament: the need for cooler interior environments. The Gulf region, in particular, has climate-related challenges such as high temperatures, maximum sun exposure, and relative humidity throughout the year. In response, a variety of greenhouse designs evolved in semi-arid and tropical countries such as India, Malaysia, Kenya, and Morocco in order to adapt to their climatic context. A notable example of a hot climate greenhouse is the Spanish Parral (Almería) greenhouse and its evolution into the multi-span greenhouse. This specific greenhouse design consists of medium-to-tall, multi-span, arch or gothic arch, gutter-connected polyethylene houses with a combination of side and roof ventilation mechanisms. The design relies on increased ventilation through shade nets and roof openings. In addition, thermal or shade screens on the roof are used to reflect sunlight and reduce the temperature inside the multi-span structure.

Recently, archeologists in the Gulf unearthed a form of cooling used in ancient interior spaces. Dating back to the seventh and eighth centuries, this form of air conditioning used a complex system of underground water canals in combination with windtowers. This method later developed into evaporative cooling, which is a mechanism that lowers the interior temperature when cool water comes in contact with warm air. In the United States, evaporative cooling was first used in Arizona, specifically in 1908, by Oscar Palmer Sr. Even though greenhouses continued to be cooled by natural or fan ventilation methods, it wasn't until 1954 that evaporative cooling took off and was used more often.

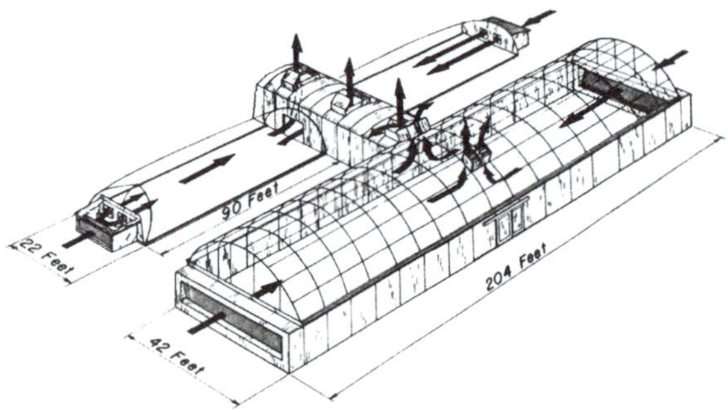


**Fig. 04a Evaporative cooling pads in greenhouses to** decrease high temperatures, Saadiyat project, Abu Dhabi, 1972, by Dr. Merle Jensen, Courtesy of UAE National Library and Archives.

Fig. 04b Drawing of greenhouses with ventilation and covered structure showing air flow, Saadiyat project, Abu Dhabi, 1972, by Dr. Merle Jensen, Courtesy of UAE National Library and Archives.

*Ibid.*

*Ibid., 49.*

*Ibid.*

*Ibid.*

## Al Saadiyat

The first greenhouses built in the UAE were models originally imported from the University of Arizona in 1967. The university was working on a unique project: fresh vegetables grown in a controlled environment in the desert using small quantities of desalinated seawater. The possibility of having fresh vegetables grown in the UAE intrigued the late Sheikh Zayed bin Sultan Al Nahyan. And so, the project began with a simple phone call from Abu Dhabi and led to the invitation of the director of the research station at the university to visit the emirate, eventually becoming the Saadiyat project of greenhouses. Even though vegetables were grown seasonally in the UAE at the time — using traditional agricultural methods in Al Ain, Al Dhaid, Liwa, Ras Al Khaimah, and Fujairah, which were rife with groundwater — large quantities of fresh vegetables were usually air-freighted into Abu Dhabi from other countries such as Lebanon. Many scientists believed that arid regions, such as the Gulf, could produce large quantities of food if fresh water could be consistently supplied, and Abu Dhabi served as the perfect candidate for the development of such a program. Scientists at the University of Arizona's Environmental Research Laboratory (ERL) were at the forefront of the development of power-water-food concepts for desert communities throughout the world, including the aforementioned Abu Dhabi experiment.

When the project was operational, one of the first vegetable crops to be harvested was cucumbers: a vegetable not often grown in Abu Dhabi due to the presence of severe plant viruses common to open-field production. It quickly became a favorite for locals. Yields for the Saadiyat greenhouse generally were much higher than field culture, which were attributed, in part, to the more ideal growing conditions in the greenhouse as well as the warm climate and the high year-round sun exposure (Figs. 04, 05).

## Greenhouses in Context

While the seed was planted with the Saadiyat project, strides in greenhouse design and architectural interventions cannot go unmentioned, especially when it comes to UAE-based experimentation with technology, climate control, and materials. Institutions at the forefront of local research in greenhouse design are most notably United Arab Emirates University (UAEU), International Center for Biosaline Agriculture (ICBA), and Silal.

A research project at UAEU, specifically at their experimental farm in Al Foah, used two greenhouses that were mirrored in layout and offered a unique approach to controlled-environment agriculture. Containing eight separate plots to experiment with, the form is bookended by two semi-circular chambers that trap the cool air that the fans pull out of the greenhouse when the evaporative cooling pads are on. This optimizes airflow and efficiency without having to re-cool fresh air.

Between 2019 and 2021, ICBA in Dubai experimented with a "low-cost proof-of-concept greenhouse design," which aimed to produce food crops by depending solely on seawater. With walls built out of salt-resistant pozzolan bricks, the greenhouse relied on an innovative pozzolan-based evaporative system to cool down the space. Fresh water for irrigation was produced by desalinated water using solar energy. A specially designed hydroponic system was also integrated, harnessing humidity from the internal air.

At Silal's innovation oasis in Al Ain, open-field trial sites and experimental structures are provided for research on crops grown in controlled environments. These sites feature an array of greenhouses equipped with a variety of cooling systems, automated irrigation and fertilization, and sensors to measure temperature, humidity, soil moisture, and other parameters, contributing to advanced analysis. Greenhouses are equipped with sensors like laser, fluorescence, and thermal imaging cameras as well as automated spray, fertilizer application systems, and crop monitoring tools, enhancing the facility's capacity for studying plant characteristics. Noteworthy would be the blueberry greenhouses, equipped with evaporative cooling pads and an internal expandable net house structure, nestled within the polycarbon-

*International Center for Biosaline Agriculture (ICBA) is an international, not-for-profit applied agricultural research center located in Dubai. ICBA works on identifying, testing, and introducing resource-efficient, climate-smart crops and technologies that are best suited to different regions affected by salinity, water scarcity, and drought.*

*Silal is working closely with farmers and local food suppliers to boost production and ensure consistent access and delivery of nourishment to the people of the UAE and is supporting the development of an enabling ecosystem for AgriTech in Abu Dhabi. It is conducting research through partnerships and collaborations with the R&D sector to develop implementable AgriTech.*

*Khalil Ammar, "Saline/Sea Water Greenhouse," **International Center for Biosaline Agriculture,** accessed September 3, 2024, https://www.biosaline.org/experiments/experiment-1.*

*Ibid.*

Fig. 05 Cucumber produce at the Saadiyat project, Abu Dhabi, 1976, by Dr. Merle Jensen, UAE National Library and Archives.

Fig. 06 Unrepaired greenhouse in Khor Fakkan, Sharjah. Photo by author.

Fig. 07 Abandoned greenhouse in Liwa, Abu Dhabi. Photo by author.

ate shell, further shielding the bushes from the harsh desert sun. In addition to greenhouse experimentation, Silal also provides guidance to local farmers by integrating their systems into the local agricultural infrastructure, enhancing their output, and ensuring a diverse landscape of locally produced crops.

**Flipping the Script**

While temperatures in arid regions such as the UAE can be adequate for traditional agriculture during winter seasons, many issues are still faced. Some of those challenges include a lack of freshwater, adequate soil, sand storms, and winds from the sea heavy with salt. Those threats make it impossible to grow vegetables outdoors along desert sea coasts.

During fieldwork, an unexpected finding was the number of abandoned greenhouses across the landscape. This left us questioning their fate and what could have led them to this state, where, perhaps, their decay offers clues about changing landscapes and the passage of time.

One of the farms visited in Khor Fakkan bears witness to the destruction of greenhouses by a recent rainstorm that the UAE weathered in April 2024. Badr, a farm owner in Khor Fakkan, mentioned that the repairs were too expensive and that he'd rather spend that money on irrigation mechanisms, fertilizer, and seeds used in open-field farming. Despite the greenhouse's ability to grow fresh fruits and vegetables all year round, Badr was one of many who chose not to repair the significant damages.

While revisiting sites in Al Zubair, we witnessed a drastic change in one particular farm. The greenhouses that were thriving in August were stripped of their enclosures and stood in the middle of the landscape as bare frames. Mohamed, the farm owner, said that they will be moving to another location due to a rent increase. Even though they only had one functioning green house when visiting in late October (to grow gherkins), he was uncertain of what the future holds for it.

Other instances in Liwa and Al Ain offered an interesting insight. Even though one of them seemed to have just crumbled, with burnt tomatoes on the ground from the sun, the other was used to still grow crops without a full enclosure. When asked about their demise, Ahmed, an Abu Dhabi farmer, referred to the lack of sufficient expertise when it comes to the required maintenance to keep them up and running. Greenhouse models are often imported, with designs that are not fit for the local environment and, as a result, fall apart quicker than others, especially if their materials become brittle in the sun. Others are erected by expensive contractors that are quite demanding in terms of cost in the long run and the yield does not justify the amount of money spent. (Figs. 06-10)

Fig. 08 Abandoned greenhouse in Liwa, Abu Dhabi. Photo by author.

### Unanswered Questions and Redefined Perspectives

Despite multiple strides in the technological advancement of food production, the architecture of these spaces and their spatial attributes remain an unexplored endeavor. During the fieldwork phase of the project, nine typologies of greenhouses were recorded to be used in the UAE (Fig. 11). The Parral greenhouse, for example, dominated the landscape and was used on multiple farms, repeatedly and regardless of the context. Others, such as the geodesic domes, were more technologically advanced and, as a result, more nuanced and used sparingly. It is also interesting to note that the same architectural form performed differently depending on the emirate where it was located. A greenhouse in Al Ain, for example, was used (and only able) to grow cucumbers. However, the same exact model was used in Khor Fakkan to grow a variety of crops, all year round, from cucumbers to tomatoes to green peppers. This begs the question of what to do when cultivated crops in greenhouses are divorced from their context and what should the response be to this predicament.

Fig. 09 Functioning Greenhouse in August in Al Zubair, Sharjah. Photo by author.

Fig. 10 Abandoned Greenhouse in October in Al Zubair, Sharjah. Photo by Ola Allouz.

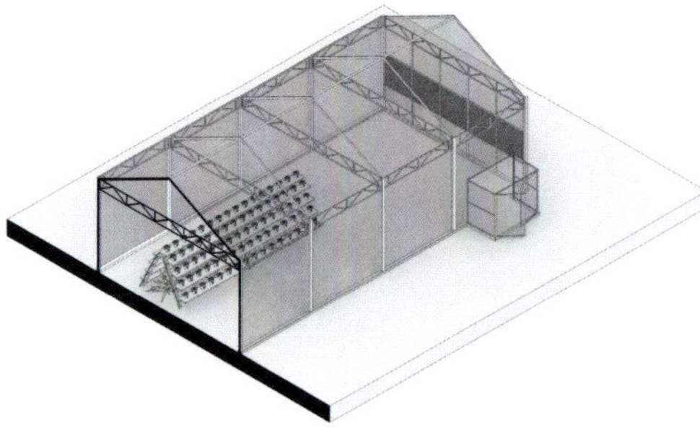

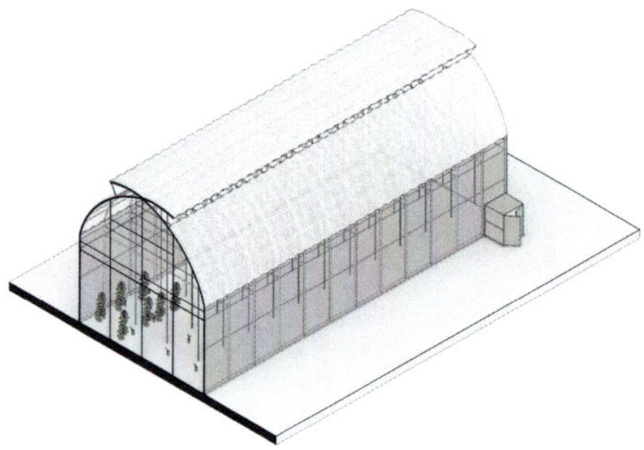

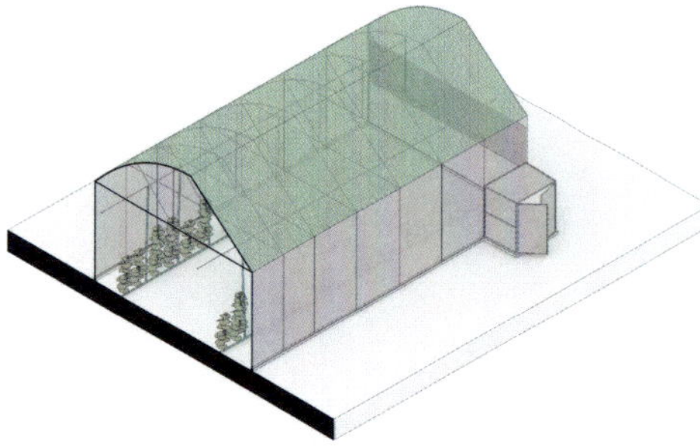

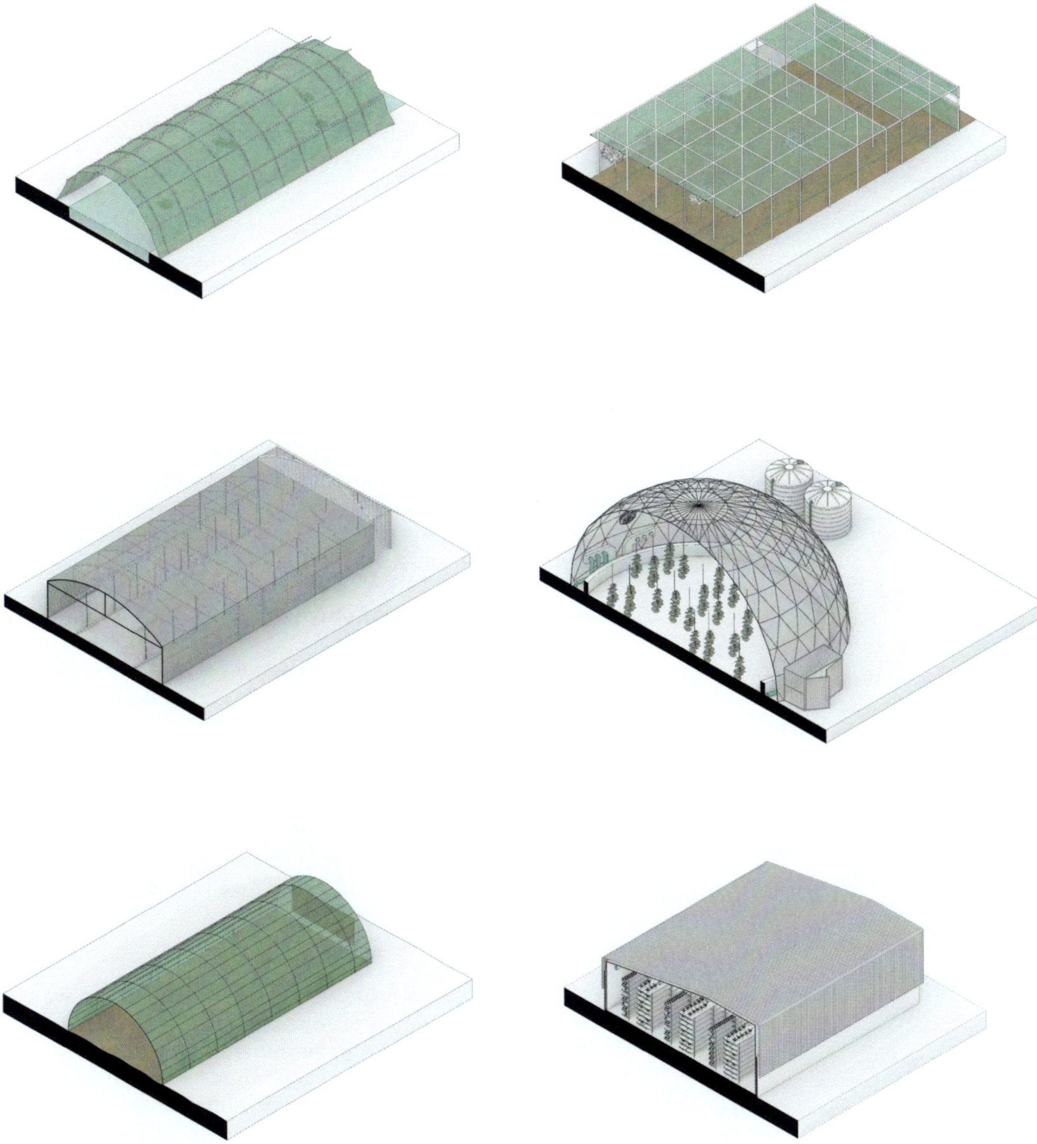

Fig. 11 Nine Greenhouse Categories in the UAE. Drawn by Noor Hamdan and Sara AlMahmoud.

*Architectural form and various models were tested using the digital tool developed by the team (Dimitri Brand, Kit Elsworth and Saeran Vasanthkumar). See:* ***It's Not the Heat, it's the Humidity: Designing for Crop Growth and Human Comfort in Desert Greenhouses*** *by Dimitri Brand and Kit Elsworth.*

*The kits fall along a scale ranging from easy, medium, to difficult based on the architectural form and the associated mechanics of its different architectural parts. Those building methods have been tested in Zayed University Dubai and can be replicated in different parts of the UAE.*

*See:* ***It's Not the Heat, it's the Humidity: Designing for Crop Growth and Human Comfort in Desert Greenhouses*** *by Dimitri Brand and Kit Elsworth.*

**Identified Challenges:**

- Lack of expertise
- Budget constraints
- Limited output and insufficient yield
- Underperforming cooling methods
- Water waste
- Not contextual

As a result, the greenhouse's architectural form was explored throughout this project in order to come up with solutions that are not only contextual but respond to the crop that it intends to grow. A variety of architectural forms were tested and retested in order to further understand their adaptability to specific locations in the UAE. Those experiments proved that architectural form does play a role in the greenhouse's performance. With all of these various models, reformulating and reintegrating the greenhouse model into the Emirati landscape circled back to an architectural question.

**Architectural Breakdown**

In order to further analyze and reconfigure the greenhouse as a typology for arid climates, the greenhouse's kit-of-parts was broken down into its basic architectural elements (roof, wall, floor, tools, and materials). Resulting in endless combinations of architectural expression, those assemblies offered a variety of responses to the identified challenges mentioned above. Each of those kits offers an affordable approach that could be easily assembled.

*Roof*

Within the context of this project, this element was divided into two separate categories: the "formal" roof attached to the greenhouse and the added "external shade" structure. Those offer different outcomes when it comes to the interior environment of the greenhouse and its performance. The "formal" roof helps with air circulation and mitigates the accumulation of hot air. It also reduces heat gain based on the angle of incidence to the sun. Meanwhile, the "external shade" decreases UV and overall sun exposure, offering shade, and aids in maintaining the cooler interior climate. This factor is also influenced by the shade net's form and net density. Using the tool to verify those results, we have tested a variety of shade forms, in order to explore shade orientations. However, the type of plant in each greenhouse will dictate the amount of sunlight needed. Eggplant, for example, needs direct sun exposure for significantly longer hours when compared to lettuce. Additionally, the shade is most effective when it's active (retractable), despite the slight increase in construction costs.

### *Wall*

Walls in greenhouses regulate the interior environment by managing light, heat, and airflow, especially in regard to orientation. While testing assemblies, we have found that greenhouse models performed better when the broad face is positioned north-south. This limited heat gain from the western sun at the end of the day. We have also experimented with the use of CMU blocks as a plinth for the greenhouse which could help moderate temperature fluctuations. This also aids in cutting down the percentage of transparent material that encloses the greenhouse, further managing sun exposure. However, seeing that planting takes place a meter away from the edge of the greenhouse's walls, this might pose an issue to some plants that require direct sun and, in turn, the plinth would need to be adjusted in height, accordingly. While the materials used for walls in this project mainly depend on polycarbonate, experiments were also conducted with UV-blocking polythene and green shade net. The former significantly influenced energy efficiency, plant health, and overall functionality of the greenhouse.

### *Floor*

Utilizing geothermal mass provides a sustainable and naturally available method for temperature stabilization by tapping into the Earth's consistent thermal energy. Soil, here, acts as an insulator, maintaining a more stable temperature compared to surface air. Subterranean spaces benefit from the Earth's thermal mass, which absorbs and retains heat during the day and releases it slowly at night, reducing the need for artificial cooling.

Additionally, the surface area-to-floor area ratio plays a variable role in the thermal performance of the greenhouse. While a square plan has a better surface area to volume ratio than a rectangular one, the rectangular form performed better while testing, which could be attributed to heat gain on the western face. Other tested structures with lower ratios, such as the fully enclosed circular form, minimized heat gain and loss, creating more energy-efficient and naturally temperate environments.

### *Tools and Materials*

In order to achieve cool internal temperatures that are suitable both for humans and plants, this project mainly depends on evaporative cooling pads and fans. While the former are relatively water intensive, in terms of usage, the project looks into experimenting with seawater on the pads to save the use of freshwater. Those pads could be rinsed at the end of the day to preserve their efficacy. Other cooling methods that were experimented with were night cooling methodologies and the inclusion of interior bodies of water.

## Kits and Assemblies

In putting together the kit-of-parts, we tested a wide array of combinations and cross-referenced climatic information from a variety of locations in the UAE. Over the course of the project, Al Ain offered the best results overall, while downtown Dubai and Sharjah had the most difficult parameters to be mitigated, such as increased humidity levels.

While an endless number of forms were tested by the digital tool, performance here is quantified based on the results we have received, especially when it comes to the number of hours the interior of the greenhouse is below 30°C in a year.

Below are some of the assemblies we tested, along with interesting findings along the way:

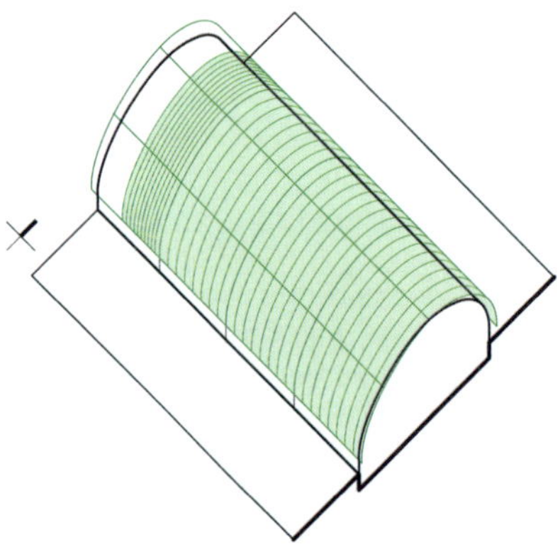

Fig. A: Axonometric drawing of Experimental Assembly 1. Drawn by author.

***Experimental Assembly 1:***

Roof: Arch + Retractable shade
Wall: Vertical polycarbonate
Floor: Grade level or below grade

Based on a commonly found form during the fieldwork phase, the arched roof, not surprisingly, performed better than a flat or pitched one. However, when dug into the ground, the extra thermal mass actually causes the assembly to perform worse when the shade is retracted. The heat gain was better mitigated by extending the shade net, while, simultaneously, digging into the ground.

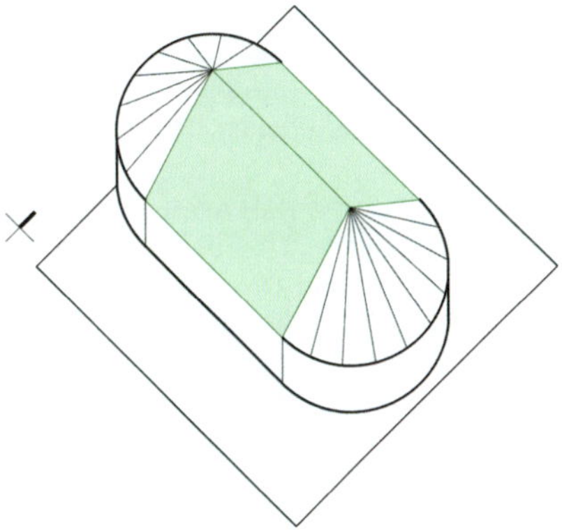

Fig. B: Axonometric drawing of Experimental Assembly 2. Drawn by author.

***Experimental Assembly 2:***

Roof: Pill-shape
Wall: Curved polycarbonate
Floor: Grade level

This form was the best performing as it reduces the amount of time the sun is shining directly on a broad surface of the greenhouse, even when unshaded. To push this experiment further, this assembly performed even better when supplemented with a full shade. This resulted in a mere fraction of days during the year when the temperature was above optimal plant growth level.

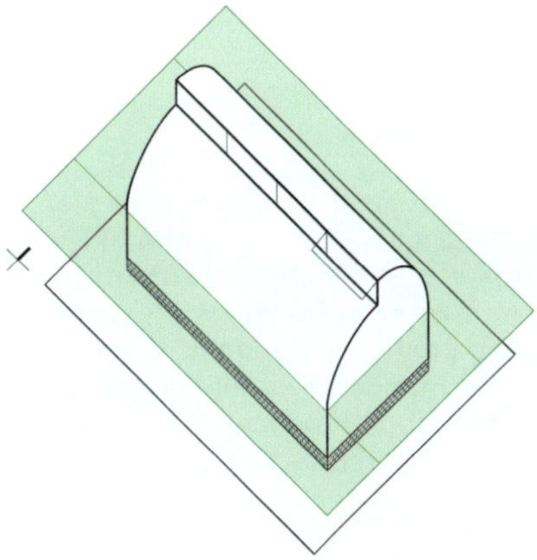

Fig. C: Axonometric drawing of Experimental Assembly 3. Drawn by author.

***Experimental Assembly 3:***

Roof: Broken arch + Perimeter shade
Wall: Vertical polycarbonate
Floor: Above grade with CMU blocks

While the broken arch roof performed almost the same as the regular arch, we wanted to explore formal options for ventilation that didn't have a negative effect on efficiency and performance. Here, panels could be operable for enhanced airflow at specific times of the year, such as fall and spring. What we also found surprising was that performance was enhanced by incorporating CMU and simultaneously shading it by extending the perimeter shade.

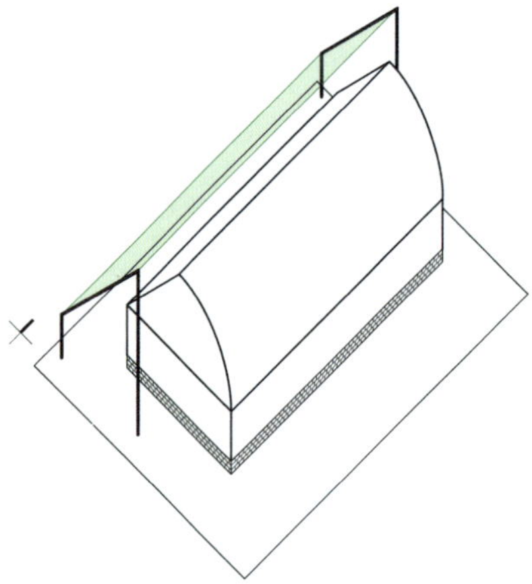

Fig. D: Axonometric drawing of Experimental Assembly 4. Drawn by author.

***Experimental Assembly 4:***

Roof: Half arch + Half shade
Wall: Vertical polycarbonate
Floor: Above grade with CMU blocks

With the combination of the half arch and the west-facing external shade, this assembly offered insights into orienting the greenhouse in the UAE. Not only did the shade protect the interior environment from excessive heat gain, but this combination performed better in comparison to the same form facing south.

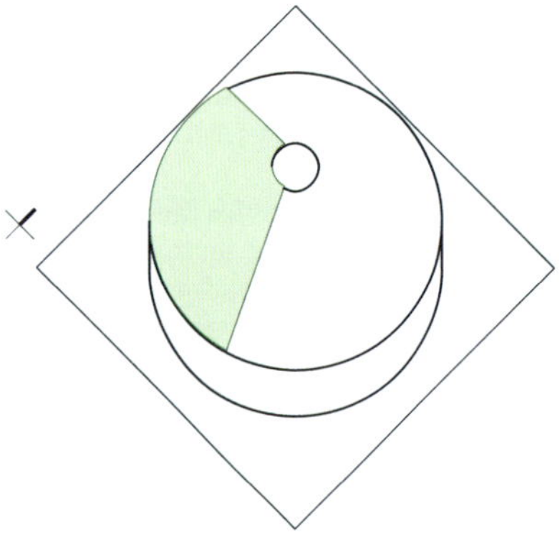

Fig. E: Axonometric drawing of Experimental Assembly 5. Drawn by author.

***Experimental Assembly 5:***

Roof: Circular Roof
Wall: Curved polycarbonate
Floor: Grade level

This experiment explores an alternative plan form: the circle. Closely following the pill-shaped kit, this assembly outperforms the arched roof, in terms of efficiency. Shading the west-facing portion helped enhance the assembly's performance. Creating a retractable opening at the top of the form also allows for an opportunity for ventilation.

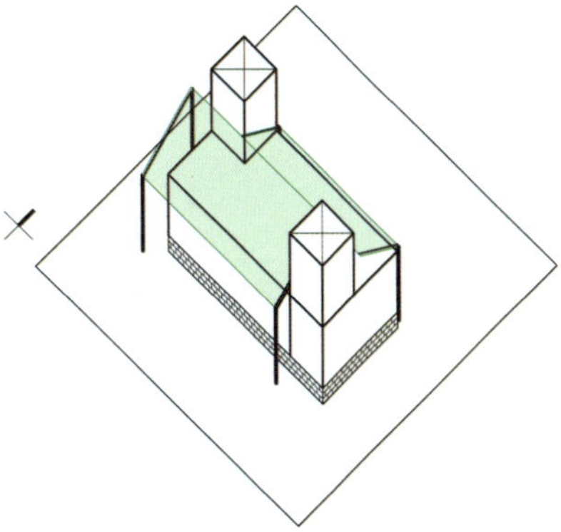

Fig. F: Axonometric drawing of Experimental Assembly 6. Drawn by author.

***Experimental Assembly 6:***

Roof: Barjeel
Wall: Vertical polycarbonate
Floor: Grade level

The *barjeel*, also known as a windtower or wind catcher, is an architectural form that is widely used in the region for ventilation and enhanced airflow. Incorporating this method could potentially cut down on expensive fan usage. We expect that a fan assist would be necessary for times when the wind is stagnant and not available. With that being said, the UAE, generally, has very consistent winds, which can be harnessed.

**Conclusion**

From the specularia of ancient Rome to today's high-tech climate-controlled structures, greenhouses have long reflected a variety of approaches when it comes to creating optimal interior environments for cultivation. Their evolution reveals not only advancements in architecture, engineering, and technology, but also shifts in agricultural practices, food security strategies, and environmental awareness.

As we face the challenges of climate change and resource scarcity, greenhouses remain vital tools for sustainable growing methods, bridging historical knowledge, local ingenuity, and future innovations. While this project experiments with architectural form as a binding agent with future speculation, the original kit was developed from local fieldwork, documenting the progress made toward food security in the UAE. By studying those forms, learning from them, and reformulating their parts, we argue that combining these kits is an architectural problem, not only in their need to be contextual, but also in terms of optimization, systematization, accessibility, aestheticization, and urban proliferation and integration. While these assemblies are experimental, their combinatory logic still provides interesting insights into how architectural form can be altered and reformulated for enhanced food production in arid environments. As such, in the UAE, food production is closely intertwined with architecture, creating a unique approach to exploring the notion of food security.

# It's Not the Heat, it's the Humidity: *Designing for Crop Growth and Human Comfort in Desert Greenhouses*

Dimitri Brand and Kit Elsworth

***Ingredients***

Seawater
Fan
Shading
Evaporative Cooling
Air Flow
Filter

---

*P. O. Fanger,* ***Thermal Comfort: Analysis and Applications in Environmental Engineering*** *(New York: McGraw-Hill, 1970).*

---

*The team was led by Holesum Studio — Dimitri Brand, Kit Elsworth, and Saeran Vasanthakumar under the direction of Azza Aboualam.*

---

*The tool uses Rhino for geometry and is built in Grasshopper using Ladybug, Openstudio, and custom Python scripts. The tool as it stands requires a working knowledge of these programs but has been simplified to the point where it is manageable by a typical design professional.*

---

*Philip Davies and Charlie Paton, "The Seawater Greenhouse: Background, Theory and Current Status,"* ***International Journal of Low-Carbon Technologies*** *1, no. 2 (2006): 183–90, https://doi.org/10.1093/ijlct/1.2.183.*

During the team's fieldwork at various greenhouses in the United Arab Emirates (UAE), we found something encouraging, and under further inspection, perhaps not altogether surprising. Even though these greenhouses were warmer and more humid than the typical indoor comfort levels (20–22°C with 50% humidity) at 30+°C with very high humidity, they still felt like thermal oases in the desert.

This experience, as part of the research conducted for the National Pavilion UAE at the 2025 Venice Biennale, put the team on a path to see how this effect could be quantified and harnessed in the support of architecture. As designers, we wanted to find a way to use the phenomena we see in local greenhouses as part of a larger architectural vocabulary while also improving the ability to option future iterations that are conceived of as spaces for both plants and people to thrive.

The team's project was to mine existing greenhouse technology used locally to develop an adaptive tool that could test different greenhouse designs in any region of the UAE and similar climates. The goal was to develop a kit-of-parts that can be assembled specifically for different locations, with an eye toward overall efficiency. To gauge and monitor the impact of these combinations, we developed a digital tool that could model the performance of each of our implemented greenhouse variations. This project is not the first exploration of these inputs and their associated outputs in this context: it builds on various hot-weather greenhouse projects including the 2006 Seawater Greenhouse by Charlie Paton and Phillip Andrew Davies, who mathematically modeled the performance of a greenhouse in Abu Dhabi, which was later constructed. Our tool is unique in its breadth of inputs as well as adaptive capabilities in which the geometry of the project can be easily edited and retested.

**What Is in a Number?**

To understand the reason for our experience in the greenhouse, one must first understand how it is that humans experience heat.

When we check our weather apps, we are generally met with two temperatures: the ambient air temperature and a "feels like" metric. While the former is a measure of the air temperature in an environment, the latter takes other factors into account to describe our experience of the environment. This "feels like" temperature takes into account a particularly important indicator of the human experience of heat — the relative humidity. This is especially important in hot climates because the human body's natural cooling method is through sweating, or evaporative cooling, and the higher the humidity, the less of this natural cooling method can take place. Additionally, wind speed is factored into the "real feel" because the more air that moves across our bodies, the more evaporation can take place and the cooler we'll feel.

However, even the "real feel" measurement is an incomplete reflection of human satisfaction as it relates to the thermal environment. For human satisfaction, we look at what is known as "thermal comfort." Historically, thermal comfort has been dependent on the metrics used in the "feels like" method: air temperature, humidity, and air speed, but also the additional metrics of radiant temperature, clothing, and metabolic rate. The human experience of temperature is a localized and relative one. Meaning, if we are in the shade with a breeze blowing, wearing loose breathable clothing, and standing next to a cool surface (such as a large rock that has cooled overnight), we will be much more comfortable than if on the same day we are in the full sun, on hot asphalt, wearing a jacket, in still air – even if the temperature and humidity are the same in both environments. Additionally, in naturally ventilated buildings our thermal comfort is related to the outdoor temperature, meaning if there is a higher temperature outside, we are comfortable at a higher temperature inside.

**What Do Plants Need?**

Cucumber: 17.5–30°C

Blueberries: 30°C +/- 3°C

Eggplant: 27–37°C

Corn: 24–31°C

Zucchini: 21–35°C

Cauliflower: 16–24°C

Thermal comfort is usually a human-centric metric; however, the primary user in a greenhouse is plants. Much of the world thinks of the greenhouse as functioning in colder climates to extend the growing season on either side of the warm summer months. In the UAE, farmers are dealing with the inverse.

Approximately, during nine months out of the year, the mean high temperature in the UAE is above the general upper limit for growing a number of vegetables and fruits found locally. That means there is a short growing season. For a crop like zucchini, one of the most heat-tolerant crops, the UAE is too hot for it to be cultivated seven months out of the year. While some crops can tolerate temperatures outside this range for a short period, it generally has neg-

*Radiant heat is defined as heat transmitted by radiation in contrast to heat transmitted by conduction or convection. In this context, it is further defined by the temperature of the surfaces in the space. Operative temperature is a metric that includes heat transferred by convection and radiation and is often used in thermal comfort analysis.* ***Merriam-Webster.com Dictionary****, s.v. "radiant heat," accessed December 20, 2024, https://www.merriam-webster.com/dictionary/radiant%20heat.*

*Metabolic rate is defined as the rate at which heat is given off by an organism at complete rest. In this context, it is further defined by the actions of the user.* ***Merriam-Webster.com Dictionary****, s.v. "basal metabolic rate," accessed December 20, 2024, https://www.merriam-webster.com/dictionary/basal%20metabolic%20rate.*

*These temperature ranges were extracted from a variety of sources and research and have been broadly confirmed by the local agricultural sector; B. R. Strain and E. L. Higginbotham, "Temperature Acclimation of Mesophyll Conductance in Cowpea,"* ***Physiologia Plantarum*** *89, no. 2 (1993): 193–198, https://doi.org/10.1111/j.1399-3054.1993.tb01737.x.*

*Yunpu Zheng et al., "The Optimal Temperature for the Growth of Blueberry (Vaccinium corymbosum L.),"* ***Pakistan Journal of Botany 49****, no. 3 (2017): 965-979., https://doi.org/10.1515/fhort-2017-0008.*

*Rolf Müller, "Advancing Sustainable Energy Transitions: A Multi-Level Perspective,"* ***Environmental Impact Assessment Review*** *110 (2024): 106796, https://doi.org/10.1016/j.eiar.2024.106796.*

*Margot E. J. G. T. Deguines et al., "Pollination and Global Change: Examining the Effect of Climate Change on Pollinator-Dependent Crops,"* ***Agriculture, Ecosystems & Environment*** *209 (2015): 106-113, https://doi.org/10.1016/j.agee.2015.04.004.*

*Deep Roots Project, "Veggie Temperature Tolerances," accessed January 15, 2025, https://www.deep-roots-project.org/grow-your-own-food-all/veggie-temperature-tolerances#gsc.tab=0.*

ative effects on their growth. For example, corn is viable up to 42°C. But when exposed to maximum daytime temperatures above 35°C, the performance of the crop is irrevocably damaged in both yield and kernel size even when returned to below that temperature. Additionally, even if temperatures are amenable for the plants' growth, the evaporation rate in high heat can make irrigation both cost and resource prohibitive.

From a technical perspective, using a greenhouse to heat a space is an easier problem to solve than using it to cool a space. There is an alignment between a plant's essential resource – the sun – and the heat it provides to the greenhouse's environment. In hot climates, however, the sun's heat can't be harnessed. Instead, it must be overcome by the hot-weather greenhouses that must cool the space to extend the growing season into the hotter months as well as preserve a precious resource: freshwater. The challenge of the hot-weather greenhouse is further complicated by high humidity levels. This reduces the effectiveness of evaporative cooling, for the same reason sweating is less effective for humans.

*Ibid.*

***Oxford English Dictionary**: Greenhouse, n, A glass building in which plants are grown that need protection from cold weather.*

*Varies depending on location across the UAE.*

*Muhammad Waqas, Wang Xiukang, Syed Zafar, Mehmood Ali Noor, Hafiz Hussain, Muhammad Azher Nawaz, and Muhammad Farooq, "Thermal Stresses in Maize: Effects and Management Strategies," Plants 10, no. 2 (2021): 293, https://doi.org/10.3390/plants10020293.*

*Food and Agriculture Organization of the United Nations (FAO), "Chapter 2: World Food and Agriculture - Statistical Yearbook 2022," accessed January 15, 2025, https://www.fao.org/4/s2022e/s2022e02.htm.*

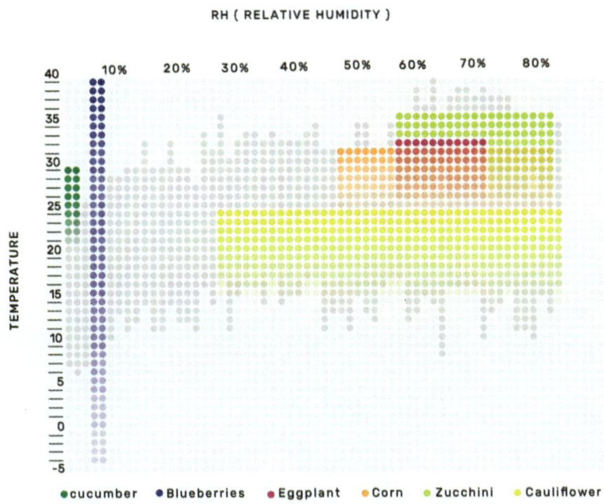


Fig. 00 Temperature and Humidity of Selected Crops. Graph drawn by Alya Alrushdi.

*Due to the novel construction of greenhouses, there are limits to how well this digital tool can verify how all the factors come together. To accurately test the performance of the kit, real-world testing needs to occur, at nearly full scale resulting in gathered data to create an even more accurate model, thereby improving its applicability.*

## What Is in Our Kit-of-Parts?

In order to develop energy-efficient greenhouse spaces for both plants and people in the UAE's hot climate, the team developed a kit-of-parts based on and expanding upon the cooling strategies currently in use in the local agricultural sector.

The UAE is aptly positioned as a lab for testing these hot-weather cooling strategies because of its two main climatic conditions: hot and dry, and hot and humid. The interior of the country, such as Al Ain, one of the UAE's oldest farming regions, has a summer ambient air temperature higher than the more populated coastal areas, but a much lower relative humidity during the hottest months.

A hot-weather greenhouse climate modeling tool was then developed by the team to explore greenhouse combinations that work for these varied climates. It looks at the effects of different modifications to the form of the greenhouse, such as roof shape, wall height, and aspect ratio, in relation to the material and construction strategies listed in the figures below. The tool allows the user to combine these approaches and maps the interactions of the various parts and strategies.

PAR is the light band plants use to perform photosynthesis.

NOAA Science on a Sphere, "ClimateBits: Solar Radiation," accessed January 15, 2025, https://sos.noaa.gov/catalog/datasets/climatebits-solar-radiation/#:~:text=According%20to%20the%20UCAR%20COMET,gamma%20rays%20and%20radio%20waves.

Second Sky is a technology that embeds a unique additive to greenhouse covers during the manufacturing process. It blocks peak NIR heat without compromising PAR light transmission https://secondsky.com/

The tool has the ability to filter out the light spectrum from anywhere from 0–100% and as such is adaptable to a range of materials.

R-value is the insulative property of a material, where the higher the value the better the insulation. It is defined as the inverse of the u-value, or the rate of thermal transmittance through a material, where the lower the number the higher insulation properties.

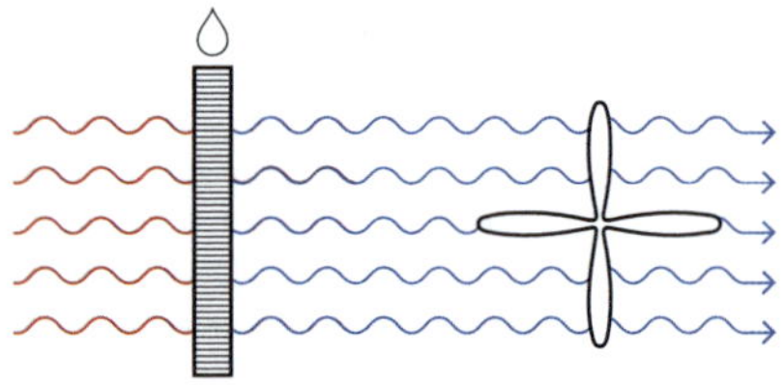

**Fig.01 Evaporative cooling**

This is a method that cools interior spaces by drawing dry exterior air through evaporative cooling pads. Typically, fans on one end of the greenhouse pull air over cardboard or metal evaporative pads that have a stream of water dripping onto them. When the water evaporates, it takes the energy (heat) out of the air.

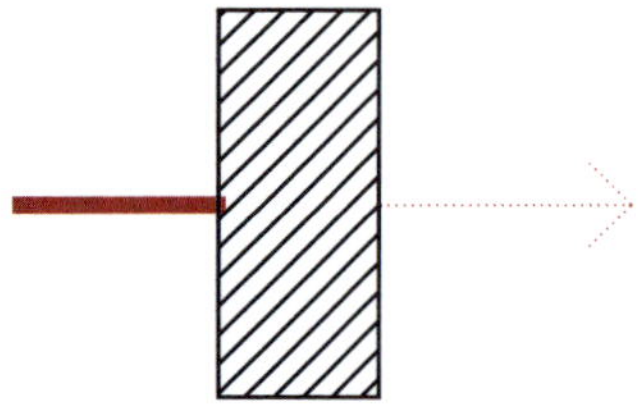

**Fig.02 Thermal isolation**

Thermally isolating materials provide protection from the heat of the exterior environment. While greenhouse wall and roof materials come in various forms, this project experiments with polycarbonate as an option in the kit. Polycarbonate offers a range of insulation values, from a double wall (which traps air between two thin sheets of polycarbonate) with an R-value of approximately 1.8 K·m2/W, to a five wall (which traps air in a crisscrossed structure) with an R value of approximately 3.2 K·m2/W. Additionally, locally available materials such as concrete blocks or rammed earth can be used and paired with insulating materials if beneficial to the project's performance.

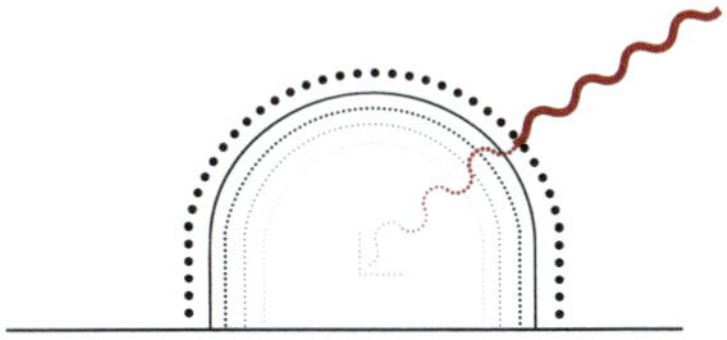

**Fig.03 Static/active exterior shading**

This method involves either static or extendable and retractable shading techniques that change depending on the time of day and heat levels. As plants have a certain level of required photosynthetically active radiation (PAR), the shades must be designed to allow enough light in. Many greenhouses in the UAE have permanent exterior shades to always reduce the sun and others include operable interior shades to shield the plants from the most direct sunlight during the hot months of the summer. However, exterior shades are more effective because they allow for variable sunlight levels while also blocking the sun's radiation before it enters the envelope of the greenhouse.

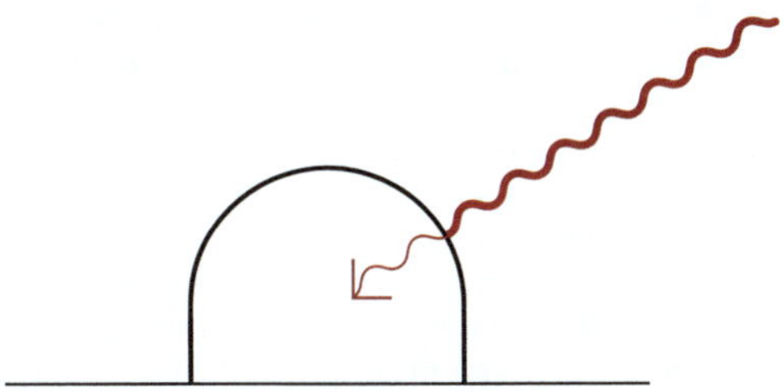

**Fig.04 Sun energy filtering**

Like shading, this method filters out the sun's energy, but in a more selective fashion. The sun's energy is expressed in its wavelength: 99.8% of the sun's energy is emitted in the bandwidth of 20-2500 nanometers (nm). Within this bandwidth there are several sub-bands, including ultraviolet at 250-350 nm which accounts for about 7% of the sun's energy (and is easily wholly filtered out). Visible light exists at 380-780 nm and accounts for 43% of its energy. Visible light cannot be wholly filtered out because it also contains the photosynthetically active radiation (PAR) that plants use for photosynthesis. Infrared is at 780 nm and above, accounts for 49% of energy, and can be mostly filtered out by locally developed materials such as SecondSky by iyris or the use of green polycarbonate.

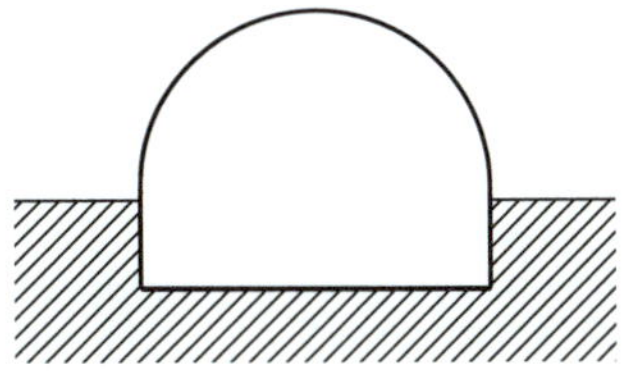

**Fig.05 Ground contact/thermal mass**

The deeper into the ground one digs, the lower and more stable the temperature of the soil. In the UAE, the benefits of this method plateaus at about seven meters. One could use buried horizontal ground tubes of geothermal wells to access this cooler ground at seven meters and below. Shallower depths still provide an appreciable benefit and are more easily constructed.

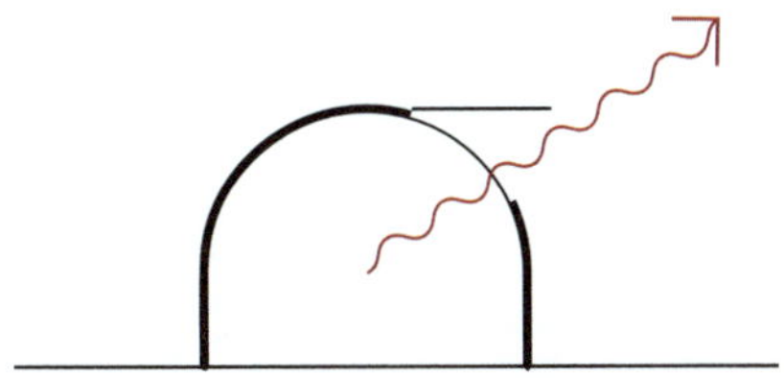

**Fig.06 Natural ventilation**

Natural ventilation allows for the heat of the greenhouse to be released when the exterior environment is cooler than the interior. This method is used most during autumn when the heat of the summer has built up in interior spaces and the exterior temperature has slightly decreased. This time of year benefits from moving as much exterior air as possible into the space to enhance airflow.

## What Is in a Metric?

The custom digital tool the team created modeled the performance of the greenhouses in various conditions in the UAE in order to test the efficacy of kit combinations tailored to hot climates. To measure the effectiveness of the different strategies for cooling across the year, we opted to track the difference between indoor and outdoor temperatures by examining the number of hours and days with temperatures exceeding our desired temperature, both inside the greenhouse and outside in the exterior environment. Additionally, we monitored what combinations of parts would require the lowest resources to operate. Therefore, we tracked the overall usage of fans and water pumps, which are used in evaporative cooling, to measure the relative electricity and water usage of each strategy against the others.

To determine our desired temperatures, we used the thermal comfort tool developed by the University of California, Berkeley's Center for the Built Environment (CBE), which is based on ASHRAE 55 and EIN 16798 standards. Since these standards were created for a primarily Western user group where temperature expectations are lower, we chose the upper limit of the CBE comfort tool as our target for thermal comfort. We assumed an air speed of 1 m/s, a standing relaxed user wearing typical summer indoor clothes standing an adequate distance from the greenhouse walls (which would have a higher radiant temperature). We compared these findings with the upper tolerance limit for many crops we identified in (Fig. 00), resulting in our determination of an upper limit of 30°C as the standard by which to measure the kit combinations success.

Additionally, on the evening of October 28, 2024, the team went out for dinner in Dubai and experienced pleasant thermal comfort and saw other customers choosing to eat outside and take leisurely walks. The temperature was 32°C with 57% relative humidity, a steady breeze and no sun exposure. This was firmly outside the thermal comfort standards set by ASHRAE 55 as outlined by the CBE tool, but clearly comfortable for the local population. This indicated that, with the correct selections, there is an even wider range of overlap between human thermal comfort and crop viability than we are using in our work.

*This was based on recent climate data from weather stations/airports collected from 2009–2023 and sourced via https://climate.onebuilding.org*

*These are standards used throughout the building industry in the United States (ASHRAE) and Europe (EIN).*

*For our model, we set a maximum air temperature of 30°C and the air speed to a maximum of 1 m/s when air movement is present with local control (meaning users can always increase the air speed to 1 m/s in their local area with controllable fans). We set the max interior relative humidity up to 80% as a baseline, but when the humidity is particularly high outside the humidity can reach upwards of 95% for limited periods, this still lands us near the upper region thermal comfort parameters of the CBE tool and most crops can withstand (and some thrive) at this humidity for limited periods of time.*

With those metrics in mind, the greenhouse kits performed the best in Al Ain, where 47.5% of the year's hours, or 4,159 hours, were above the threshold of 30°C. Here, we could reduce the number of hours above 30°C to only 4.4% of the hours in a year (389 hours). In locations like Sharjah, which is a more difficult location because of the higher humidity, we still had significant, albeit more limited, success with a reduction from 3,791 hours above 30°C to 1,618 hours, or 18.4%. In all successful combinations, we saw a reduction in the overall high temperature from approximately 48°C to 35°C.

The tool may be increasingly applicable in the UAE because development and urban growth there are currently pushing inland toward less humid zones, where the kits work particularly well. Using weather data in the digital modeling tool, the greenhouse kit performed worse in Abu Dhabi than in less humid Al Wathba, which is approximately 10 km further inland and is rapidly developing. We see a 58% reduction in hours above 30°C in Abu Dhabi (1,649 hours from 3,930 hours) but a 69% reduction in Al Wathba (1,200 hours from 3,929).

Because the digital tool provides a certain level of data, farmers could also use it to more granularly plan crop rotations for different times of the year in accordance with seasonal temperature and humidity fluctuations. For example, a user wanting to grow cauliflower during the shoulder seasons at the lowest cost would have a different set of criteria than a user looking to rotate crops in every season based on the conditions in the most effective greenhouse.

**What's Next?**

We believe this work is a step toward more efficient, lower-cost crop yields and the creation of new types of inhabited oases in the Gulf and comparable climates. The adaptiveness of the tool allows the greenhouse to be right-sized based on a variety of factors including location, up-front cost, operational cost, crop type, and material availability. For example, a potential greenhouse user can look at startup (construction) costs for the project as well as the operational costs (in the form of water and electricity) against the production capacity of the greenhouse. They may then choose a less expensive option that either provides more limited crop options or isn't operable for part of the year. The ability to create these conditions at a low cost with relatively simple technology has, in our opinion, the capacity to reshape both the agricultural and public landscape of hot portions of the globe.

Currently, our work is a proof of concept that we believe indicates the viability of the methods and a path for further research and refinement. There are a number of areas where this project could continue to be developed. For example, the consistent winds of the Gulf region point to the potential for fans to be replaced with natural ventilation. The traditional architectural form of the barjeel, which we used in our kit-of-parts, is particularly promising, but more work would be required to map and verify the viability of a wind-driven or hybrid fan wind-driven approach.

# Living Machines

HOME-OFFICE
(Daniel Jacobs and Brittany Utting)

***Ingredients***
Palm
Greenhouse
Care
Environment
Life Support

The contemporary industrial greenhouse is a sensing and sensorial machine: calibrating interior atmospheres, initiating thermal shifts, creating artificial suns, and adjusting fertilizer, water, and humidity. Through its climatic systems and chemical additives, the greenhouse and its sensing technologies simplify complex environmental relationships to produce a perpetual growing season. While these horticultural infrastructures are increasingly essential for global food supplies, their architecture reproduces the extractive logics and resource-driven practices of global capitalism: transforming landscapes of food production, relying on fossil energy, satisfying market demands, and creating excessive waste.

Greenhouse infrastructures mobilize technology and architecture to abstract climatic conditions to accelerate plant growth. This tendency toward abstraction produces artificial environments characterized by uncanny haptic and sensorial conditions: pink artificial suns, misting valves, humming systems, and observant machines. These conditions are byproducts of the care and maintenance of living organisms, requiring heat, water, nutrients, air, light, and soil, as well as the technical – yet intimate – labor of tending and nurturing. Instead of optimizing horticultural productivity, can these architectures instead embody new models of cultivation and care for multi-species life? Because greenhouse technologies simulate living ecologies, they have the capacity to produce aesthetic effects that directly tie a climatological condition to an experiential one, suggesting alternative relationships between humans and the environment. This essay explores how the greenhouse – as both an architectural type and technical form – can be reoriented toward projects of climate care and the development of new environmental sensibilities.

Fig.01 HOME-OFFICE (Daniel Jacobs and Brittany Utting), *PALM-HOUSE*, 2020. Installation view. Digital prints on aluminum-mounted acrylic panels. Courtesy of the artists.

*Mae-ling Lokko, "Hot Air Rising,"* ***e-flux Architecture: Digestion****, September 2022. https://www.e-flux.com/architecture/digestion/487068/hot-air-rising/.*

*Maria S. Giudici, "Cultiver Notre Jardin: On the Park as a Civic Space," in* ***Into the Great Wide Open****, ed. Andreas Rumpfhuber (Barcelona: dpr-barcelona, 2017), 142-165.*

*Georg H. Kohlmaier, and Barna von Sartory,* ***Houses of Glass: A Nineteenth-Century Building Type*** *(Cambridge: MIT Press, 1991), 1.*

*See the "Tulipomania" chapter in Charles Mackay,* ***Extraordinary Popular Delusions and the Madness of Crowds*** *(London: Richard Bentley, 1841), 89-97.*

*Catherine Horwood,* ***Potted History: How Houseplants Took Over Our Homes*** *(London: Pimpernel Press, 2020).*

*According to the MarketsandMarkets™ 2023* ***Commercial Greenhouse Market Size*** *report, "Global commercial greenhouse market size was accounted for USD 39.6 Billion in 2023 and is expected to hit around USD 68.7 Billion by 2028."*

*Keller Easterling, "El Ejido," in* ***Manual for a Future Desert****, eds. Ida Soulard, Abinadi Meza, and Bassam El Baroni (Milan, Nantes: Mousse Publishing, Beaux-Arts Nantes Saint-Nazaire, 2021), 205.*

*Barry James, "World Uses Ground to Deserts,"* ***The New York Times****, April 5, 2002.*

*Antonio Fernandez, "La Junta Vigila el Crecimiento de los Invernaderos en Marruecos,"* ***La Voz de Almería****, December 10, 2018.*

## Simulated Worlds

Mobilized by a network of colonial extraction in the nineteenth century, large-scale greenhouse structures emerged from the reciprocal development of wrought iron and plate glass building technologies and mechanized environmental systems such as steam heating. As European colonial empires accumulated land and extracted wealth and natural resources, they built structures to house botanical species collected overseas. These collections developed alongside new architectural forms and environmental systems for cultivation and display. Greenhouses such as the Palm House at Kew Gardens, designed by Decimus Burton and constructed by Richard Turner in 1848, were public vivaria that exhibited the living products of imperial accumulation. Such highly engineered and grandiose displays of tropical plant specimens served as a visible proxy for colonial reach and power. Often situated in parks and gardens, these climate machines created an immersive nature, bringing the botanical spoils of the empire to the public eye. Critically, the inclusion of "natural" environments such as greenhouses, parks, and gardens in the nineteenth-century city also functioned as a release valve for the rising industrial working class, offering both a pacifying respite from the intense conditions of production as well as a space of social education. Immersing visitors in a riot of palms, ferns, and orchids, this "theater of nature" fanned a type of collective fantasy and escapism, offering alternative sensoria in the toxic and crowded spaces of the emerging industrial city. These captured worlds triggered intense public desires, leading to phenomena such as "orchidelirium" and "pteridomania" (or fern fever) when colonial plant hunting and importing was at its height. Combined with greenhouse technologies, such manias and deliriums also transformed the domestic interior. Bay windows, sun porches, and hothouses brought more sunlight into domestic spaces, allowing for the indoor cultivation of imported tropical plants.

Since the mid-twentieth century, these greenhouse technologies have evolved into a logistical landscape of horticultural production. Built on consumer desires for exotic plants and demands for dependable off-season produce, contemporary greenhouse infrastructures form an often unseen regional network providing consumers with tomatoes in the winter and tropical flowers at any local grocery store. To supply a sharply increasing demand for stable food sources, driven by both climate change and population stressors, the large-scale greenhouse industry is projected to increase dramatically over the coming decades. However, consolidating horticultural production into regional distribution centers disrupts local food networks and increases reliance on food imports. Although such high-intensity production might be a necessary response to global food precarity, it also serves to further abstract the relationship between consumer, producer, and environment. Alongside the explosion of fulfillment centers on urban peripheries, these sprawling greenhouse infrastructures constitute a radical reorganization of both the countryside and the city.

For example, the province of Almería on the southern coast of Spain has become known as the Mar de Plástico – or "Sea of Plastic" – referring to the vast concentration of greenhouses blanketing the region. Covering 100,000 acres of land, it is among the largest aggregation of hothouse structures in the world, swallowing towns and the burgeoning city of El Ejido, clinging to the Sierra Nevada Mountains to the north, and stretching south to the Mediterranean coast. As architect Keller Easterling describes in her essay "El Ejido," these landscapes constitute a "plasticulture urbanism," a formless mat consuming all available surface area to capture the region's abundant sunshine for the plants housed within. In addition to cheap solar energy, this landscape also relies on access to an extensive immigrant labor force from North African countries who maintain the greenhouses.

While the traditional Almerían low-tech greenhouse type, known as the *Parral*, was first developed in the region, today, Almerían growers often use high-tech and ultra-calibrated hydroponic systems, chemical fertilizers, and nutrient-rich substrates to enable, enabling the abundant production of year-round produce in what is effectively a desert. The scale of this landscape has drastic consequences on the ecosystemic health of the region, including increased soil salinity, desertification from overdrawing the aquifer for irrigation, pollution caused by the chemical fertilizer and pesticide run-off, and the immense waste of discarded plastic. A mirror industry has emerged across the Mediterranean in Southwest Morocco. In the Souss-Massa-Draa region, the production of hothouse agriculture has outpaced that of Almería, signaling the expansion of the desert hothouse typology.

Marina Otero Verzier, "Cartesian Enclosures," ***New Geographies 12: Commons***, *edited by Mojdeh Mahdavi and Liang Wang (Cambridge, MA: New Geographies Lab, Harvard University Graduate School of Design, 2021), 44.*

*For example, Priva's PAR, or Photosynthetic Active Radiation sensor system constantly monitors the optimal light spectrum for photosynthesis and communicates with the mechanical systems of the architecture: automating shade curtains, CO2 diffusers, and lighting to reduce labor costs and optimize yields. Phenospex's PlantEye creates constant 3D scans of each plant, monitoring health through morphological and spectral analysis. The various software allows growers to create data-rich models of the entire crop that integrate factors such as leaf area, projected biomass, and hue average into yield analysis software, calibrating the greenhouse's environmental systems, gantries, and sensor infrastructures.*

*William Alexander, "Indoor Farming Is a 'No-Brainer.' Except for the Carbon Footprint,"* ***The New York Times***, *June 21, 2002.*

*Merve Bedir, Ludo Groen, Marten Kuijpers, Victor Muñoz Sanz, and Marina Otero Verzier, "Introduction: Automated Landscapes and the Politics of Collaborative Public Research,"* ***Automated Landscapes***, *edited by Merve Bedir, Ludo Groen, Marten Kuijpers, Victor Muñoz Sanz, and Marina Otero Verzier (Rotterdam: Nieuwe Instituut, 2023), 6.*

***PALM-HOUSE*** *was exhibited at Citygroup Gallery in New York City from November 2020 through February 2021. The design and research team for this project included Daniel Jacobs (Co-Director, HOME-OFFICE), Brittany Utting (Co-Director, HOME-OFFICE), Jianing Cui, Leah Hong, Tiffany Xu, and Clara Núñez-Regueiro. The authors would like to acknowledge the support of the School of Architecture at Rice University and the Taubman College of Architecture and Planning at the University of Michigan in the realization of this project.*

Fig.02 Westland Greenhouse Interior, 2020. Luca Locatelli/Institute.

The industrialized landscape is not exclusive to the desert. In the Netherlands, the horticultural industry has further abstracted the greenhouse interior from its exterior climatic conditions. The Westland region of the Netherlands – within the Randstad Megalopolis, south of The Hague – hosts one of the world's largest networks of high-tech, state-of-the-art greenhouses. The urbanization patterns of the Dutch greenhouse landscape reflect a centuries-long process of land reclamation, or poldering, in which bodies of water are enclosed by networks of dikes and drained to create arable land. Initially, small polder farms were created through a democratic policy of equal land distribution for farming families. After years of neoliberal land governance, however, these farms have been consolidated into vast agricultural tracts owned and operated by large multinational companies. In contrast to the loose and formless urbanism of the Almerían hothouses, the Dutch greenhouses compose a rigid array of self-contained and tight-enveloped prisms gridded across the polder landscape. These vast greenhouses cover more than 100 square kilometers of the Westland polders, feeding a global supply chain of vegetable produce, cut flowers, and ornamental plants.

Unlike the "seas of plastic" in Almería and Souss-Massa-Draa, the climatic conditions of the Netherlands are largely irrelevant to the growth of the plants housed within. The controlled atmospheres of the typical Venlo-type Dutch greenhouse – steel structures featuring multi-pitched roofs with operable ventilation and horticultural float glass enclosures – can temper any local, seasonal, or climatic shift. Manufacturers of these technologies advertise that the greenhouses are rapidly approaching full automation: pink grow lights produce a perpetual state of photosynthesis, hydroponics optimize water usage and chemical additives, and integrated sensors autonomously monitor the environment.

Architect Marina Otero Verzier argues that these spaces are "Cartesian Enclosures" in which "data, technology, and energy fuel the maximization of the land for year-round crops." The latest generation of greenhouses incorporates automated logistics platforms that provide complete biological, computational, and climatic control: drones, sensors, and mechanical systems analyze plant health and calibrate growing conditions. Although optimized for efficient land, water, and fertilizer use, these high-yield grow spaces are often energy-intensive and their central role in global food distribution networks further contributes a significant carbon footprint. By concentrating the means of food production into fewer and fewer hands, these proprietary greenhouse technologies contribute to the loss of local food autonomy by disrupting smaller-scale food networks that are informed by a region's geography, seasons and climates, farming methods, and flora and fauna. Furthermore, although these greenhouses are advertised as increasingly automated, many aspects of their production lines still require human labor. They create the illusion of abundance, hiding the environmental and social costs of such forms of production.

**Sensing, Caring, Living Machines**

From empire to industrial-scale cultivation, the scale of current greenhouse landscapes reflects the significant influence that our habits of consumption have on the global movement of resources and capital that sustains them. In this context of increasingly closed, automated, and extractive worlds, can the same technologies and sensibilities of the greenhouse be reimagined to create sensing, caring, and living machines? The project *PALM-HOUSE* (2020-2021) by HOME-OFFICE, a research and design collaborative led by the authors, explores what it means to preserve an organism, redeploying greenhouse technologies to imagine new life support systems in a changing climate. The project asks: In the face of extinction, what are the costs, means, and methods of perpetual environmental care? The project is a speculative design proposal for the Orto Botanico, a garden and herbarium in Padua, Italy.

The Orto Botanico was founded by the University of Padua in 1545 for medicinal plant research. Located along the city's Santa Chiara Canal south of the Basilica of Sant'Antonio, the herbarium encloses a circular garden divided into four quadrants, each containing a precisely curated arrangement of specimens. The herbs and plants in the garden, imported from all over the world, were used to train medical students to identify species for medical and therapeutic remedies, a difficult practice in which mistakes could lead to incorrect dosages or fatal ingredients. The specimens in the garden also served to maintain the herbarium's plant stock for the Venetian Republic's emerging pharmaceutical trade. Owing to the rarity and high value of the specimens housed within, the Orto Botanico was fortified against theft with a circular stone wall.

Such Renaissance botanical gardens sought to rationalize the natural world into an organized collection of specimens, embodying the structure of pharmaceutical knowledge in the sixteenth century. According to botanist Andrea Savoia, the four quadrants of the garden reflected either "the four Aristotelian elements (earth, fire, water and air) or else the four curative properties Galen identified in plants (dry, humid, hot and cold)." Regardless of the mythic origins of the garden's design, the geometry of the contents of this *Hortus sphaericus* was not only tied to the pedagogical apparatus of medical training, but was also a direct representation of the power of scientific knowledge: knowledge that was protected, coveted, and proprietary to the Venetian Republic.

In the northeast quadrant of the Orto Botanico survives the oldest of the garden's specimens: a 450-year-old Mediterranean palm, or *Chamaerops humilis*. This palm, a species native to southern Europe and North Africa, was included in the garden's collection owing to its various traditional medicinal uses. Known more famously as Goethe's Palm, it served as a primary inspiration and subject for Johann Wolfgang von Goethe's theory on botanical morphology, enumerated in his essay "The Metamorphosis of Plants" from 1790. In this text, Goethe outlines a proto-evolutionary theory describing the relationship between a plant's environmental conditions and its patterns of growth and development.

---

*Vittorio Dal Piaz and Maurizio Rippa Bonati, "The Design and Form of the Padua* ***Horto Medicinale****,"* ***The Botanical Garden of Padua*** *1545-1995 (Venice: Marsilio Editori, 1995), 44.*

---

*Dal Piaz and Rippa Bonati, "The Design and Form of the Padua* ***Horto Medicinale****," 54.*

---

*Andrea Ubrizsy Savoia, "The Botanical Garden of Padua in Guilandino's Day,"* ***The Botanical Garden of Padua*** *1545-1995 (Venice: Marsilio Editori, 1995), 173.*

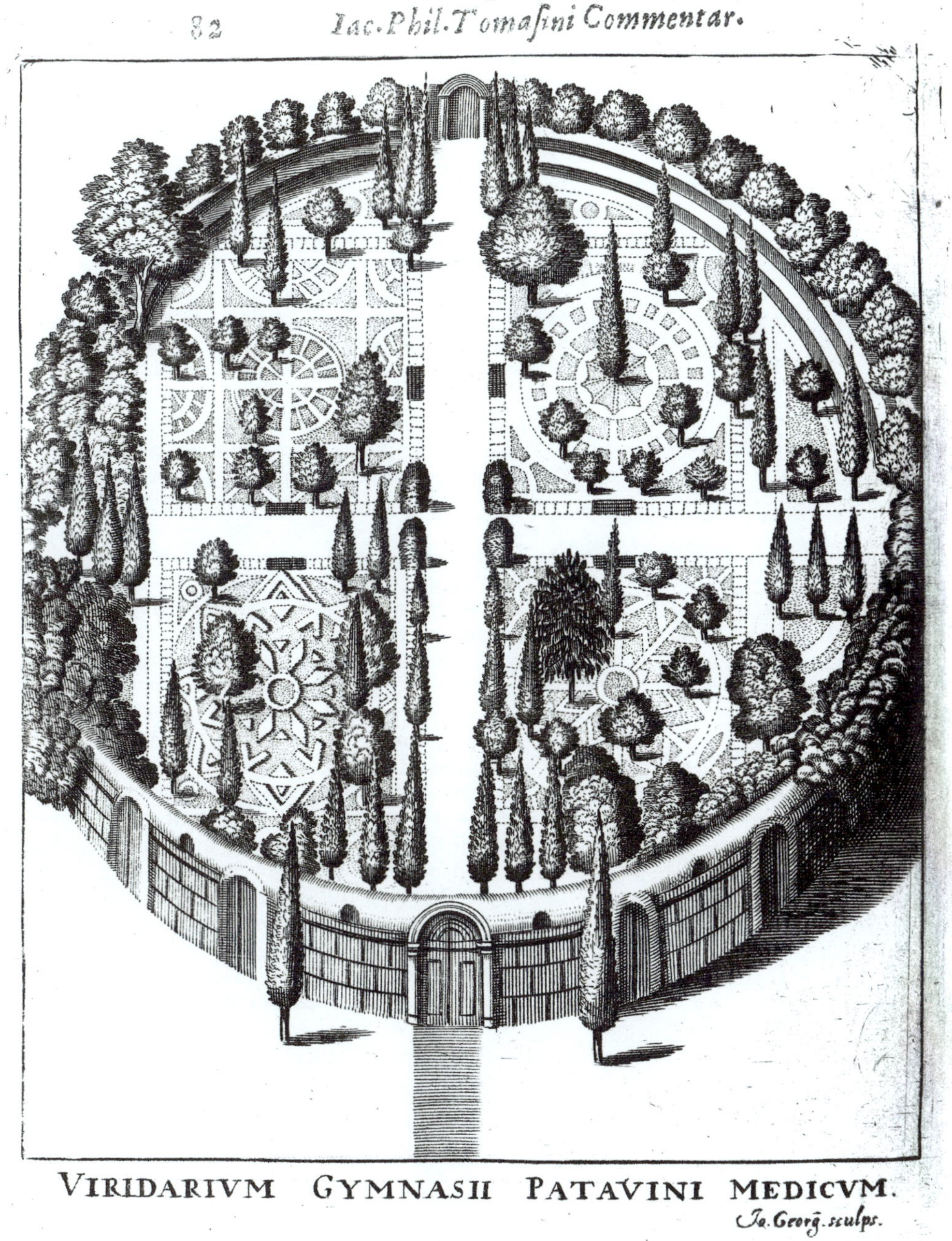


Fig.03 Drawing of Orto Botanico, in *Gymnasium patavinum* by Jacopo Filippo Tomasini, 1654.

The theory argues that within each plant, there exists an *urform*, or original archetypal model, that drives the plant's structure and form. According to Goethe, this internal morphological impulse is in constant tension with the plant's environmental conditions. Through direct observation of the palm, Goethe expanded theories of botany to include a plant's habitat, such as climate, soil composition, and water availability, setting the groundwork for future theories of ecology. As Gordon L. Miller argues, "Goethe's emphasis on the interdependence of organism and environment, as well as organism and organism... presents a view that can surely be described as ecological, seventy-five years before German biologist Ernst Haeckel coined the term." ■

To protect this scientifically and culturally valuable specimen over the centuries, university gardeners constructed a series of temporary, and ultimately permanent, palm houses to shelter and display Goethe's Palm. Early etchings reveal elaborate structures built each winter and removed in late spring. The earliest photographic evidence of a palm house structure depicts an ornate wood and glass shelter designed and built in the 1870s. This structure was later replaced by an operable concrete, steel, and glass greenhouse in the 1930s after a cold snap in 1929 almost killed the palm. The current structure, a renovation in the early 2000s, transformed the palm house into an operable enclosure featuring radiant heating and large panes of glass that open and close depending on the ambient temperature. This evolution from a primarily open-air structure to an environmentally contingent enclosure serves as an architectural index of the tightening strictures of environmental control and display. Each technological stage of the palm house evolution reveals the changing relationship between a living organism and its environmental contexts.

■

*Gordon L. Miller. Introduction.* ***The Metamorphosis of Plants*** *(Cambridge: The MIT Press, 2009), xxi-xxii.*

Fig.04 Postcard depicting Goethe's Palm in the Orto Botanico in Padua, Italy, circa 1895.

*PALM-HOUSE* steps into this long history of cultivation and examines the relationship between Goethe's Palm, the gardeners who maintain it, and the architecture that houses it. Continuing the four centuries of cultivation that began in 1585 with the planting of Goethe's Palm, *PALM-HOUSE* proposes three possible prototypes to house this specimen. While greenhouse architectures, such as the Palm House at Kew or the Westland greenhouses in the Netherlands, often represent a complex interplay between resource exploitation and ecological optimization, can an alternative deployment of the tectonic and climatic systems used for horticultural care instead be used to promote a renewed awareness of planetary ecology? In search of new modes of mediation between architecture and its environments, these three structures reveal the ecosystems of care and curation that implicate the viewer, the specimen, and the maintenance worker in the daily life of the palm.

Fig.05 HOME-OFFICE (Daniel Jacobs and Brittany Utting), *PALM-HOUSE*, 2020. Digital rendering of PALM-HOUSE 01. Courtesy of the artists.

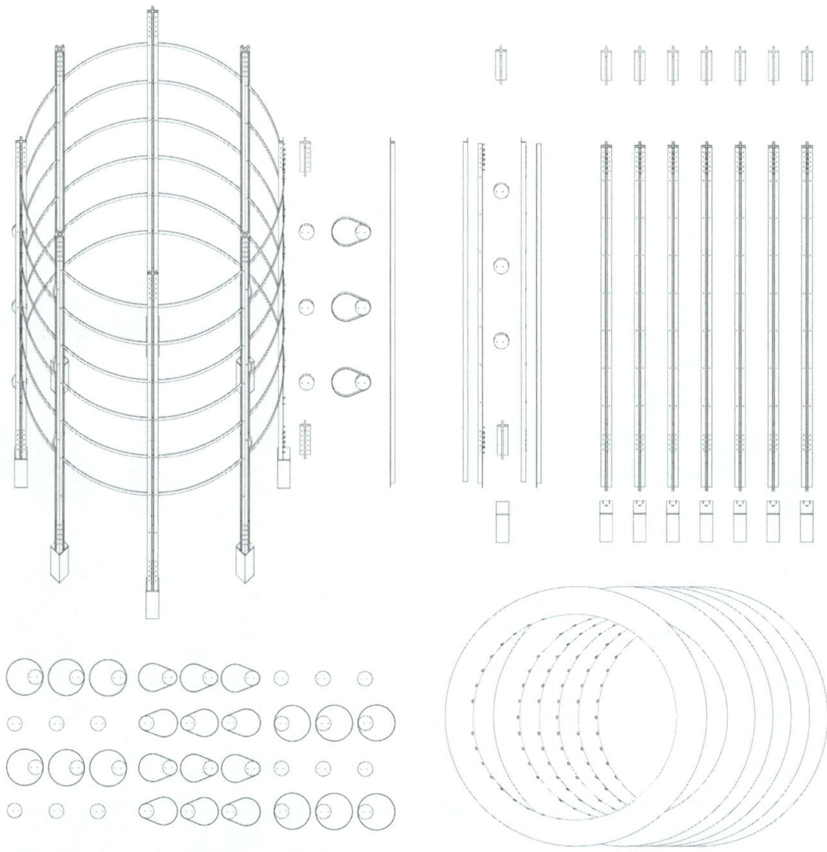

Fig.06 HOME-OFFICE (Daniel Jacobs and Brittany Utting), *PALM-HOUSE,* 2020. Axonometric drawing of PALM-HOUSE 01. Courtesy of the artists.

PALM-HOUSE 01 is a circular steel structure suspending a series of fabric air ducts around the palm. Each duct connects to a supply of water, nutrients, and natural pest deterrents controlled by a daily maintenance schedule designed by the palm's caretakers. When threatened by drought, clouds of water vapor envelop the fronds, adjusting the humidity of the enclosure's microclimate. The structure can exhale aerosolized essential oils to mitigate fungal infections and dissuade invasive species from tunneling into the trunks of the palm. Caretakers can also program the structure to release nutritional sprays, including manganese, potassium, magnesium, and iron, to revitalize the soil, aid root growth, and strengthen the palm's leaves. The structure breathes – inhaling, exhaling, misting, and sighing – becoming an extension of the plant's ecology.

Fig.07 HOME-OFFICE (Daniel Jacobs and Brittany Utting), *PALM-HOUSE,* 2020. Digital rendering of PALM-HOUSE 02. Courtesy of the artists.

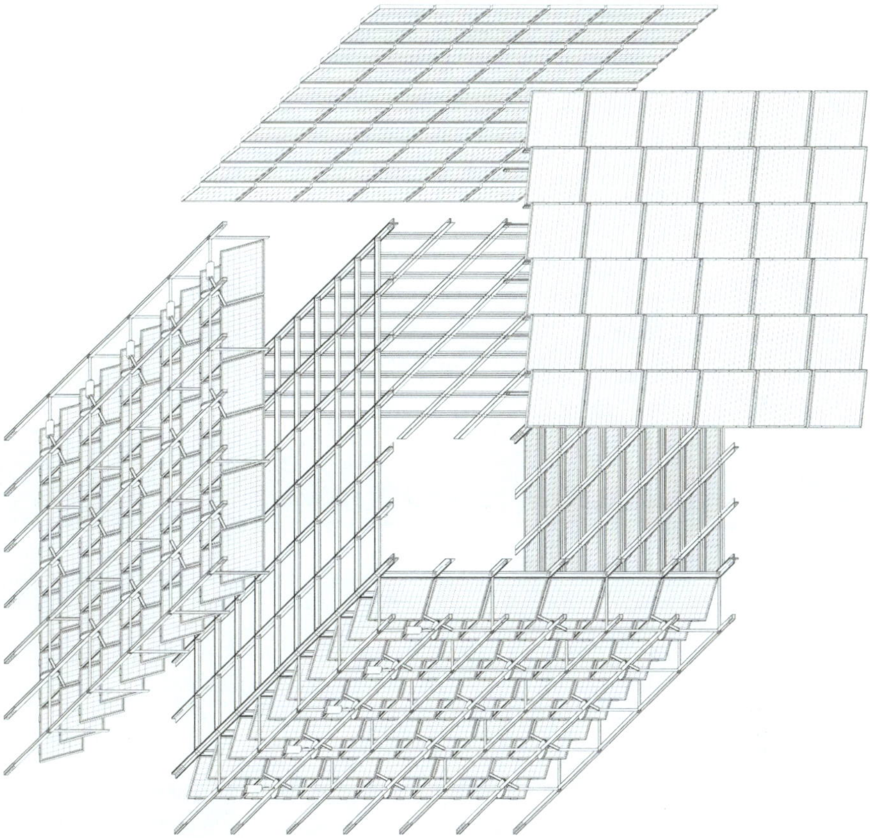

Fig.08 HOME-OFFICE (Daniel Jacobs and Brittany Utting), *PALM-HOUSE,* 2020. Axonometric drawing of PALM-HOUSE 02. Courtesy of the artists.

PALM-HOUSE 02 responds to the increasing concentration of environmental pollutants that threaten to overwhelm the palm's natural osmotic defenses. Composed of an infrastructure of filtration panels, the wall assemblies open and close with a motorized gear system, limiting the infiltration or increasing the passage of airborne particulates. Botanical caretakers maintain the shingled and breathable envelope: monitoring atmospheric systems, replacing spent filter units, and adjusting the facade's permeability to increase pollination rates. When the structure buzzes and hums to life – gears turn, and filtration panels close – it can calibrate the palm's immediate atmosphere to counter dangerous particulate clouds, molecular swarms, and synthetic compounds.

Fig.09 HOME-OFFICE (Daniel Jacobs and Brittany Utting), *PALM-HOUSE,* 2020. Digital rendering of PALM-HOUSE 03. Courtesy of the artists.

---

*Note: This essay builds upon our previous research on greenhouse architecture and includes excerpts from the chapter "Life Support: The Greenhouse as an Architecture of Survival," in* ***Pedagogical Experiments in Architecture for a Changing Climate****, edited by Tulay Atak, Luis Callejas, Jonathan Scelsa, & Jørgen Johan Tandberg (Routledge, 2024).*

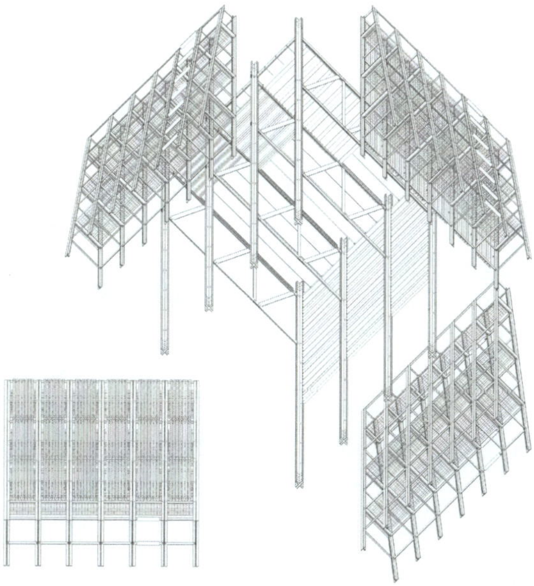

Fig.10 HOME-OFFICE (Daniel Jacobs and Brittany Utting), *PALM-HOUSE,* 2020. Axonometric drawing of PALM-HOUSE 03. Courtesy of the artists.

PALM-HOUSE 03 enables botanical technicians to adjust the palm's exposure to heat and light, protecting it from extreme temperature fluctuations due to climate change. The structure is an open armature that deploys lightweight solar greenhouse curtains to regulate the palm's exposure to light while also providing a thermal barrier. A secondary structure of movable wall panels of grow lights and heat lamps can be repositioned to mitigate cold snaps and supplement solar energy during the winter months. The structure emits an uncanny glow – the steel reflects pink, whites become green, and greens transform into a dull and ruddy crimson.

By adjusting these assemblages, botanical technicians can continuously calibrate the enclosures to mitigate the deteriorating environmental conditions of the specimen. While the elaborate assemblies of the PALM-HOUSES reveal the *degree* to which we have profoundly altered planetary ecology, they also express the ongoing practices of maintenance and tending required for a species' survival. Critically, the structures are not closed worlds creating ideal interior climates, but rather, they allow pollinators, atmospheres, and the increasingly hostile environment to continue to shape a living organism. *PALM-HOUSE* reimagines the historic preservation of a plant – not by recreating a past climate but by demonstrating the life support systems necessary for its future survival.

# *Meal Kits & Prep*



Illustrations by Khalid Mezaina

*Chapter* **04**

# Future Speculation:

## *Live, Grow, Eat in an Emirati Neighborhood*

Azza Aboualam

***Ingredients***

Urban
Domestic
Center
Edge
Backyard

*On October 5, 2024, Sheikh Mohammed bin Rashid, Vice President and Ruler of Dubai, unveiled "Plant the Emirates," an initiative launched to boost agricultural development and enhance the nation's food security. "The national programme aims to spread the culture of agriculture in every school and home, and in our new generations. The programme aims to increase our food security, develop our agricultural technologies, build new partnerships with the private sector and spread the green area in our country to ensure its sustainability." See: "Sheikh Mohammed announces Plant the Emirates project to boost agriculture in UAE," in* ***The National****, October 6, 2024.*

*Salwa Tohme Tawk, Mounir Said, and Shady Hamadeh, "Urban Agriculture and Food Security in the Middle Eastern Context," in* ***Beyond the City: Resource Extraction Urbanism in the Middle East,*** *ed. Nelida Fuccaro (Oxford: Oxford University Press, 2014), https://doi.org/10.1093/acprof:oso/9780199361786.003.0007.*

*Katy Gillett, "UAE primed for desert expansion and 15-minute cities to keep pace with population boom," in* ***The National****, December 4, 2024.*

## Introduction

My grandmother's chickens were so important to her. So important, in fact, that when my family would travel abroad for the summer, she called daily (internationally, back when landlines were the only link) to check in on them. She never bought eggs from the supermarket and what came out of her backyard was sufficient for a family of seven at the time.

Scales of participation in food security and sufficiency are largely varied. If I plant mint on my balcony, I am contributing to food security at the scale of a room. If I grow one kilo of cucumbers in my backyard, I am doing it at the scale of a household. If I have a farm with fruit trees and a chicken coop, sharing crops and eggs with my neighbors, I am doing it at the scale of the neighborhood.

Agriculture — and its association with other food production practices — is a much-celebrated part of the local food movement and is ingrained in the daily practices of many individuals in the United Arab Emirates (UAE). However, its impact on reducing food insecurity in Emirati cities remains understudied, given its informal nature and small-scale output. I am not sure that growing broccoli or the occasional palm dates in one's backyard can affect food security at the scale of the country. However, these small steps are worth exploring, especially as part of their integration into a larger strategy.

Despite ongoing local efforts on an individual level, questions arise in terms of what happens when the strategy is scaled up to be integrated into a larger scheme, tapping into the existing infrastructure. While the concept of feeding neighborhoods from within themselves presents many challenges, this essay speculates: How can neighborhoods be planned with productivity as an inherent part of them, while retrofitting others?

## Urban Sprawl and Urban Agriculture

The Middle East has one of the highest global urbanization rates, with a direct relationship to the increasing demand for land and water. Cities in the UAE have undergone noticeable growth in recent years. Dubai's population, for example, is expected to almost double by 2040. In the first three months of 2024, 25,700 people moved to the city, while Abu Dhabi and Sharjah have also reported an increase in residents in the same year. With a steadily growing world population, it is expected that most of this growth will be concentrated in urban areas. Within the context of the UAE, this urban sprawl constitutes expansion into the desert, farther away from the coastline. This presents a number of challenges and assets. While urban sprawl overtook agricultural land in some emirates, the drier desert air presents a unique climate for the kit-of-parts that we have been experimenting with, as the assemblies performed better in less humid climates.

Sparking increased interest, urban agriculture has witnessed a significant growth spurt, especially when it comes to framing self-sufficiency within the urban context. While urban agriculture includes city greening and beautification, other factors include improved nutrition, enhancing local food security, community building, and economic development. Urban agriculture has been defined as "reconnecting with the community through food, jobs and economic development." It is extremely heterogeneous, with a diverse landscape that evades a singular definition, scale, and means of measuring its success. It encompasses vertical and rooftop farming, urban foraging, community and residential gardens, and commercial urban farms. Here, urban agriculture is defined as the endeavor of growing food in an urban context, encompassing a range of activities that are related to food production, including self-production and subsistence agriculture on the scale of the neighborhood.

## Scales and Approaches

One of urban agriculture's benefits is to re-engage city-dwellers with the educational and community-building side of food production. The systemization and integration of the built environment and food production is not a novel approach. Across North America, most are launched in collaboration through lease agreements with public agencies, private landowners, or land trusts. While its impact on urban diets and income is still being studied, urban agriculture has constituted a local asset due to its potential to address multiple needs, such as supplying fresh produce, and offering opportunities for employment, education, and recreation.

In the case of Oakland, in particular, the city is considered to be a food desert not due to the lack of food, but rather because of the limited access and affordability to healthy and nutritious options. In response to high rates of food insecurity in East Oakland, for example, Freedom Farm has 28 wooden boxes that anyone can use to grow food, where soil, seeds and water are provided. In tandem, Phat Beets Produce is an organization that revitalizes gardens in the city by emphasizing the community aspect within the urban garden model. Gardens are managed collectively by community members and volunteers with specific guidelines to regulate their activities. This includes what crops can be grown and the sharing of responsibilities for watering, weeding, and maintaining the space.

---

*Sarah Meehan, "Urban Farm Coming to Former Sparrows Point Steel Mill Site in Baltimore County,"* ***Baltimore Sun****, May 8, 2018, accessed May 10, 2018, http://www.baltimoresun.com/business/bs-md-sparrows-point-farm-20180508-story.html.*

*Urban is of, relating to, or constituting a city or town. See https://www.collinsdictionary.com/dictionary/english/urban.*

*"Urban Gardens,"* ***Phat Beets Produce****, accessed January 19, 2025, http://www.phatbeetsproduce.org/urban-gardens/#dover.*

*Andrea Basche, "Urban Farm-Fed Cities: Lessons from Cuba's Organopónicos,"* ***SAGE Magazine****, accessed January 19, 2025, https://sagemagazine.org/urban-farm-fed-cities-lessons-from-cubas-organoponicos/.*

*Ibid.*

*"About Food Tech Valley,"* ***Food Tech Valley****, accessed January 19, 2025, https://www.foodtechvalley.ae/node/9.*

*"ReFarm Global, IGS break ground on GigaFarm project in Dubai,"* ***Oil and Gas News****, OGN, January 2025 (Volume: 42 / Issue: 1).*

*The Sustainable City, "Dubai," accessed January 6, 2025, https://thesustainablecity.com/cities/dubai/.*

The organopónico in Cuba presents another approach. Plots of land that were used for construction staging were converted into urban farms in the early 1990s after the collapse of the Soviet Union. The loss of imports affected the Cuban diet, which saw a 30% deficit in calories, as it lost its supply of wheat, beans, and oil almost overnight. In response to issues of food access, organopónicos are located in areas of high population density from surrounding high-rise buildings, placing the farms within walking distance for the majority of the population. Individuals can farm the land to make a living while producing fresh food in the center of the city. Each one has a market stall, which acts as an essential piece in the success of Cuba's organopónico system, positively affecting the immediacy of this food transfer. Produce is sold by the people who work the garden and get to keep half of the sales revenue.

While those Western-based case studies offer insight into the overlap of the urban fabric and agrarian practices, contemporary projects in the UAE provide an alternative take. Food Tech Valley is a UAE-based initiative aimed at rethinking the overlap of food production, consumption, and innovation. In addition to designated residential areas with single-family homes, the development is divided into four main "productive" zones, which is referred to as its "ecosystem." Those include: a food production zone with advanced farming techniques, a logistics zone for processing and distribution, a business park for food and agritech operations, and an innovation and an R&D (research and development) center for developing technological solutions in agriculture. The project has partnered with Badia Farms, the Middle East's first high-tech indoor vertical farm, to integrate advanced models using hybrid farms that employ sustainable practices, reducing water usage by 90% and utilizing clean energy, to grow pesticide-free, high-quality produce year-round. It also partnered with Tadeling, a local e-commerce platform, to distribute and sell the produce in the UAE. The project aims to eventually grow more than three million kilos of produce annually and offset 1% of the country's fresh produce imports.

The Sustainable City has projects in the Middle East with locations such as Sharjah, Abu Dhabi, and Yeti, Oman. Specifically, The Sustainable City Dubai incorporates innovative food production systems to promote self-sufficiency. The development features urban farming initiatives, including biodomes and vertical gardens, that provide residents with fresh, locally grown produce year-round. Located along a central green spine, it incorporates a strip of communal greenhouses, urban farming plots, and hydroponic systems. The biodomes, where residents can grow their own vegetables, are designed by Alesca Life Technologies & Trotec, an AgriTech company based in Dubai, Tokyo, and Beijing. Specializing in vertical farming, they utilize advanced techniques such as hydroponics and aquaponics, which require less water and land when compared to traditional farming.

## Potentials for Crossover

The aforementioned examples offer insights into operation, scale, and user interface with urban agriculture. While almost all of them are located within a dense residential urban setting, each case study offers its own unique insights into how those practices can be reimagined within the context of an Emirati neighborhood. The case studies in Oakland, for example, provide opportunities for residents to learn about the food system and become active participants in agricultural practices. This also provides a learning ground for knowledge sharing, especially when it comes to passing on intangible heritage manifested in adaptive practices developed by residents in response to different locales, like the arid climate in the UAE. This is further emphasized by the immediacy of food transfer in the organopónico as well as revenue reallocation. Sales from food production zones could inform a systemization of operation, where profit can go back into the greenhouse, supporting personnel working on its maintenance and upkeep. This allows for expansion by the ideas raised by Food Tech Valley which partners with local food suppliers and distributors to sell the produce. And finally, the centrality of the green spine in The Sustainable City physically situates the architectural element in the center of the neighborhood, creating a formal impact and a social space.

## Speculations

What if urban agriculture was viewed as an activator of interstitial space, where traditionally private spaces associated with domestic home activities cross the boundary into public space? The following speculative future of Emirati neighborhoods demonstrates a redefinition of conventional enactments of public and private property through personal relationships based on an ethic of care for the land and social enactment of space. When urban food production crosses into the public realm, it inherently introduces a domestic element, thereby forcing us to re-examine preconceived notions of commerce and domestic caring as well as the rethinking of the separation between private/domestic activities and public uses of land. Striking a balance between the use of the domestic space and the public realm is key.

We examine a new take on urban agriculture in a unique setting like the UAE in addressing food insecurity from a systems perspective: one that takes into consideration scale and human participation but also the policies that govern the process in which food is produced, processed, distributed, and consumed. Using imaginative scenarios, how can architecture contribute to greater food security and new conceptions of space?

While the typical urban dweller today has little understanding of where or how food is produced and distributed, this project aims to integrate architecture and food production into the Emirati urban fabric, proposing a third space: where food production and social fabric interact, allowing UAE residents to become active participants in achieving food security goals.

Expanding on the kit-of-parts, a few neighborhoods were identified in response to the project's application and imagined as possible venues of proliferation. This includes an experimentation of integration on the scales of the household and neighborhood. When the urban strategy was studied and outlined, the following locations were selected due to certain characteristics where a multitude of experimental scenarios could take place, reflecting the kit-of-parts' versatility and adaptability to the urban context in an arid environment. They allowed for retroactively integrating those kits into their existing infrastructure. Not only was the overall neighborhood layout and its spatial planning compatible with the project's integration, but also each one contained sufficient lot sizes as well as existing infrastructure, such as parks, that have irrigation systems that could be tapped into.

**Al Safa 2, Dubai:**

Unique characteristics: Variety of residential lots

Typical plot size: 1134–1395 $m^2$

Infrastructural and public spaces: Umm Suqeim Girls School and Safa Park 2

Zoning: Mixed-use

Fig. 01 Map of Al Safa 2, Dubai, with potential allocations of the kit-of-parts. Drawn by author, and Noor Hamdan.

Figs. 02, 03 Selected sites in Al Safa 2, Dubai, with potential allocations of the kit-of-parts. Drawn by Noor Hamdan, Nourhan Rahhal and Sara AlMahmoud.

Figs. 04, 05 Axonometric of Al Safa 2, Dubai, with potential allocations of the kit-of-parts. Drawn by Noor Hamdan, Nourhan Rahhal, and Sara AlMahmoud.

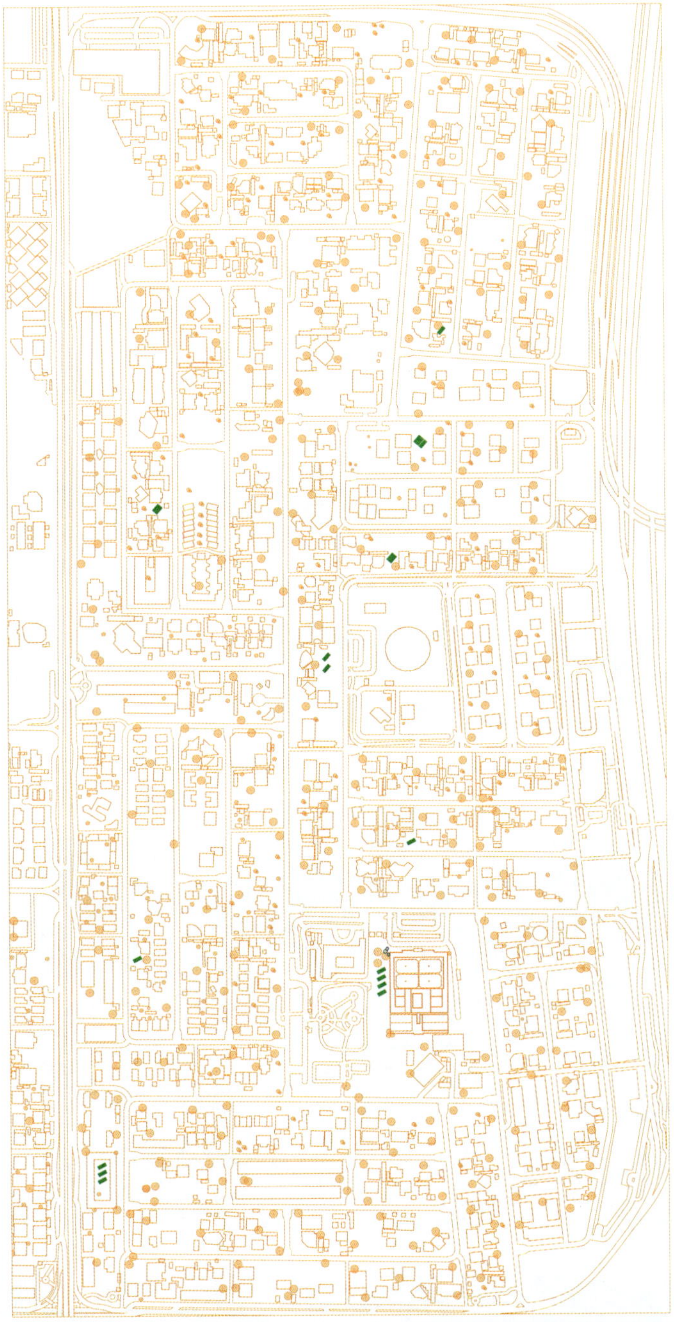


01

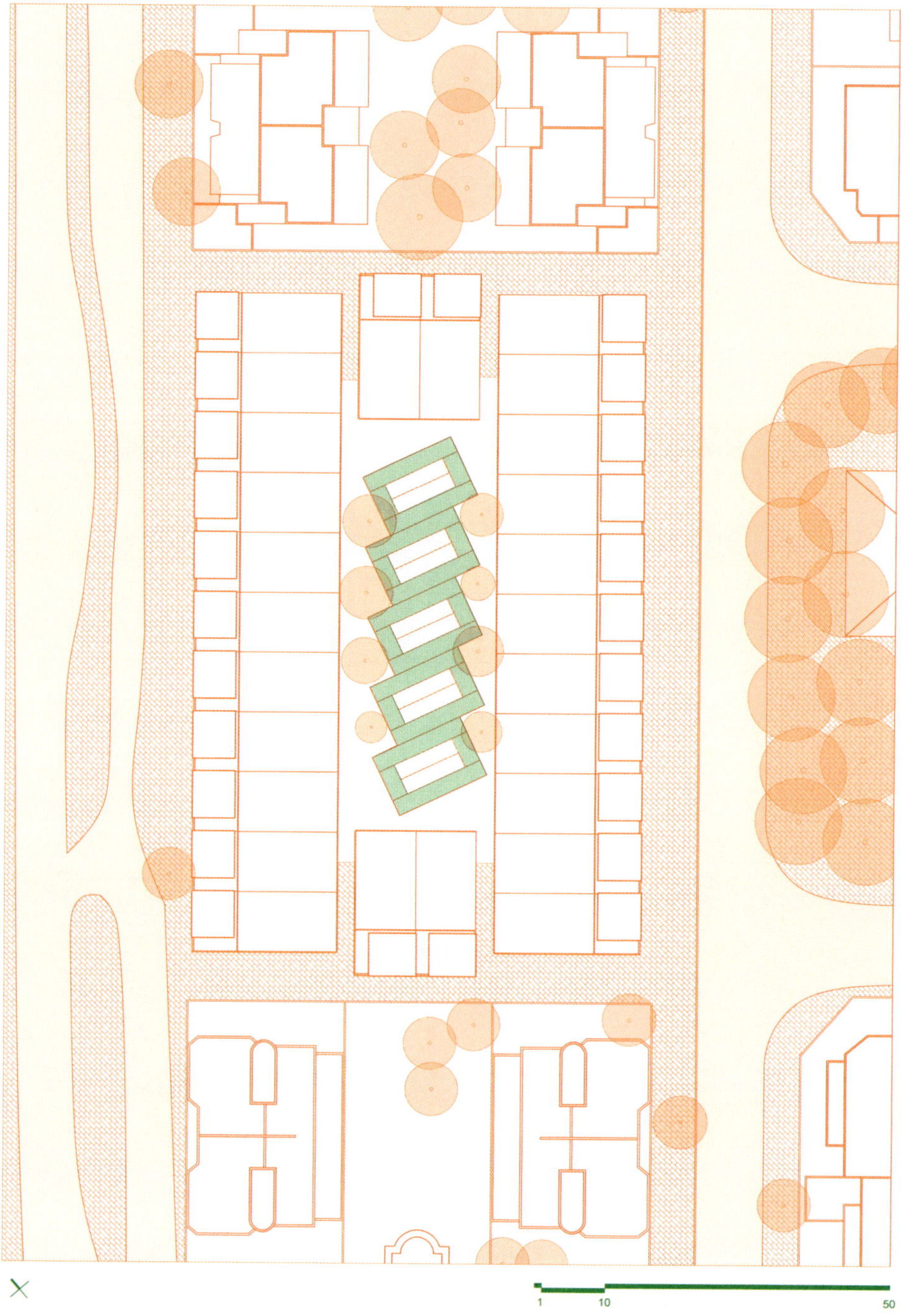
1
10
50

1
10
50

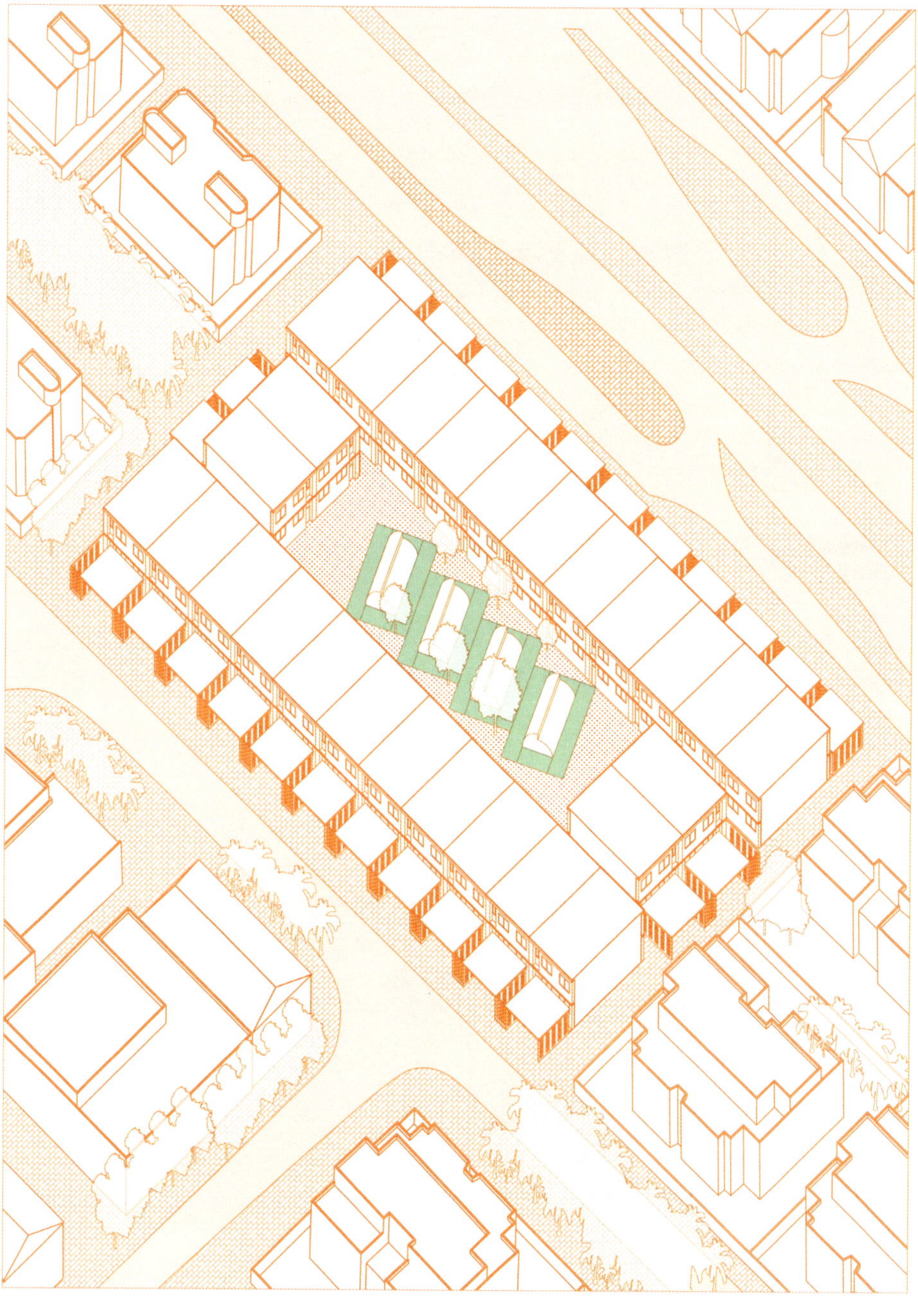


04

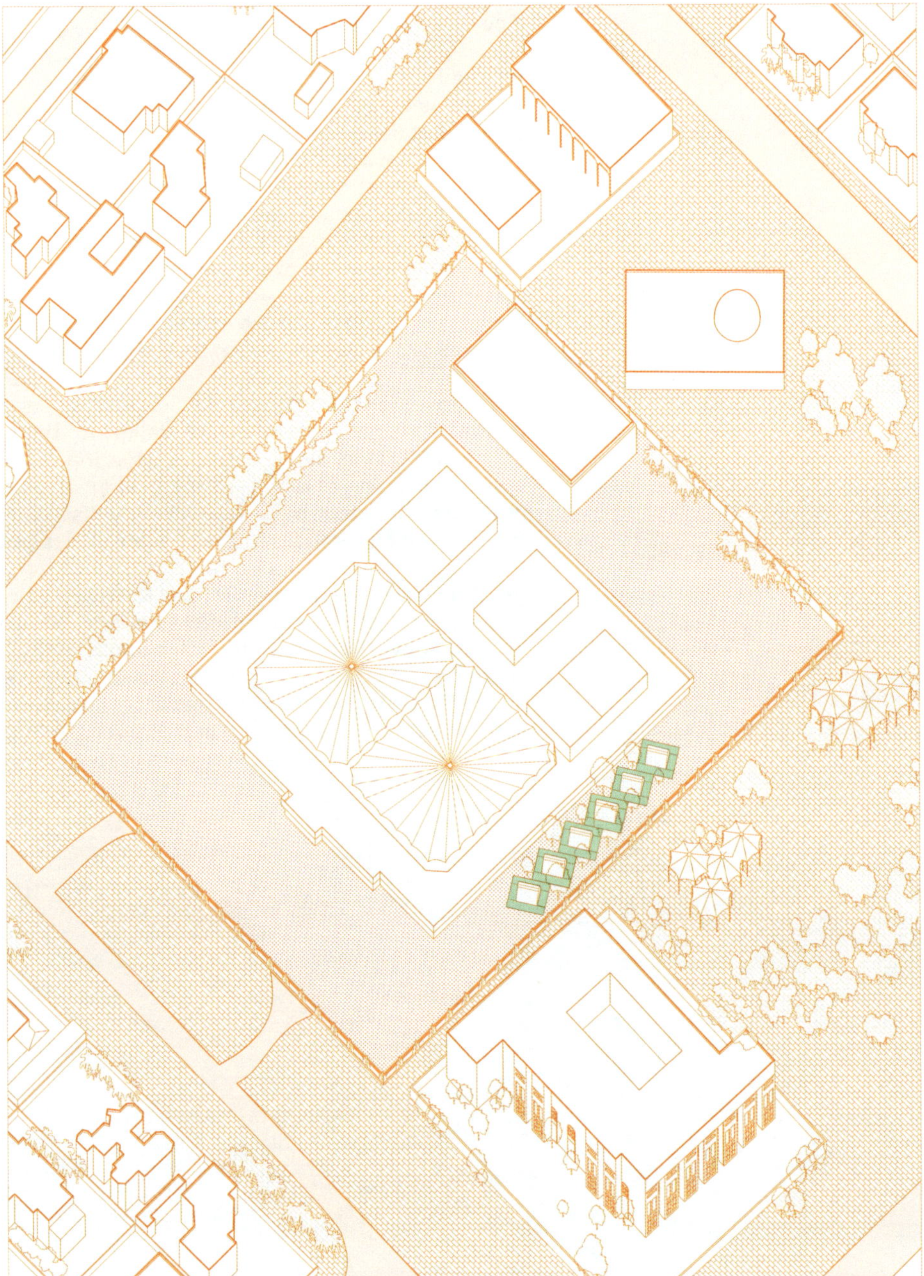
1 10 50

## Speculative Scenario 1: **Backyard**

It's the first week of July: a week of cucumber harvest. The splashing of children in the pool has fallen silent after a hot day in the sun. Amina, a resident in Dubai, walks out her back door with her son and heads to the greenhouse to collect their share for the month. This greenhouse assembly belongs to the residential compound and is maintained by a regular service fee included in her rent to supplement electricity and water usage. Families take turns tending to it, pruning leaves, checking moisture levels, and ensuring that the fans are turned on when they should be.

Walking under the retractable shade, she hears the bustle of the harvesters as she walks into the cooler interior space, along with the whirring of fans and the dripping of water on the evaporative cooling pads. The neighbors have already distributed most of the cucumbers in the residents' designated baskets. Along the wooden table in the interior, her neighbors are slicing cucumbers for fresh salads, while others are swapping pickling jars. "Mom, did you know that cucumbers are some of the only crops that can survive the UAE's heat in a greenhouse?" asked her son as he toyed around with the long vines. "Can we grow green peppers, tomatoes, and lettuce when the weather gets better, like we did last year?"

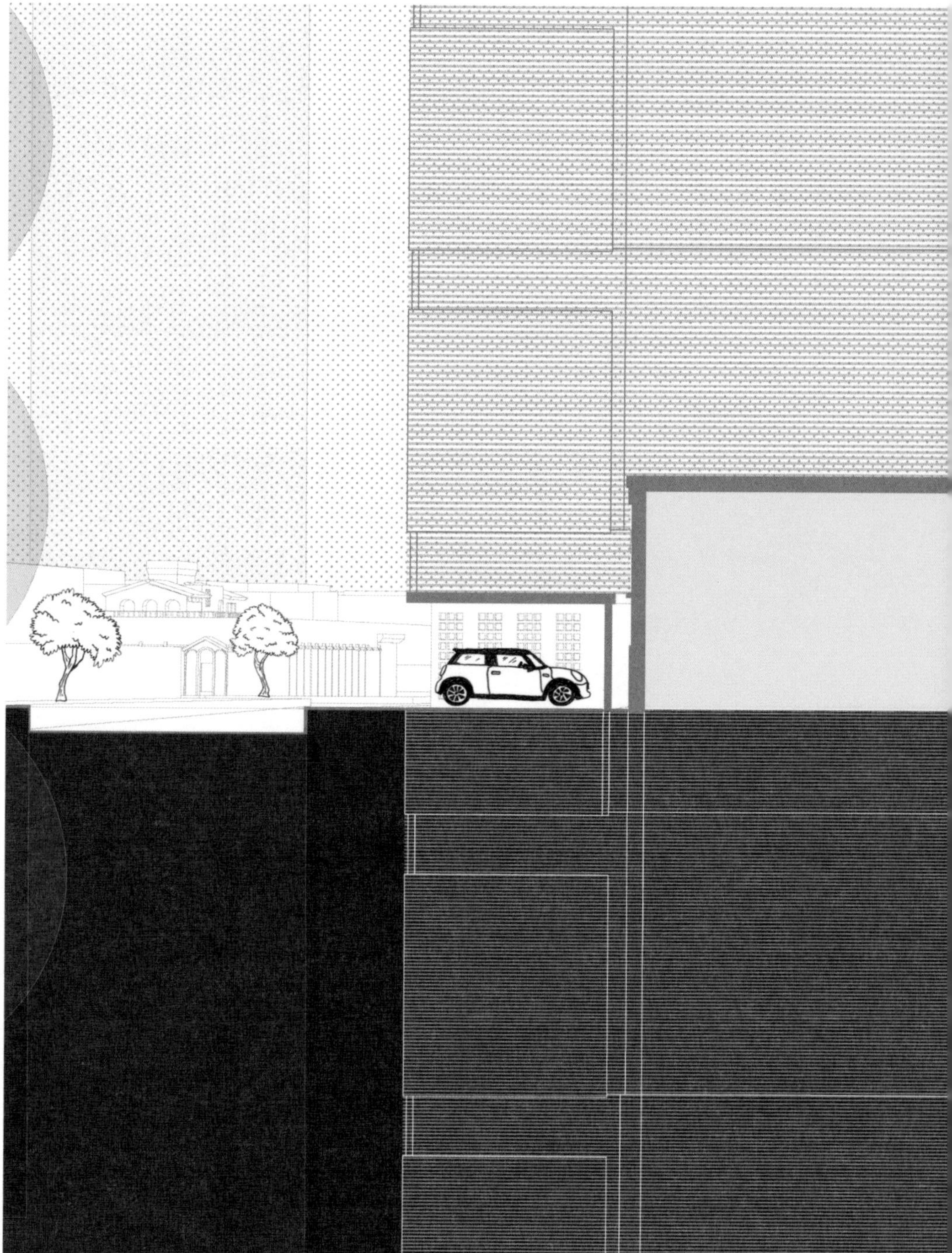

Fig. 06 Section perspective drawing of Arenco 26 villas in Dubai. Drawn by author and Noor Hamdan. I

rations by Khalid Mezaina.

**Al Shahba, Sharjah:**

Unique characteristics: Residential center with a green spine on the east border and retail on the west border

Typical plot size: 450–2000 m$^2$

Infrastructural and public spaces: Taryam Omran Secondary School, Ibn Seena English High School and Shahba Park

Fig. 07 Map of Wasit suburb in Sharjah, with potential allocations of the kit-of-parts. Drawn by author and Noor Hamdan.

Figs. 08-10 Selected sites in Wasit suburb in Sharjah, with potential allocations of the kit-of-parts. Drawn by author and Noor Hamdan.

Figs. 11-13 Axonometric of Wasit suburb in Sharjah, with potential allocations of the kit-of-parts. Drawn by Noor Hamdan.

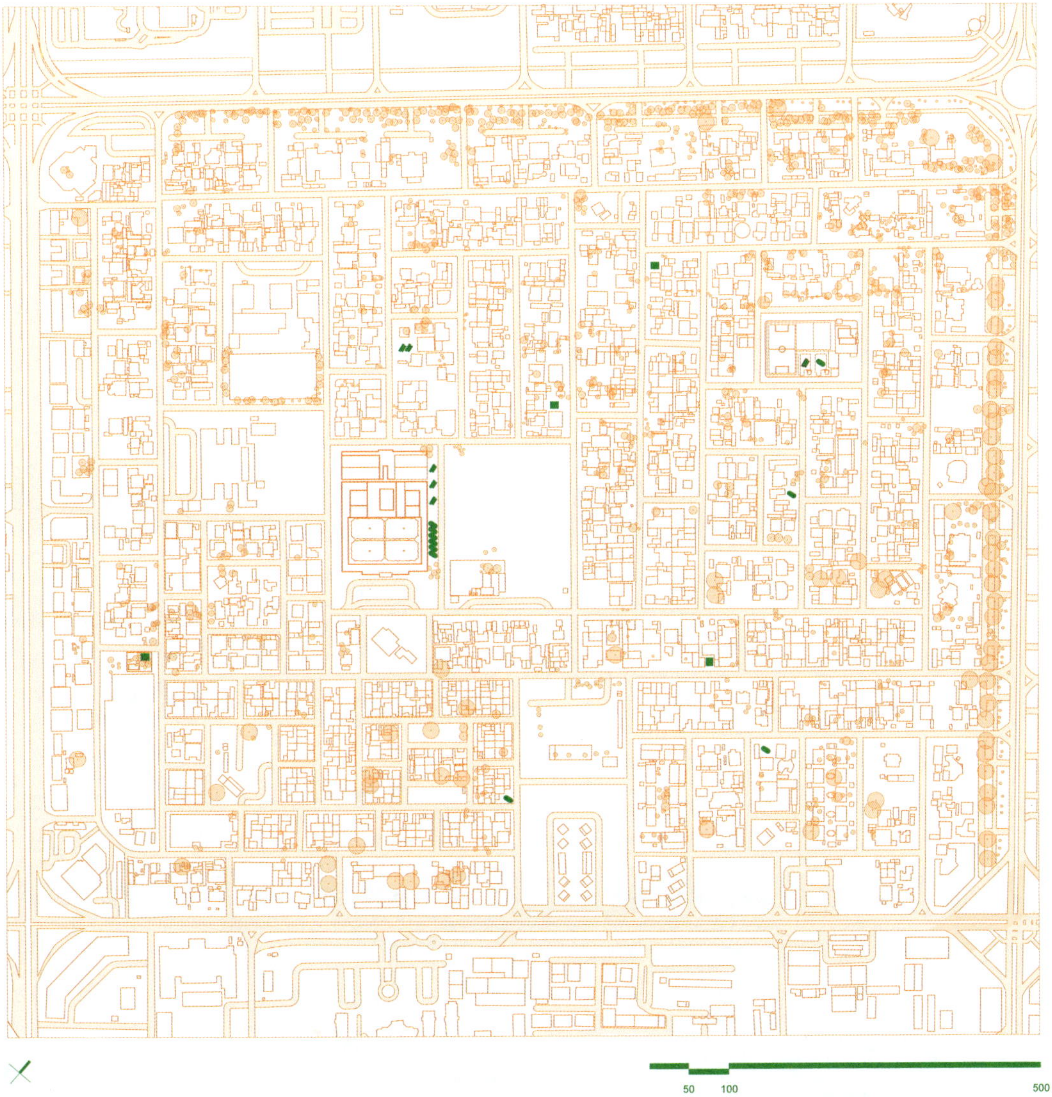


07

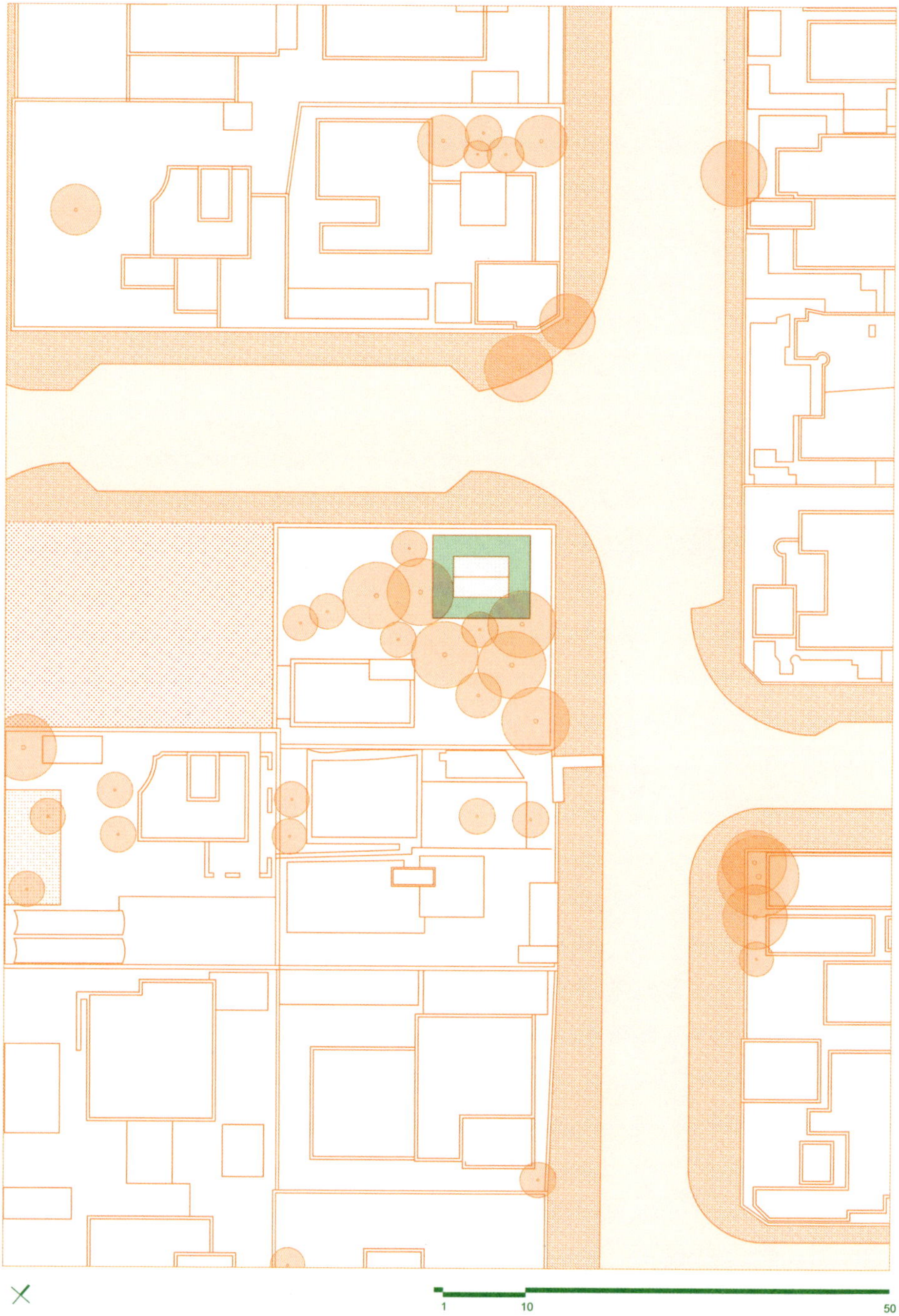
1
10
50

1
10
50

1
10
50

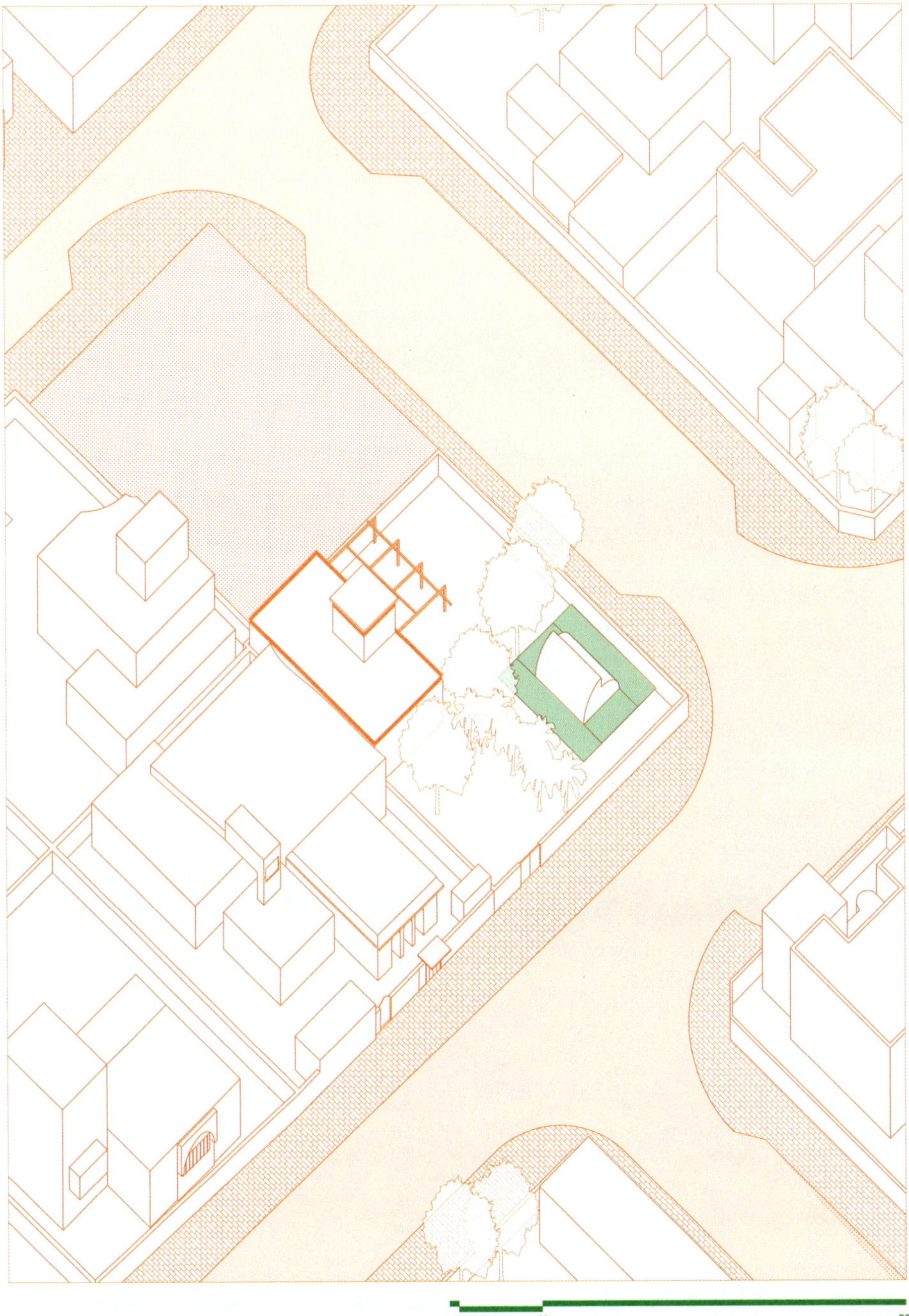
1
10
50

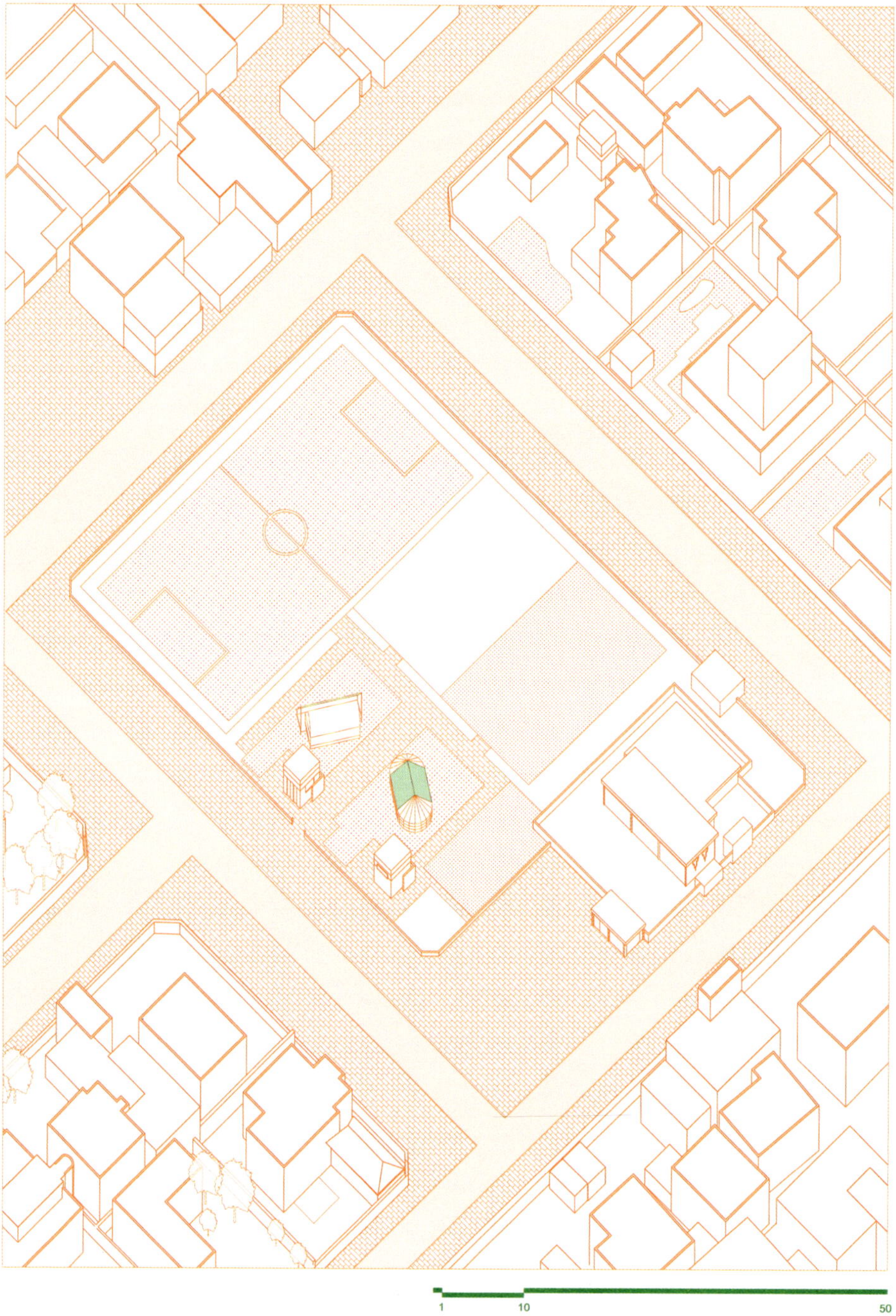
1
10
50

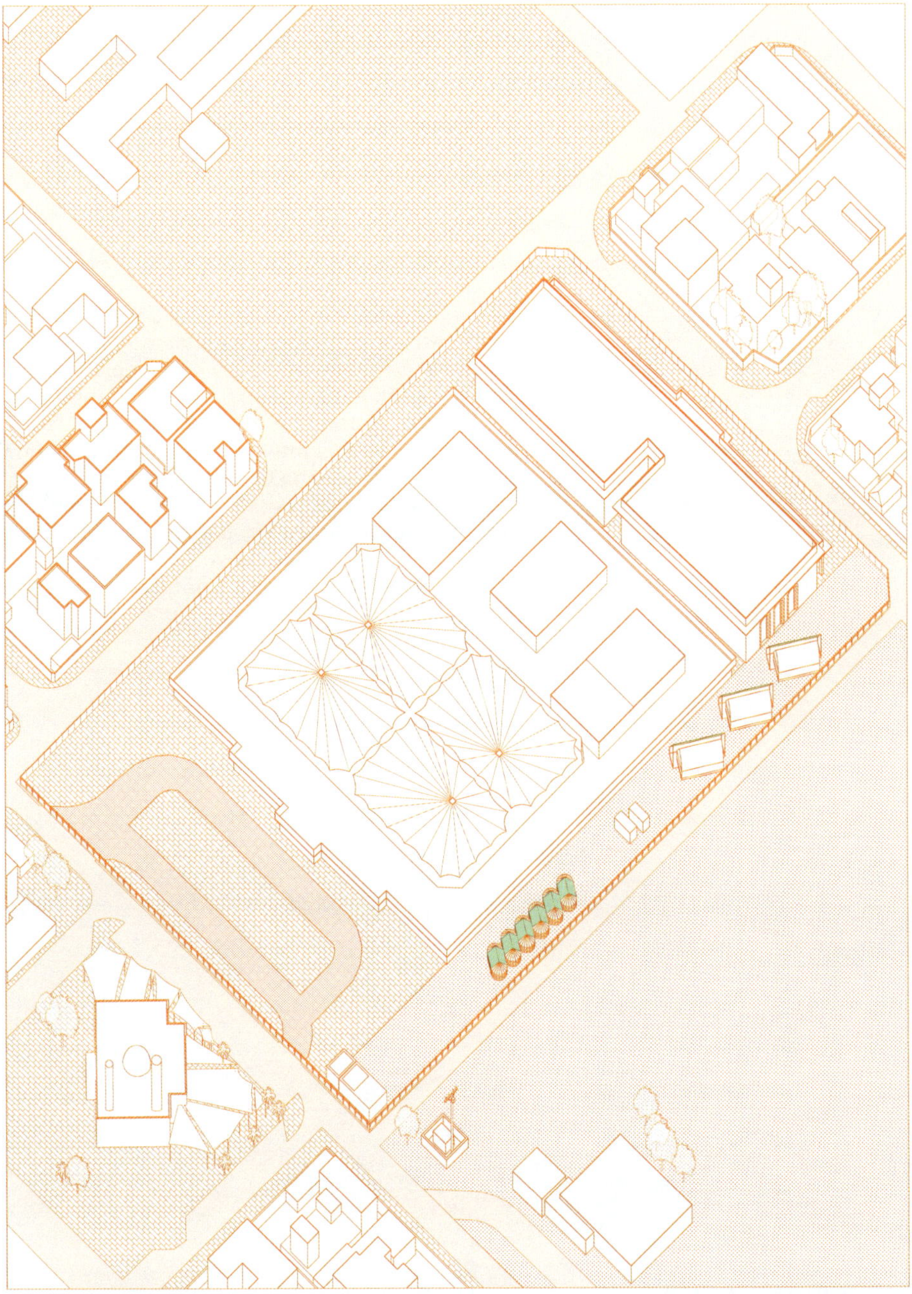
1
10
50

Zoning: Mixed-use
Speculative Scenario 2: **Edge**

Late November usually marks the beginning of the season for vegetable sharing in the UAE. Since the new greenhouse assemblies were installed in the neighborhood, one for each interested family, Salem took on managing an assembly for his household consumption. He inherited his love of agriculture from his late father, who was an Al Dhaid native.

While he helped with putting up some of the greenhouse structures himself, his nightly routine now involves checking on the greenhouse, turning off the pump for the evaporative cooling pad, and opening roof panels so cooler autumn air can circulate during nighttime. His daughter, who was helping him that evening, made sure to unfold the green shade net so it could shield the leaves from the morning sun. She brushes her hands along the rough CMU surface that hasn't fully cooled down yet as they head home. "Dad!" she exclaims, "we forgot the box of zucchini

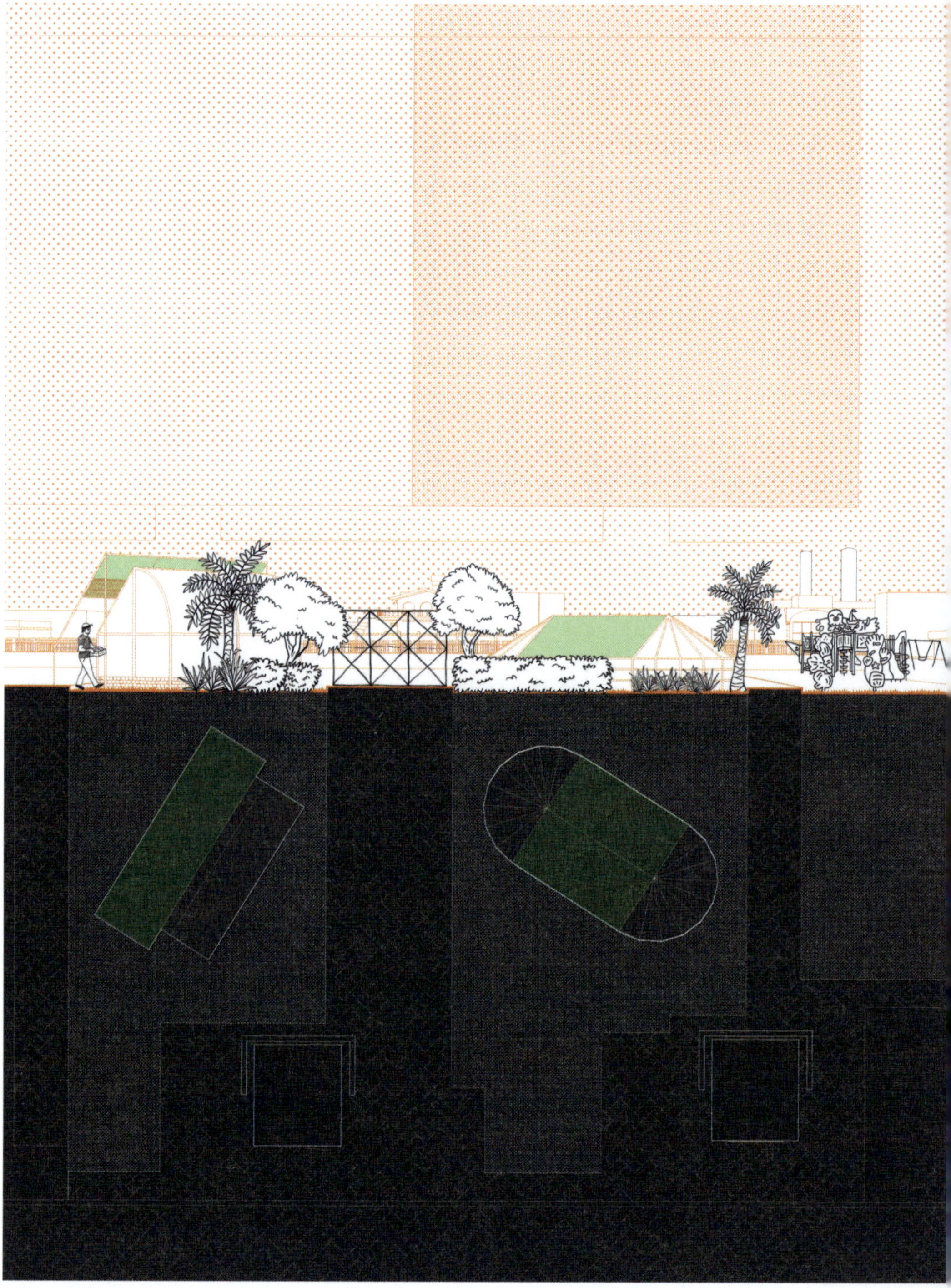

Fig. 14 Section Perspective Drawing of Wasit suburb's green edge in Sharjah. Drawn by author and Noor

ndan. Illustrations by Khalid Mezaina.

for Auntie in the greenhouse."
**Mohamed Bin Zayed City (Z31), Abu Dhabi:**

Unique characteristics: Typical residential lot

Typical plot size: 2025 m$^2$

Infrastructural and public spaces: Al Angham Park (contains a cafeteria and a mini market) and Al Wahah Park

Fig. 15 Map of Mohamed Bin Zayed City (Z31), Abu Dhabi, with potential allocations of the kit-of-parts. Drawn by author , Noor Hamdan, and Nourhan Rahhal.

Figs. 16, 17 Selected sites in Mohamed Bin Zayed City (Z31), with potential allocations of the kit-of-parts. Drawn by author, Noor Hamdan, and Nourhan Rahhal.

Figs. 18, 19 Axonometric of Mohamed Bin Zayed City (Z31), Abu Dhabi, with potential allocations of the kit-of-parts. Drawn by author, Noor Hamdan, and Nourhan Rahhal.

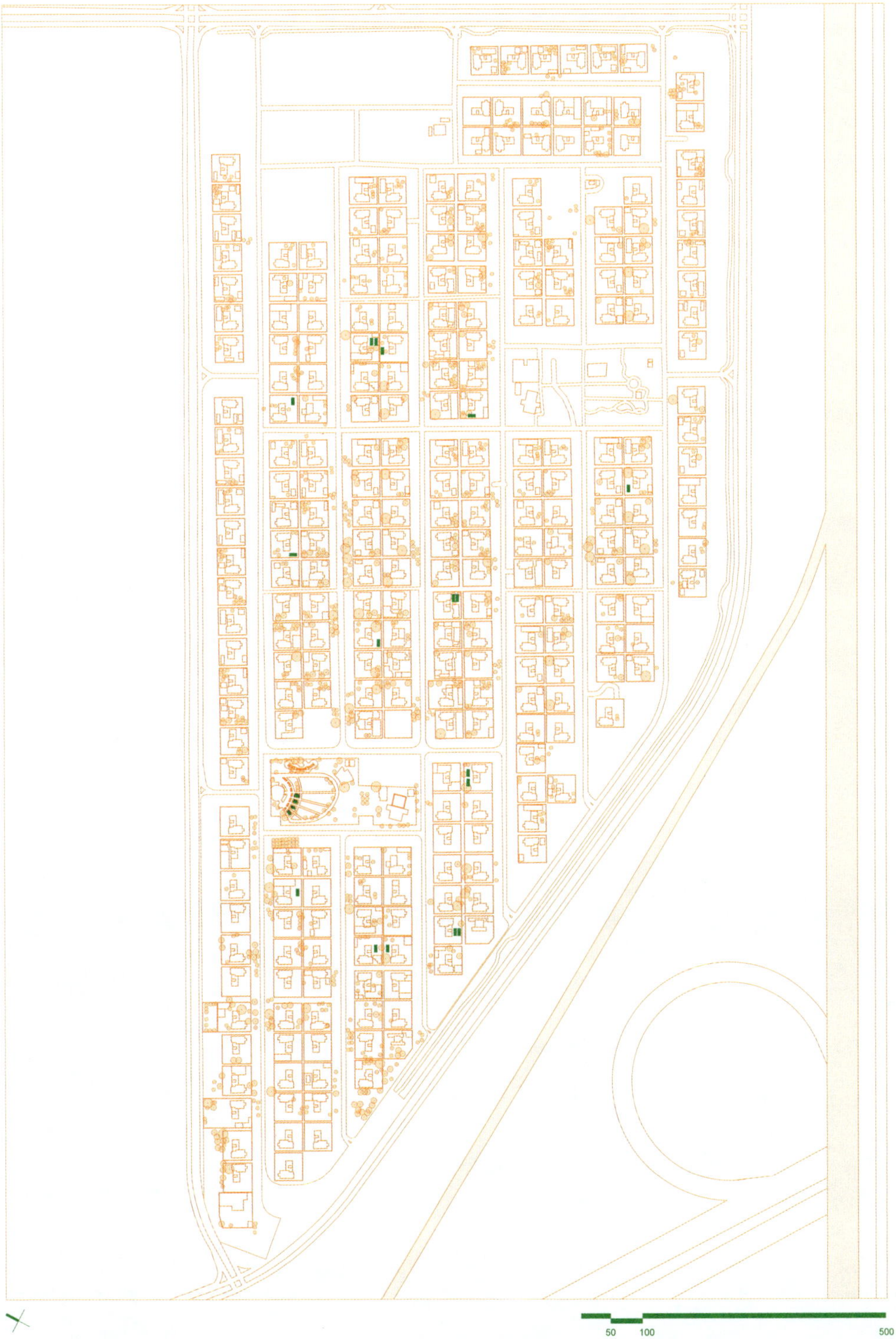


15

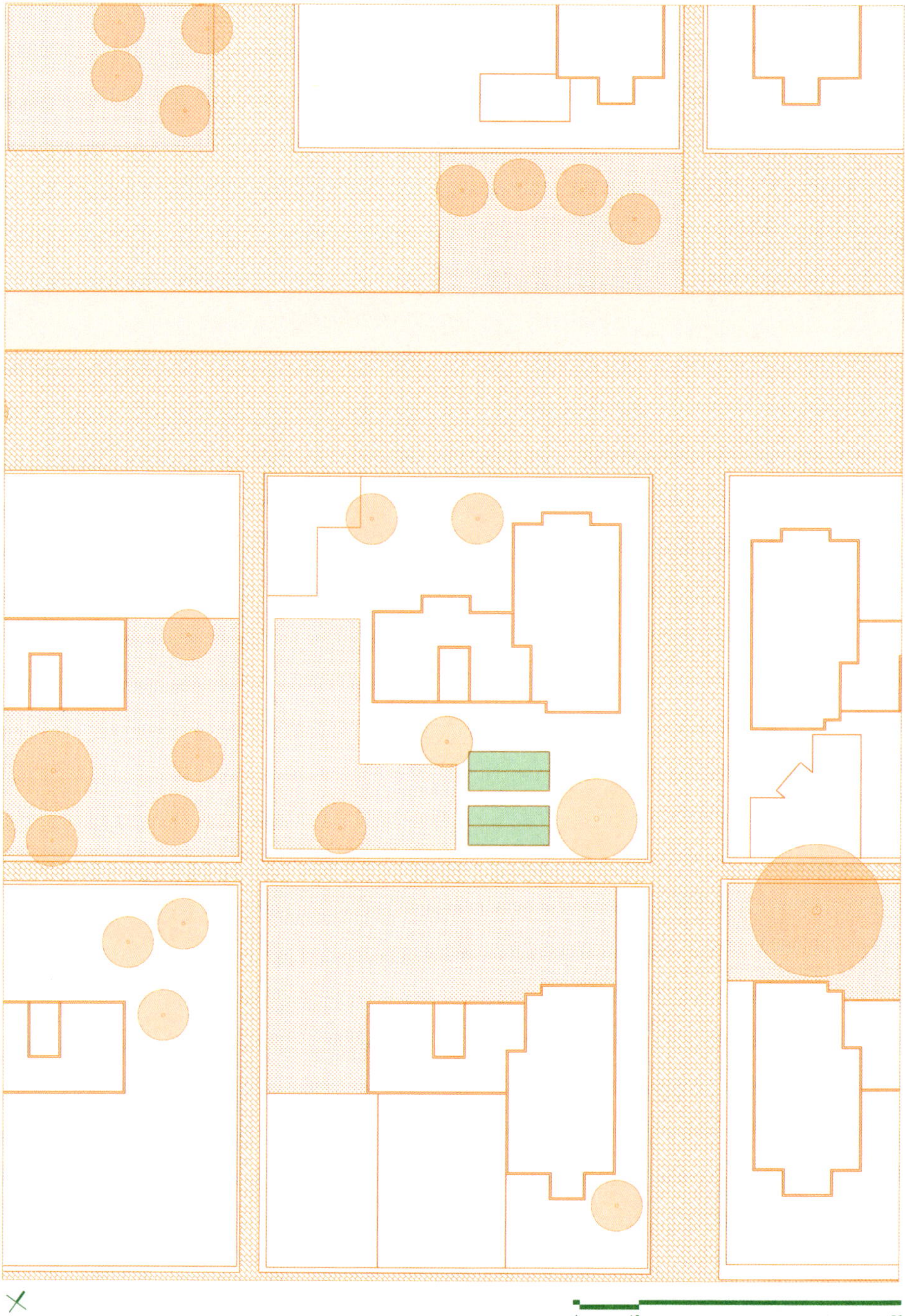

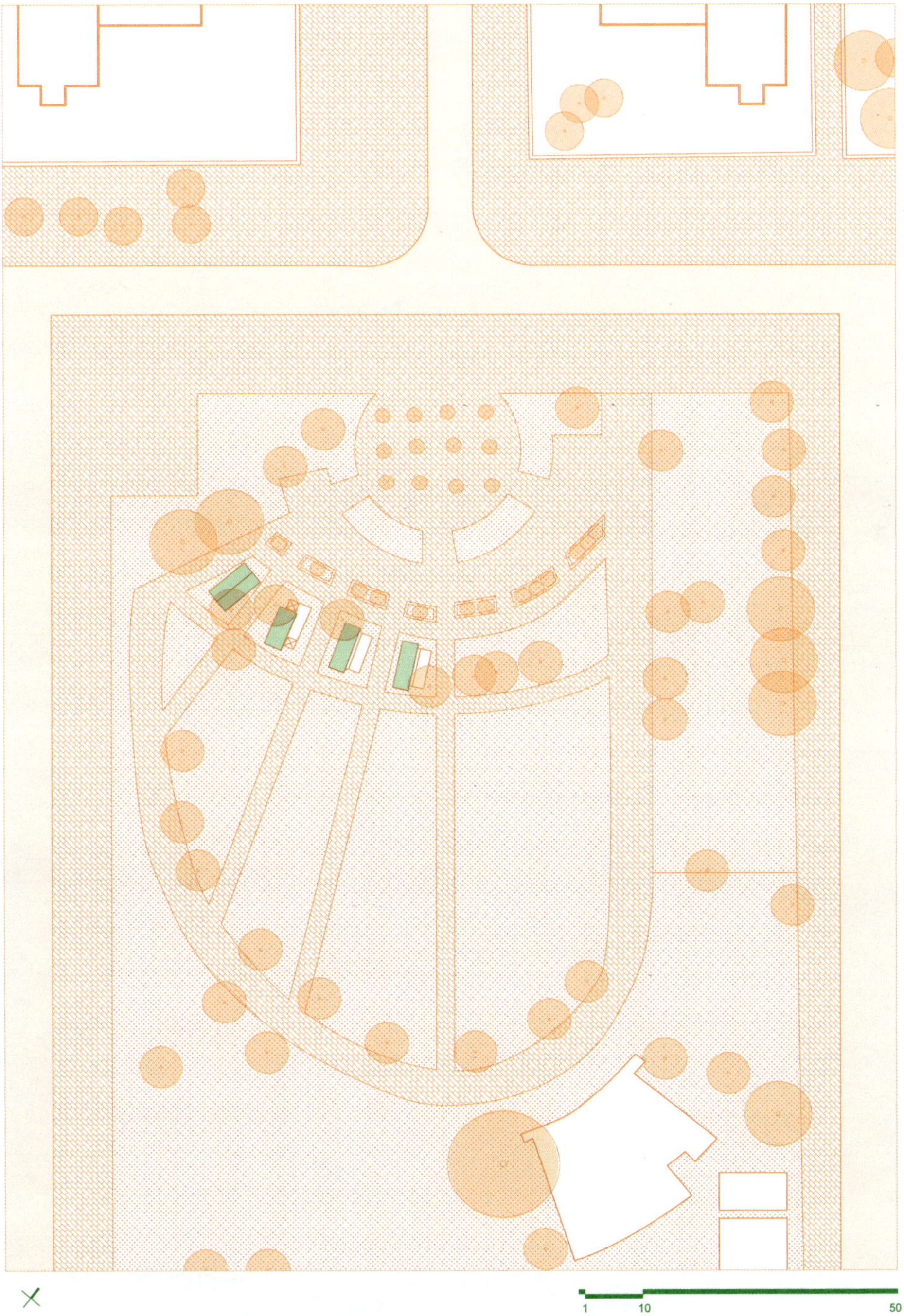
1
10
50

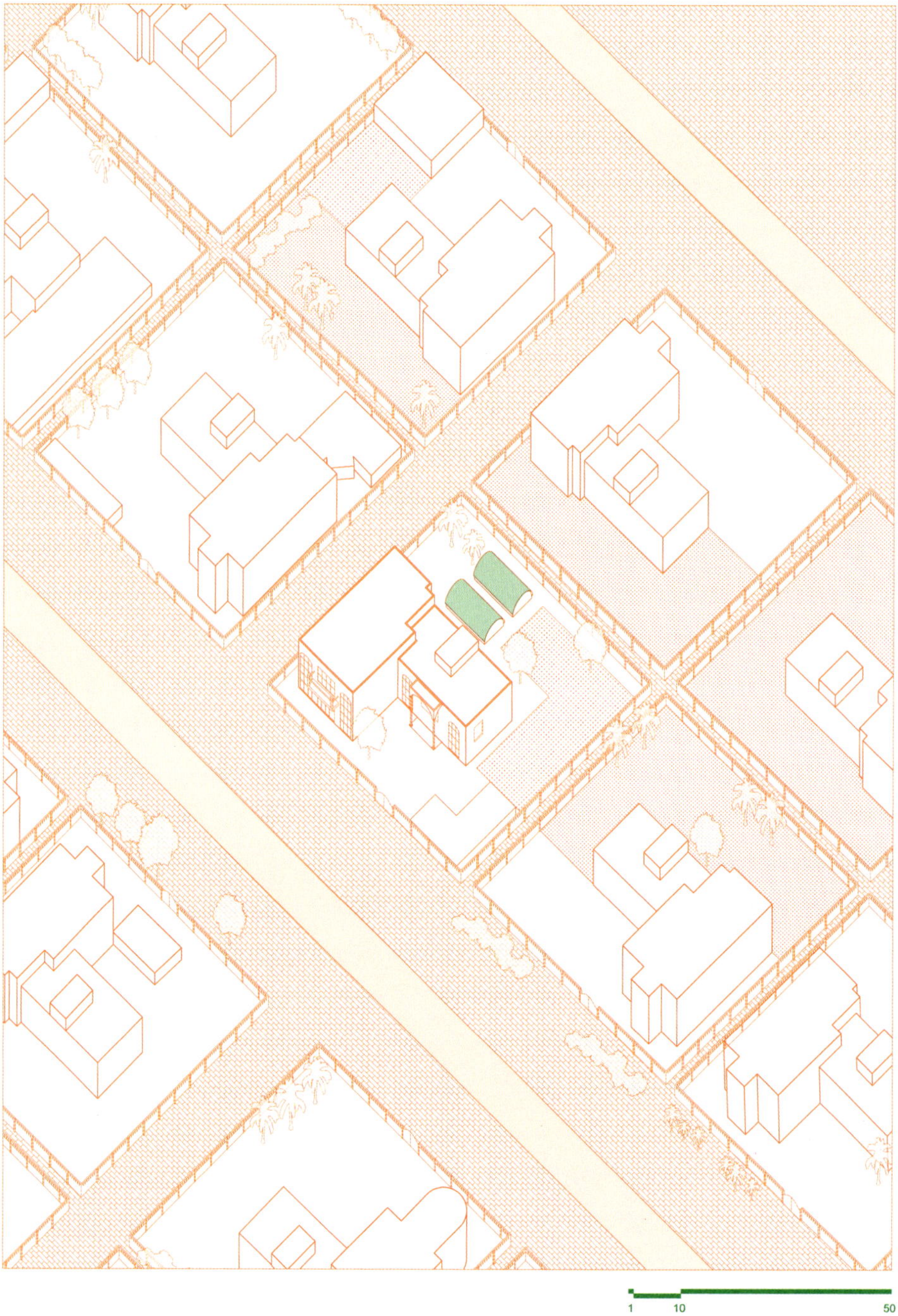
1
10
50

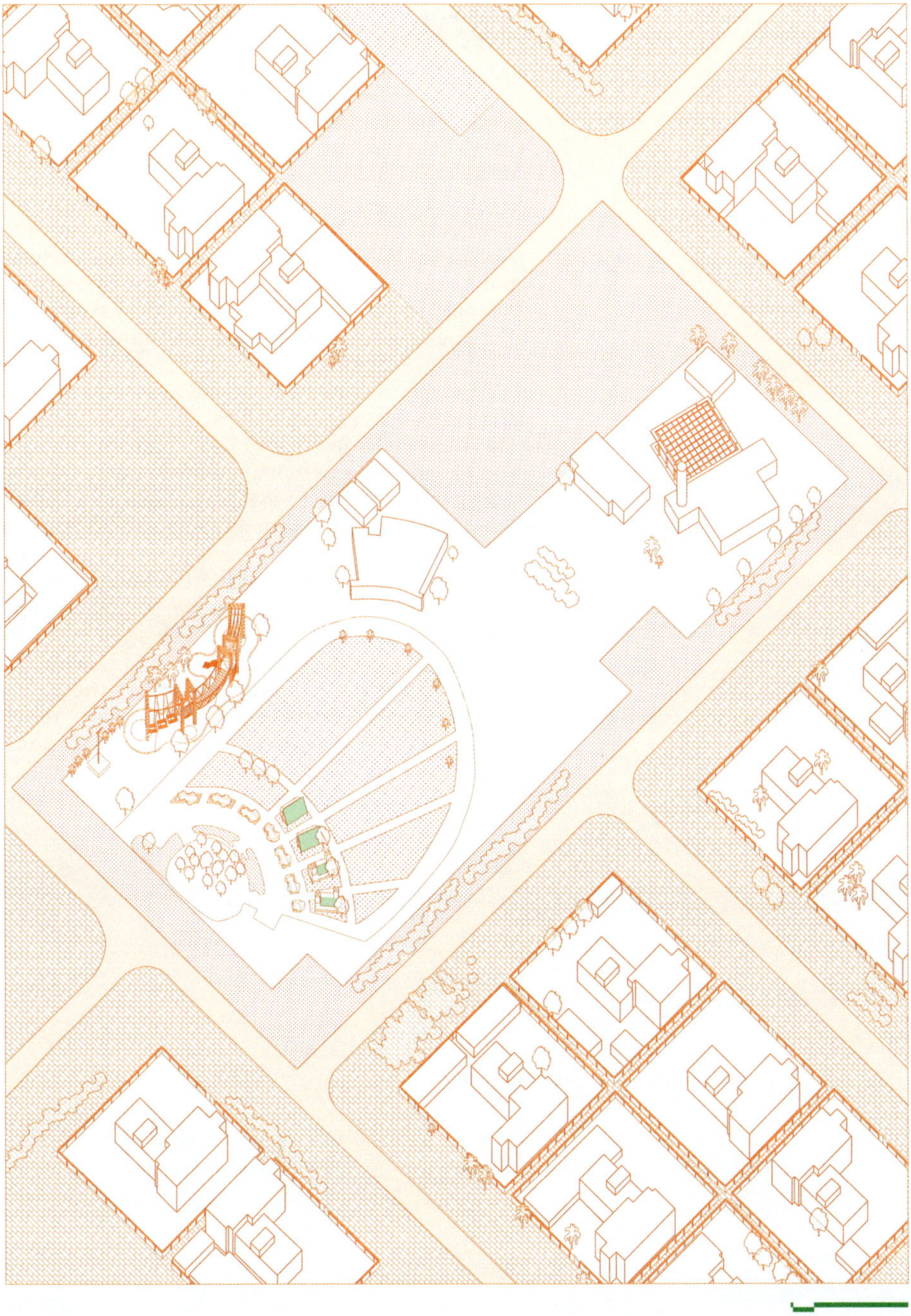
1 10 50

Zoning: Residential
Speculative scenario 3: **Center**

On Friday afternoons, Moza picks up her younger sister Fatma after school. They make a weekly visit to the local park that has integrated a greenhouse in their neighborhood in Abu Dhabi. This project is part of a larger scheme, a collaboration between the municipality and the Agriculture and Food Safety Authority. While Fatma and Moza used to visit the park sparingly in the past, their weekly visits have become routine, especially when they started buying the park's local produce for their family.

It's the middle of February and a crisp breeze rustles the tree's leaves in the park. As the girls park the car, Fatma can see her cousins waiting for her by the greenhouse with its green shade net down. She was excited for this week's harvest: strawberries from Greenhouse Assembly A. While all the greenhouse assemblies in the park grow crops in rotation, this one is nearing the end of the berry season. She always looks forward to papaya, grapes, and pineapples in the summer, but the fresh eggs that come out of Greenhouse Assembly C are her favorite. "Don't forget to get the eggs for Mom from the *dukan* before we go home," Moza reminded her. "You know how particular she gets about the park's eggs."

---

*Neighborhood scale convenience store in UAE neighborhoods.*

Fig. 20 Section Perspective Drawing of Al Angham Park in Abu Dhabi. Drawn by author and Noor Hamdan.

strations by Khalid Mezaina.

## Conclusion

The story of how our food is grown and gets from farm to plate is an important one. While vertical farms claim that they can "feed the world in the twenty-first century," those instances often follow a specific food system model of profit maximization and resource use efficiency, subscribing to specific logics that usually prioritize yield and performance. [■] The rise of urban agriculture cannot go unnoticed as a vital strategy for building the resilience of a city's food supply. In the West, classic definitions of urban agriculture increase employment and improve nutritional outcomes. While urban agriculture is not considered a foolproof strategy, when combined with effective city-region planning, the food production system can more efficiently meet the needs of populations residing in urban areas.

The UAE currently hosts more than 200 nationalities who live and work in the country. While the Emirati population constitutes 11.6% of the total population, the South Asian contingent constitutes 59.4%, which includes Indian 38.2%, Bangladeshi 9.5%, Pakistani 9.4%, other 2.3%). [●] One of the conversations that I had with Dr. Majid Al Qassimi, from Soma Mater, illustrated an interesting analogy with regard to knowing when the UAE has achieved its intended food security: making sure it sufficiently produces the ingredients needed for biryani and karak, or maintains adequate reserves for its production. Even though this analogy provides insight into how elusive the definitions of food security and self-sufficiency can be in the UAE, there is something to be said about activating underutilized public spaces in neighborhoods as systemized sites of food production. The expansion of new residential communities allows us the opportunity to rethink the structure of a residential neighborhood, all the while harnessing the nation's natural resources and keeping pace with a continued population boom and surging demand for housing and infrastructure. This speculation takes a moment to reflect on the future of Emirati neighborhoods, offering new generations new modes of living among sites of active food production.

[■] *Alana Siegner, Jennifer Sowerwine, and Charisma Acey, "Does Urban Agriculture Improve Food Security? Examining the Nexus of Food Access and Distribution of Urban Produced Foods in the United States: A Systematic Review,"* ***Sustainability*** *10, no. 9 (2018): 2988, https://doi.org/10.3390/su10092988.*

[●] *Central Intelligence Agency, "United Arab Emirates,"* ***The World Factbook****, last updated January 9, 2025, https://www.cia.gov/the-world-factbook/countries/united-arab-emirates/.*

# Reviving Self-Reliance:

## *The Resurgence of Backyard Farming and Livestock Management in Emirati Suburban Villas*

Rashed Almulla

*Erhard F. Gabriel, **The Dubai Handbook**, Dubai Petroleum, 1985.*

*Dawn Chatty, "Culture Summary: Bedouin," **Human Relations Area Files,** (New Haven, CT: Human Relations Area Files, 2009), https://ehrafworldcultures.yale.edu/document?id=mj04-000.*

*Ibid.*

*Evelyn A. Early, review of Aesthetics and Ritual in the United Arab Emirates by Aida Kanafani, **Middle East Studies Association Bulletin** 18, no. 2 (December 1984): 183–185, https://www.jstor.org/stable/41887992.*

*Juma Khalifa Ahmed bin Thalith Al-Himyari, **Encyclopedia of the Emirates Wildlife: Part One** (Dubai: Knowledge and Human Development Authority, 2013), https://altibrah.ae/book/16538.*

*Arabian Gulf Digital Archive, **Internal Political Situation in Muscat and Oman** (FO 371/120542), 1956, https://www.agda.ae/.*

***Ingredients***

Camel Milk
Foraged Plants
Chicken Feed
Backyard
Animal Pen
Almond Tree

## Introduction

The Omani farmer Ibrahim AlSanani shares his techniques on Instagram for growing a variety of produce with his 200,000 followers, many of whom live in Dubai. In the United Arab Emirates (UAE), Halal 2020 organizes online livestock auctions where followers bid on Australian goats and Pakistani sheep. Meanwhile, Kuwaiti gardener Alzainah Albabtain, with her 1.2 million followers, challenges narratives of farming limitations in the desert by proving that backyard gardening is a viable hobby across the region. Coupled with the recent COVID-19 pandemic, the rise of these influencers across social media platforms from the Gulf Cooperation Council (GCC) region led to the revival of old habits: the resurgence of backyard utilization as a means to forming self-sustaining mechanisms. While these habits saw a decline in the past two decades, due to government restrictions and lack of time, these reshaped habits, routines, and behaviors influenced how Emirati families perceive and engage with their domestic spaces. This research delves into the origins of animal husbandry and growing produce in Dubai's suburbs, articulating its origins, peak, downfall, and recent revival.

## A Self-Sustaining Start

The juxtaposed nature of urban and rural Dubai can be further understood from the practices of produce and livestock management in the domestic space. Prior to the UAE's union in 1971, Dubai's urban residents grew their own produce, whether it was in their limestone and mud dwellings or palm frond structures. Simultaneously, on the outskirts of the city, Emirati Bedouins shared similar traits of self-reliance that their pastoral nomadic lifestyle supported. Animals were commonly used to provide milk, eggs, fur, or hair, and most importantly, meat as a form of sustenance. Each of those activities was associated with its architectural counterpart. Every Bedouin commune had a *zarb* or *zerb* (animal pen) or its counterpart in the mountains called *dars*.

Other structures included the *hadheera* (open-air enclosure) circled by *areesh* (palm fronds), which was used as a place for men to gather. Bedouins moved outward during winter to find new wells, settle in warmer dunes, and search for local flora which was crucial to feed the animals. Some groups even adapted to the hot summers by feeding fish to their sheep, which resulted in saltier meat — a culinary nuance rooted in environmental adaptation. Livestock and their management remained essential to these communities, connecting families through shared practices of animal care and trade across the Arabian Peninsula.

Camel herding, for example, remains a cultural touchstone across the UAE. Historically, Bedouins traveled between Al Ain and Dubai, trading livestock, dates, and other local goods with urban merchants. These exchanges created a cycle of self-sufficiency that bridged rural and urban lifestyles, allowing Bedouins to influence city dwellers' customs and diets.

A. Abdulrahman, **Between Sips of Coffee** (Esdarat - Department of Culture and Tourism, 2014).

Marvine Howe, "Abu Dhabi adapting to Modern World," **The New York Times**, January 14, 1972.

Yasser Elsheshtawy. "Research Materials," in **Transformations: The Emirati National House**, Ed. Yasser Elsheshtawy, (Abu Dhabi, National Pavilion United Arab Emirates la Biennale di Venezia, 2016), 93.

Ibid, 97.

Ibid.

Yasser Elsheshtawy et al., "'Transformations: The Emirati National House': Inside UAE's Pavilion at the 2016 Venice Biennale," **ArchDaily**, August 22, 2016, https://www.archdaily.com/789101/transformations-the-emirati-national-house-inside-uaes-pavilion-at-the-2016-venice-biennale.

Yasser Elsheshtawy. "The Al Meqbali House: A Case Study," In **Transformations: The Emirati National House**, Ed. Yasser Elsheshtawy, (Abu Dhabi, National Pavilion United Arab Emirates la Biennale di Venezia, 2016), 238.

Rashed Almulla, The Rise, Demise, and Possible Revival of Al-Hamriyah (Deira), **Dubai: Land Policies, Social Cohesion, and Possible Reforms**. Unpublished Thesis. (2021).

For centuries, Bedouins have cherished camel milk. In the early hours of dawn, a camel caretaker takes the herd and wanders into the desert. Back at the farm, the owner collects camel milk and shares it with family and friends, while the surplus is sold. A Bedouin elder, the late Rashid bin Ghilaita Al Qamzi, from Hili village in Al Ain, speaks of the cultural and nutritional value of camel's milk. At 125 years of age, Al Qamzi attributes his longevity to his traditional lifestyle, which included camel herding. "My life has always been rooted in caring for these animals and drinking their milk," Al Qamzi explains, noting that his days included trips to Al Ain market to buy fodder for his herd of over 2,000 camels. (Fig. 01)

Fig.01 A greenhouse at a farm in Al Khawaneej, Dubai. Photo by author.

## Modernity in Flux, Traditions Anchored

The 1960s marked a turning point in the Gulf, as economic prosperity fueled urban growth across the Arabian Peninsula. To accommodate shifting lifestyles, the UAE's government introduced the *sha'bi* (pl. *sha'biyaat*, adj. *sha'abiyah*) housing typology, or "the people's house," designed to settle the transient populations living in areesh houses at the time. Japanese architect Kisho Kurokawa, after visiting Abu Dhabi's outskirts, observed an unexpected use of sha'biyaat, saying: "The owners set up tents outside for themselves and kept their livestock in the houses. The concrete structures were ovens, trapping the day's heat, so they found it more comfortable to live outside," signaling that it was not designed with Bedouin traditions in mind.

By the 1970s, urban homes were increasingly designed to incorporate animal spaces, either as pens in the backyard or as enclosures that were attached to the main house. A 1972 *Aletihad Newspaper* article celebrated a new sha'abiyah housing development, noting that "the outdoor spaces are left open to raise chickens and cultivate a vegetable garden." In 1974, another article in *Aletihad newspaper* mentions that a field visit was conducted by the minister of housing in Fujairah to a dwelling that consisted of two bedrooms on a plot of land that was 1829 square meters (6,000 square feet). The vast land was provided to encourage agricultural and self-reliance habits. Furthermore, the chicken pens that were not physically connected to domestic spaces have now been integrated. Both articles exemplify how traditional animal rearing and gardening practices were preserved in the face of rapid urbanization in the UAE.

## Building a Community

The sha'abiyaat were relatively dense neighborhoods with plots averaging around 380 square meters (1246 square feet), which encouraged family cohesion. Livestock management and farming were important aspects of community building, especially when it came to sharing goods with neighbors, such as dates from palm trees, eggs from chickens, and Eid meat. In "Transformations of the Emirati National Housing," Yasser Elsheshtawy examines Al Meqbali house as a case study, mentioning the adjustments that were made to the sha'bi house to include chickens, goats, and sheep.

"Most Emirati families have their own animals such as chickens and goats or cows. At the back of the house, they built a closed area from concrete for the animals." In an interview with Shaabiyah Al-Hamriyah's residents in Deira, built in the 1960s, many interviewees mentioned that chickens and, to some extent, goats were common. It was considered a way of life that was inherited from their ancestors and would be passed onto future generations.

*Khaled Alawadhi, **Lifescapes Beyond Bigness** (Artifice, 2018).*

## Inherited into Late Modernity

To further understand the relationship between architecture and food production in Dubai's domestic spaces, 30 interviews were conducted to fully paint a picture of life back then, specifically between the 1980s and the 1990s. The rapid and fast-paced urban development that began in the late 1970s and the 1980s resulted in the expansion of Emirati cities, with their size increasing multifold. In addition to plot sizes increasing significantly, a number of changes were introduced such as electric house appliances, the use of cars, and concrete as a building material. However, cultural traditions such as gifting home-cooked meals, livestock, and produce have certainly continued. The detachment of the domestic space from the boundary walls that surrounded the villa affected the selection of amenities that were later included in the plot. Those were customized to the land-owner's needs and inclinations, such as a pool, pergola, or outdoor seating. This was further supported by water and electricity subsidies provided by the government. An interviewee mentioned that the freedom to design their backyard felt like a Lego puzzle, emphasizing the unlimited choices one had within the spacious lot. In response, animal pens were constructed to accommodate chickens, goats, or sheep, in various sizes and materials. Some of those included fenced open-air structures with chain-link fencing, triangular *shinko* (corrugated steel), flat sheds, or fabric roof coverings.

The types of architectural interventions to host animals were:

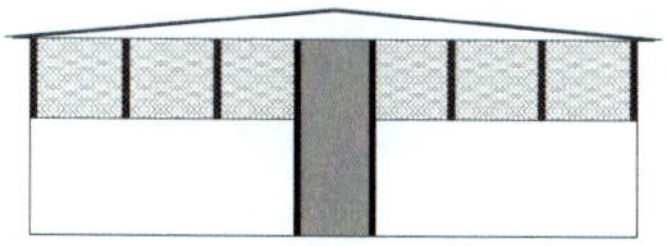

Fig.02A Cement and steel enclosures
- Steel fencing covered with green fabric
- Wooden modules for water, feed, and rest

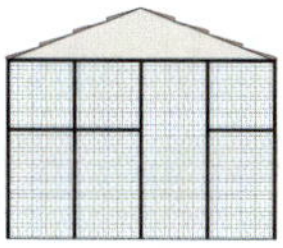

Fig.02B Triangular sheds with red shinko

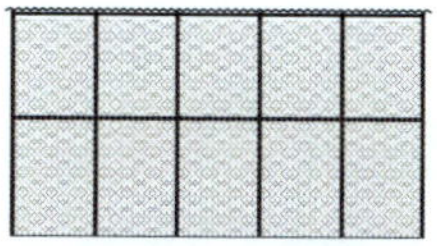

Fig.02C Flat-roofed sheds

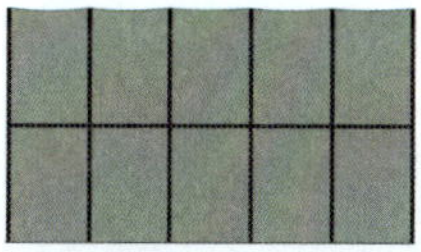

Fig.02D Cloth-based coverings for the roof

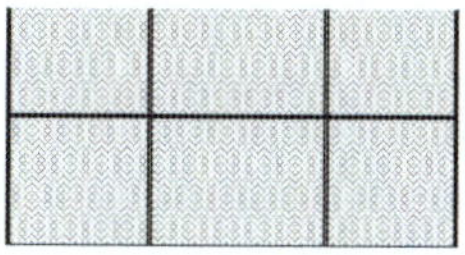

Fig.02E Roofless enclosures

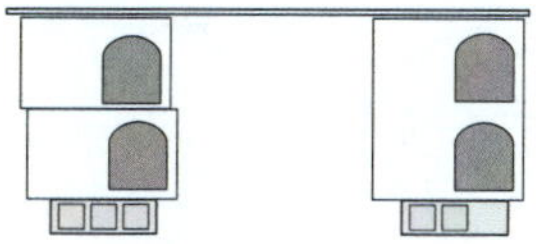

Fig.02F Birdhouse remodeled to host chickens

Fig.02: Diagrams of multiple villas in the UAE. Drawn by Noor Hamdan.

Interviewees living in neighborhoods such as Jumeirah 2, which was planned in the late 1980s, felt that allowing the chickens to roam freely in the early morning hours was a good neighborly practice. Most of those who had livestock in their homes in the 1980s inherited such practices from their parents, while others were inspired by their friends who practiced at the time. An interviewee mentioned: “My late grandmother was the one with the idea, which inspired my mother to carry on the tradition in my parent’s house.” (Figs. 03, 04)

Fig.03 A herd of goats and sheep in a pen structure in Al Ruwayyah, Dubai. Photo by Ola Allouz.

Fig.04 An unused animal pen located outside a residential house in Al-Awir, Dubai. Photo by Azza Aboualam.

## To Regulate a Backyard

As the late 1990s progressed, interviewees mentioned that moving to a new house in a new neighborhood affected social cohesion negatively. This was, in part, attributed to the new norms of a busy urban life, which has evidently impacted the rate of sharing produce and livestock among neighbors. The decline in cohesion led to an increased number of complaints, such as odor or noise, between neighbors. Two of the interviewees mentioned that raising the phone to call the municipality was the easiest way to deal with problems. As a result, in 2003, the government of Dubai, through the Dubai Municipality, revised all laws pertaining to public health. This led to the official prohibition of raising animals in residential areas. The ban did not include pets or those that were kept indoors. After the law's enactment, enforcement began in the form of knocking on people's doors and asking them to discard their livestock. Out of the 30 respondents surveyed and interviewed, a fifth mentioned that they stopped raising livestock due to the newly enforced regulations, leading to the reduction in the number of houses with goats, sheep, or chickens. The law was not the first of its kind but it certainly was the most impactful.

*Government of Dubai and Dubai Municipality, **Public Health and Safety of the Society in the Emirate of Dubai,** (Local Order No.11 of 2003), 2003, 6. https://www.wkcgroup.com/wp-content/uploads/2023/04/Local-Order-No.-11-of-2003-Concerning-Public-Health-and-Safety-of-the-Society-in-the-Emirate-of-Dubai.pdf.*

أمل الفلاسي، «حظر تربية المواشي في الأحياء السكنية»، **صحيفة البيان**، 7 نوفمبر 2007، مأخوذ من *https://www.albayan.ae/across-the-uae/07-11-2007-1.805734.*

*Ibid.*

*Ahmed Bin Darwish, "Residents in Al Twar complain of free roaming livestock," **Emarat Al Youm**, March 18, 2013. Retrieved from https://www.emaratalyoum.com/hotline/2013-03-18-1.558327.*

*Sajila Saseendran, "Top 3 Reasons Why Dubai Residents Complain About Their Neighbours," **Gulf News**, June 14, 2017. Retrieved from https://gulfnews.com/going-out/society/top-3-reasons-why-dubai-residents-complain-about-their-neighbours-1.2043514.*

*Jumana Khamis, "'Grow Your Food Event' Encourages Home Farming," **Gulf News**, October 14, 2016. Retrieved from https://gulfnews.com/going-out/society/grow-your-food-event-encourages-home-farming-1.1912573.*

Numerous municipal orders ensued, abolishing backyard farming for good. In 2007, Amal Al Falasi, a journalist for *Al Bayan* newspaper, investigated residents who regularly complained about animals' presence in domestic spaces. One of the interviewees, Umm Essa, said:

> "I tried multiple times to talk to them nicely but there was no use, we resorted to calling the municipality. The government gives them space for *izzab* (animal enclosures in the deserts) and farmlands to move their livestock there. A residential neighborhood is not the right place."

Another interviewee, Umm Ali, said: "The presence of such animals can bring harmful infectious diseases to us, such as scabies. During the winter season, odor spreads with the strong winds. Animals walking on the streets aren't a good sign of cleanliness."

Hashem AlAwadhi, then Director of Veterinary Services at Dubai Municipality, stated that the ban started as a warning, escalating to confiscation, and if the offense is repeated, a fine was issued. In 2013, an article published in *Emarat Al Youm* described the plight of the residents of Al Twar in Dubai who illegally host livestock. Laila Khalifa, a resident, states: "The chaotic goats run around littering our streets, eating the trees, and entering our private backyards to eat up our flowers."

Khaled bin Darwish, a Dubai-based journalist, mentioned multiple car accidents that occurred during the early hours of the day or later in the evening caused by people crashing into the roaming goats. The neighborhood's residents did not know who owns them but they were certainly unhappy. Finally, in 2017, a survey released by the Dubai Municipality, which collected over 700 responses, stated that one of the top three reasons for neighborhood-based complaints was due to the presence of illegal animals in private backyards. (Figs. 05, 06)

## The Resurgence of Self-Reliance

It is worth noting that the downfall of livestock management in domestic spaces and suburban areas quite oddly coincides with the increase in growing fresh fruits and vegetables in households. For example, "Grow Your Food," a campaign first launched/ introduced by the Dubai Municipality, encouraged schools and households to grow their own produce. The campaign that started in 2015 sheds light on the ways that architecture and growing produce overlap, whether through traditional methods or hydroponics. Balcony gardens, for example, have been utilizing small-scale garden setups, growing multiple species of fruits and vegetables. In Dubai's domestic spaces, an average of 140 square meters (459 square feet) of the garden has been dedicated to fruits, vegetables, and spices, which roughly accounts for 10% of the total residential plot size. The campaign was an attempt to combat the reliance on food imports, raise awareness on growing organic produce, and try to build self-reliance in the city.

Fig.05 A flock of chickens in a large pen, Al Khawaneej, Dubai. Photo by author.

Fig.06 A flock of pigeons and chickens outside a house in Al Safa, Dubai. Photo by author.

Fig.07 A herd of cows between houses in Kabir, Umm Al Quwain. Photo by Azza Aboualam.

Fig.08 A group of camels between houses in Al-Awir, Dubai. Photo by author.

*Monica Hamburgh, "Get a Pet to Boost Your Child's Immune System," **Orlando Health**. June 17, 2021. Retrieved from https://www.orlandohealth.com/content-hub/get-a-pet-to-boost-your-childs-immune-system.*

Two years later, the Ministry of Food Security was established, which was spearheaded by Her Excellency Mariam AlMheiri, who was appointed in October 2017. This marked the beginning of multiple government strategies, policies, regulations, and campaigns to further bolster the reduction of the UAE's reliance on imported food products. This also prompted recreational farm owners to rethink the role of their land, exploring its potential for producing fresh fruits, vegetables, and animal products, such as eggs and meat.

When the COVID-19 pandemic hit, multiple interviewees mentioned how this marked the beginning of their journey into gardening, caring for animals, dusting off their backyards, and reassessing their food purchase choices to support the local economy. They expressed that even though those small endeavors started as experiments and hobbies, they later expanded to include carefully calibrated methods through trial and error. Access to content on social media and the wave of information through the internet meant that they no longer required specialized training. These habits were also supported by the rise of gardening and livestock management Instagram accounts that helped facilitate purchasing, growing, and harvesting, which resulted in benefits such as fresh produce and animal products. Overall, the value chain for growing, producing, and raising animals has changed post-COVID-19, with many citing it as a start to rethink their backyards. Residents have managed to achieve their goals of reducing grocery purchases and increasing self-sufficiency by utilizing their backyards to their fullest capacity. (Fig. 07)

**Conclusion**

The revival of self-sustaining practices in Dubai's domestic spaces reflects a combination of traditional values, digital influence, and post-pandemic consciousness. While government initiatives have played a supporting role, some of the most notable drivers of this movement stem from community members, influenced by social media and motivated by the desire to take control of their food sources. As residents reconnect with nature through backyard gardening and rediscover the benefits of self-reliance, they are preserving a core part of Emirati culture that has adapted to modern life. Ultimately, the surge in homegrown food and backyard farming symbolizes a grassroots transformation that values health, community, and tradition. This revival, born out of a digital and social renaissance, illustrates the UAE's unique ability to blend heritage with progress, cultivating a future where self-sustenance and community resilience thrive together.

# Form, Pattern, Rule:

## *Reading Carbon Form at the Territorial Scale*

Elisa Iturbe

*"Form Pattern Rule" is part of a larger body of work titled Confronting Carbon Form, consisting of eleven original works by Stanley Cho, Elisa Iturbe, and Alican Taylan that explore the unique spatial and formal characteristics of the carbon age. These works originally took the form of an exhibition titled Confronting Carbon Form, which was shown at The Cooper Union, Roger Williams University, and Cornell University with the support of The Cooper Union's Architecture Archive, Graham Foundation, NYSCA, and Anyone Corporation. The drawings reproduced here were made with the invaluable assistance of Adare Brown.*

---

***Settlement pattern*** *is used here as a generic term for the shape of any human-produced built environment.*

---

*The term* ***carbon form*** *refers to the formal and spatial configurations unique to the fossil fuel era. See Elisa Iturbe, "Architecture and the Death of Carbon Modernity," Log 47 (Fall 2019), 10-23.*

---

*The term* ***energy transition*** *refers to the process of changing a society's primary energy source. These processes are complex and variable, lasting from decades to millennia. According to Vaclav Smil, "The term energy transition is used most often to describe the changing composition (structure) of primary energy supply. Transition from traditional biomass fuels (wood, charcoal, and crop residues) to fossil fuels (coal and hydrocarbons) has been the most important, and universally experienced, example of this process." Vaclav Smil,* ***Energy Transition: Global and National Perspectives*** *(Santa Barbara, CA: Praeger, 2017), ix. Today,* ***energy transition*** *has also come to refer to the process of shifting away from fossil fuels toward renewable energy sources.*

### *Ingredients*

Spatial Order
Footprint
Production
Abstraction
Hypothetical Resident

## Introduction

Under the influence of fossil fuels, the built environment has undergone a dramatic transformation. At the building scale, industrial and commercial activity placed new demands on buildings, instigating the development of new typologies — factories, worker housing, skyscrapers, department stores, shopping malls, highway motels, big box stores, and distribution centers, to name a few. These building types have become the building blocks for the settlement patterns of the carbon age, from suburbs to high-rise districts. These, in turn, are linked by vast infrastructural networks such as railroads, transit stations, highways, and airports. In the aggregate, these configurations constitute a specific spatial order — *carbon form* — that not only *indexes* energy use but also *sustains* and *intensifies* it. As such, any conversation around energy transition and climate must pay close attention to contemporary spatial arrangements, which are, in and of themselves, one of the causal forces behind the current ecological crisis.

Considering this, learning to recognize carbon form is of critical importance. However, the scale and specific geometry of carbon form can vary greatly, demanding analytic methods that go beyond the cataloging of *instances* of carbon form and instead aim to distill and discern this spatial order's inherent characteristics. This essay — a combination of text and drawing — offers one such method, deploying drawing as an analytic instrument by which to study the patterns that emerge within carbon form at the territorial scale.

The analysis consists of a comparison between three urban settlement patterns of different densities, each of which possesses a distinct spatial character and hosts different social practices. Three sets of comparative drawings (titled *Form*, *Pattern*, and *Rule*) lay the groundwork for perceiving form on these sites, showing the constitutive elements of the settlement pattern, such as building footprints, property lines, zoned uses, and road networks. From here, the study uses diagrams that trace the spatial footprint of a hypothetical resident, illustrating how a life lived within each site produces repeating patterns and logics, despite differences in scale and specific form (*Logic*). The last series increases in scale, recontextualizing the study within a vast network of energy infrastructure that operates at the territorial level (*Territory*).

Ultimately, all three sites show a high degree of separation between the various activities that sustain human life — from wage labor and commodity production to the extraction of natural resources. By noting the separation between these, a shared spatial logic emerges across all three sites, despite differences in scale and specific form: highly specialized environments are deliberately kept apart, connected instead via vast territories of energy-intensive infrastructure.

## The Sites

The Brickell neighborhood of Miami, Florida, has a population density of 42.6 people/acre. Built over soft limestone and a high water table, developments in Brickell are built on piles set deeper than their towers are tall. Known for its cultural diversity, vibrant food scene, and active nightlife, Brickell represents a high-density urban model.

Chula Vista and Bonita are two adjacent suburban settlements in southern San Diego County, California. Chula Vista has a population density of 8.6 people/acre while Bonita, an unincorporated area, is host to 4.19 people/acre. The area has been continuously inhabited by the Kumeyaay people for at least eight millennia. Both suburbs are known for their strong cultural ties to Tijuana, Mexico, which is a fifteen-minute drive away.

Hardin County, Iowa, has a population density of 0.2 people/acre. Its geological features were born from the Wisconsin Glaciation 65,000 years ago and its present form is defined by the Jeffersonian grid imposed during American colonization, as well as intensive agricultural production, continuous since the railroad entered the territory in the late nineteenth century.

*An acre equals approximately 4047 square meters.*

## Analysis

*Form*

The forces that shape urban form are numerous, and the tools for perceiving them are just as varied. Cadastral maps subdivide land, making it legible for the purposes of taxation, wealth accumulation, and control. Buildings also hold space, and their proximity, density, and scale define the nature of any settlement pattern. Together, the parcel and the building work in tandem to separate public from private, interior from exterior, and passable from impassable.

KEY

Building Footprints, Area of Study

Building Footprints, Context

Parcels, Area of Study

Parcels, Context

SOURCES

A1. Microsoft/Building Footprints. 2018. Reprint, Microsoft, 2022.
B1. Microsoft/Building Footprints. 2018. Reprint, Microsoft, 2022.
C1. Microsoft/Building Footprints. 2018. Reprint, Microsoft, 2022.
A2. State Land Records. Shapefile. Florida Dept. of Environmental Protection. Accessed June 17, 2022.
B2. San Diego Association of Governments. "SANDAG /SanGIS Regional GIS Data Warehouse Open Data Portal." Accessed September 24, 2021.
C2. US Dept. of Agriculture. Tomer, Mark, and David James. "Agricultural Land Use by Field: Iowa 2010-2019." Ag Data Commons, December 1, 2020.

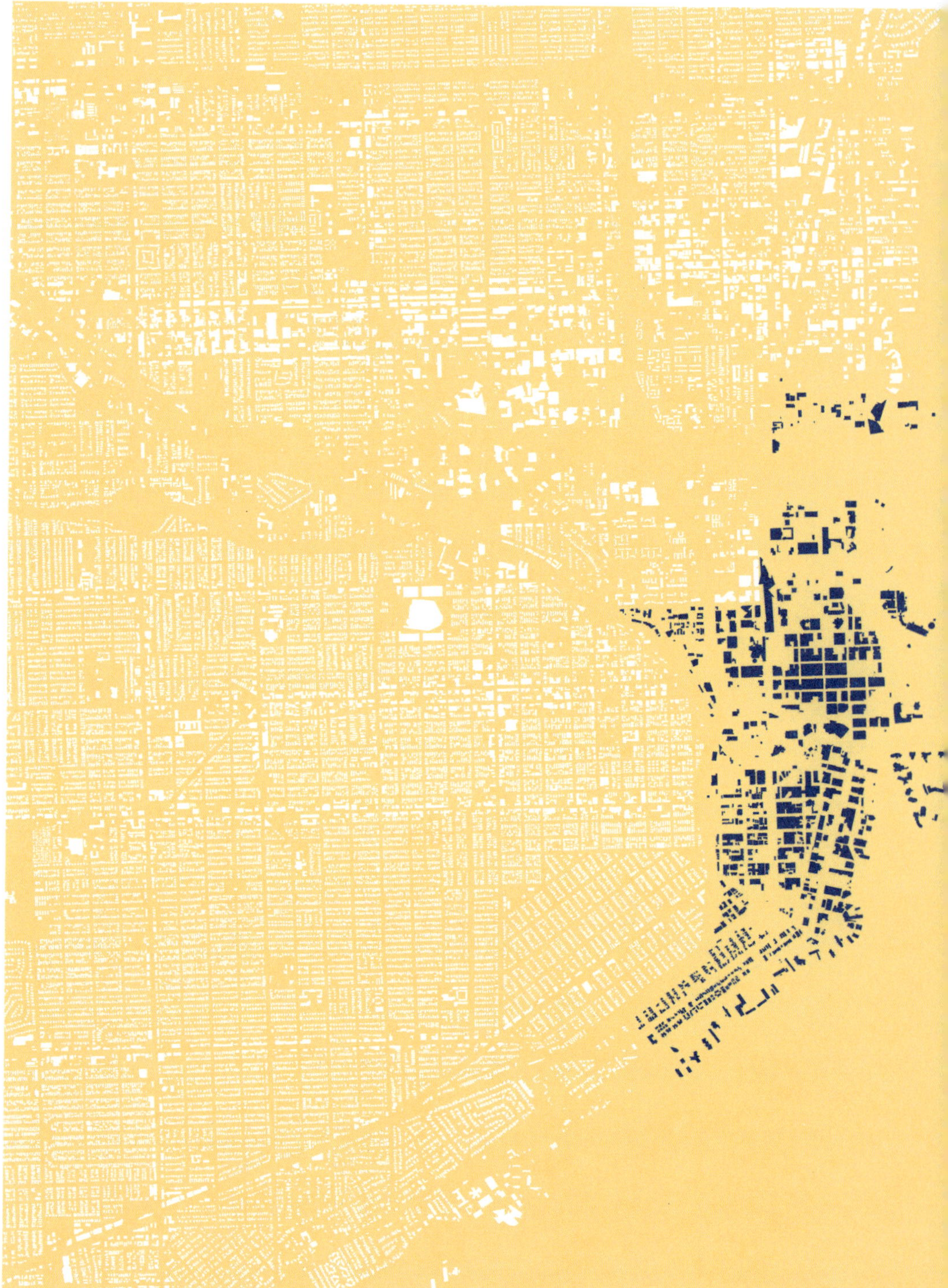

A1 - Footprints

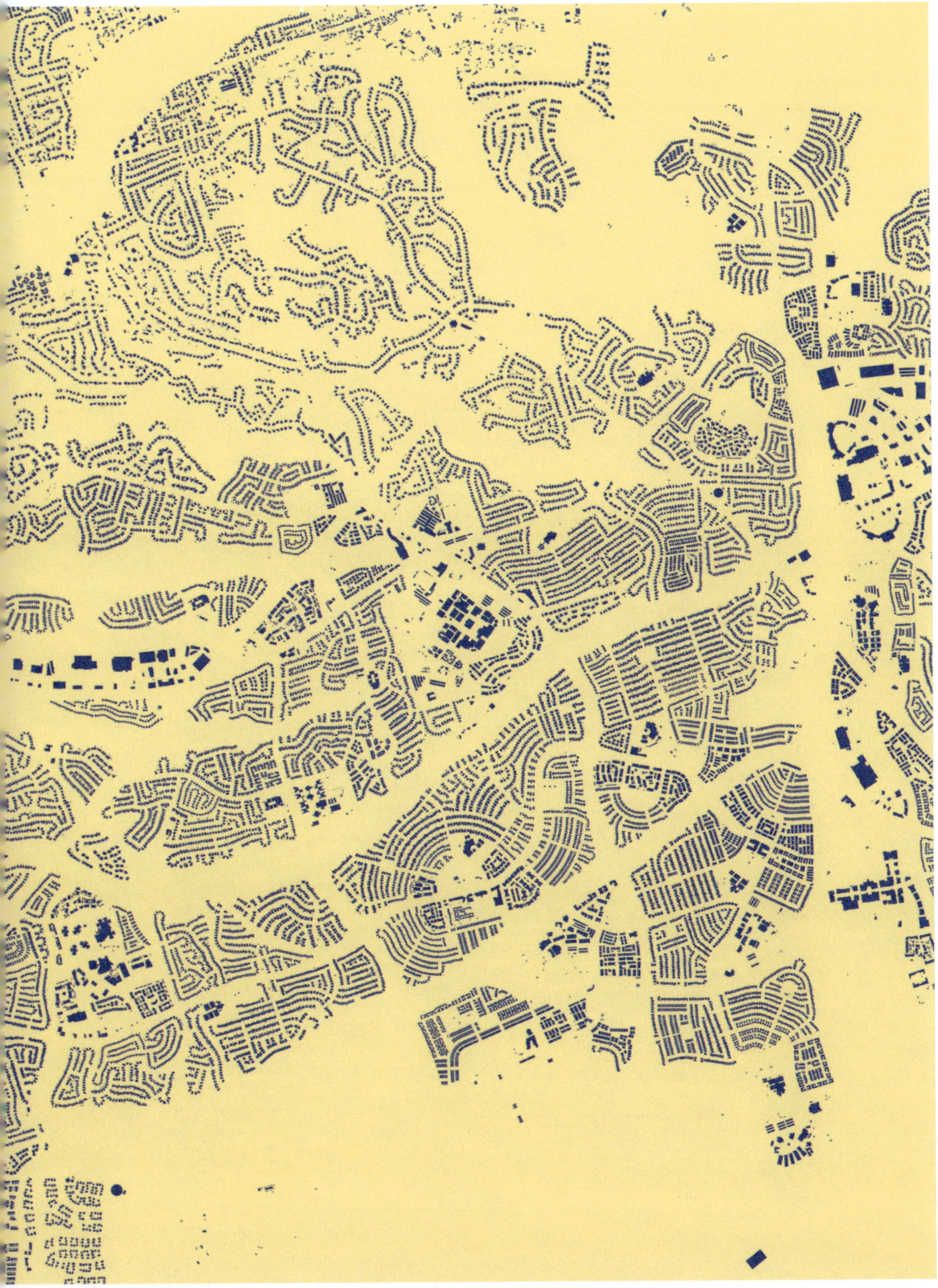

C1 - Footprints

A2 - Cadastral

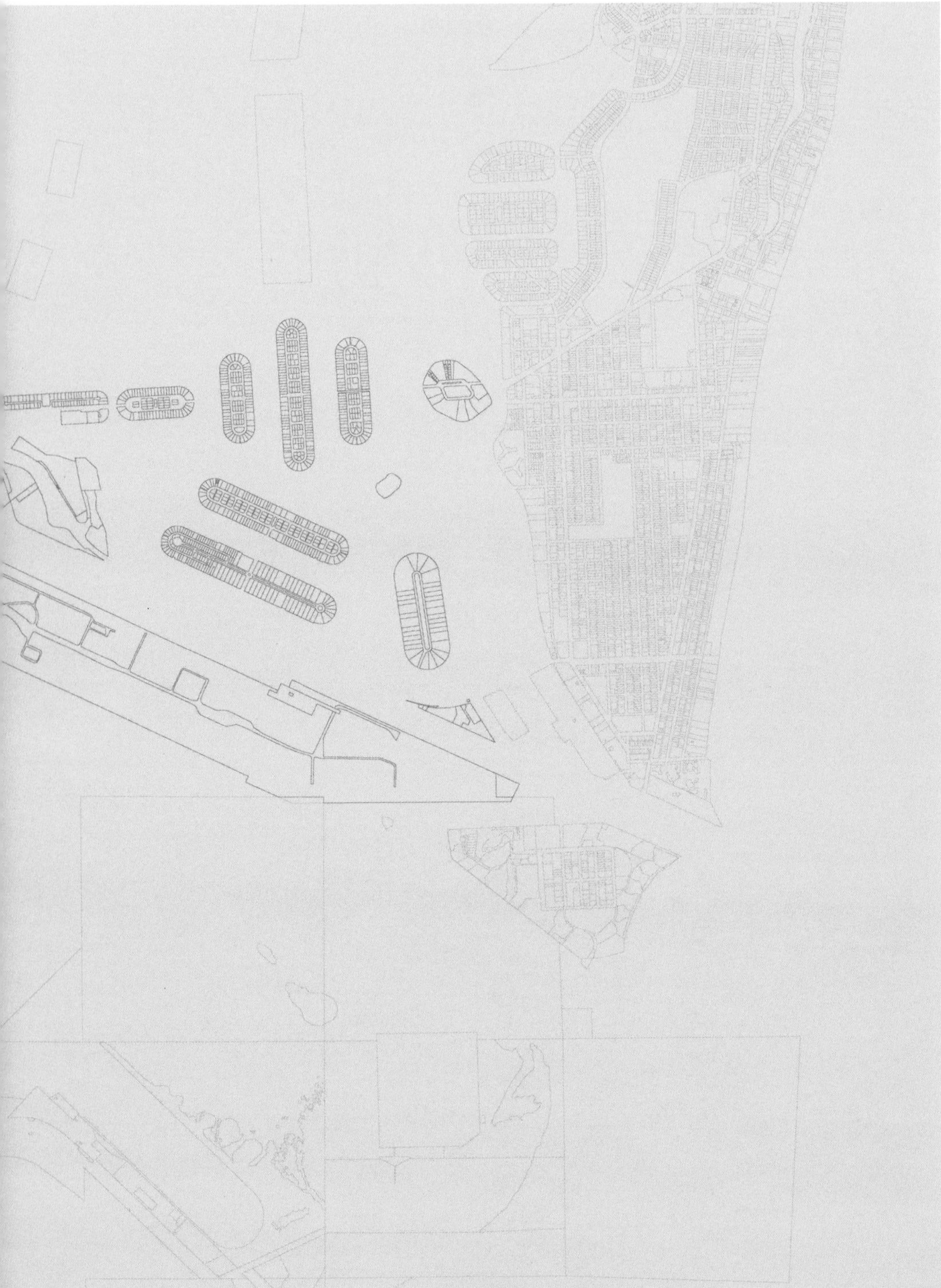

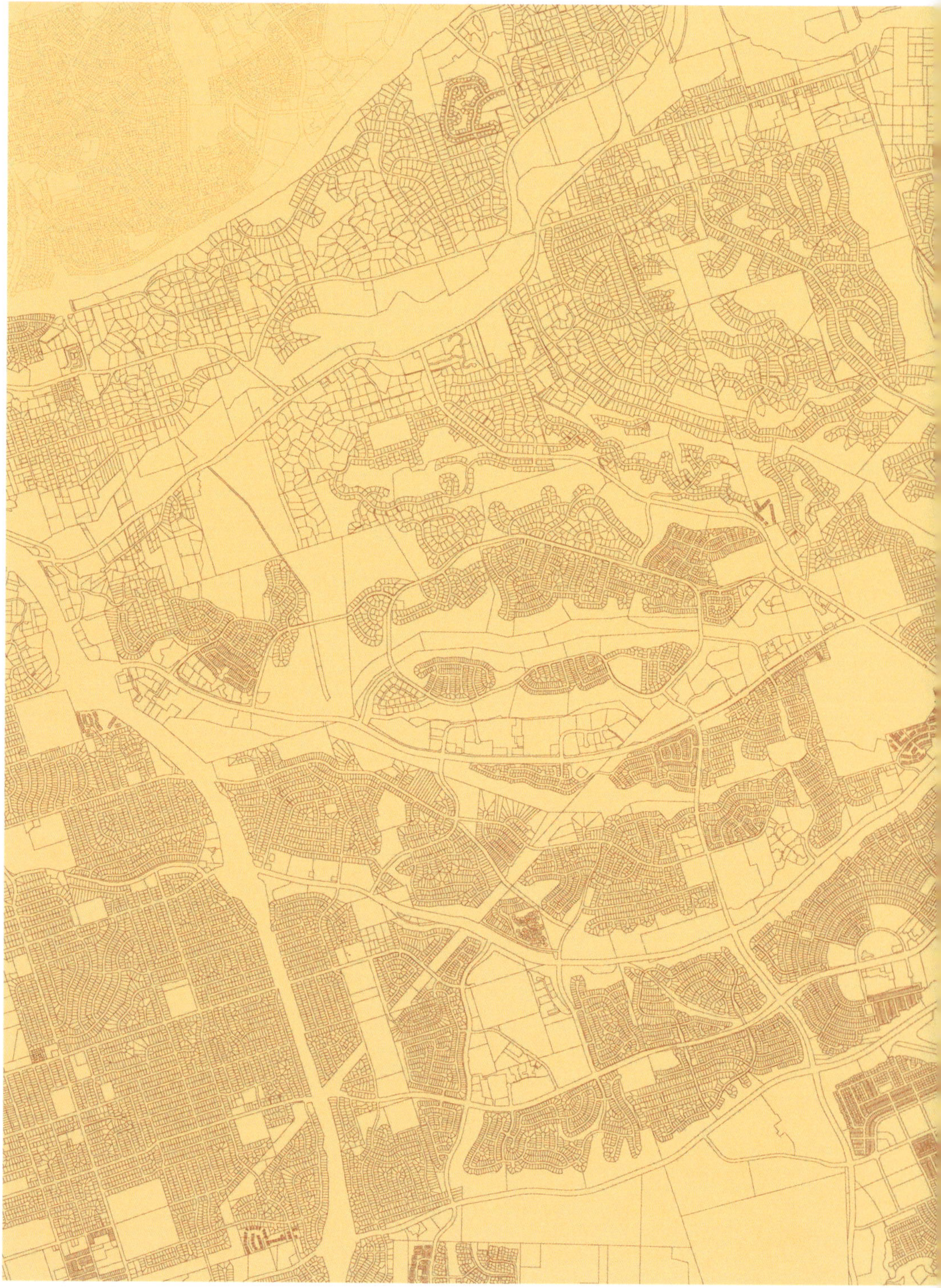

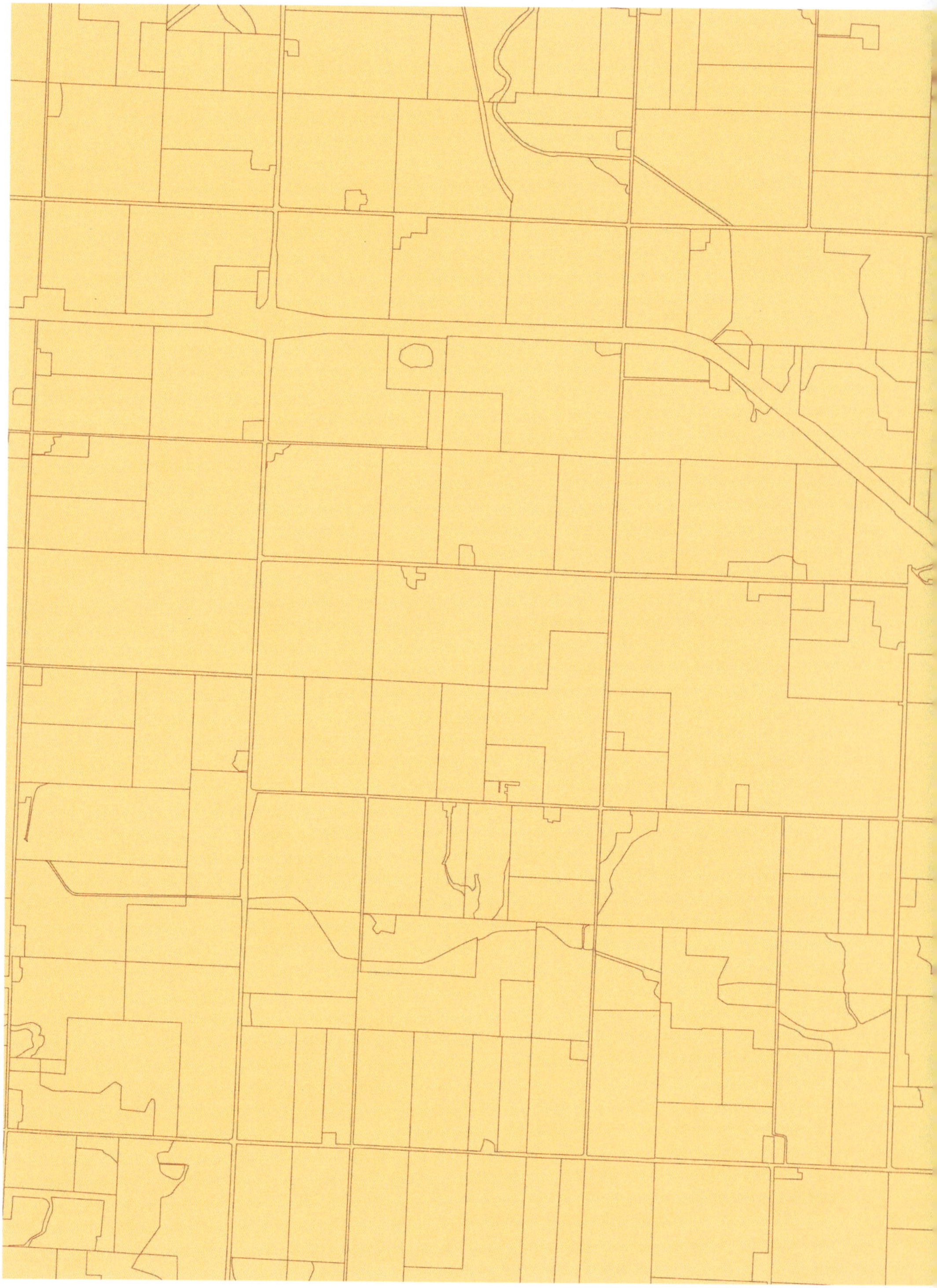

C2 - Cadastral

*Pattern*

The patterning of space goes by many names: planning, development, or zoning are common examples. They were originally invented to provide healthier environments to urban dwellers during industrialization. These instruments were developed to keep productive zones and residential areas separate. Today, they create stark spatial delineations that separate productive, commercial, and residential activities. Exacerbated by energy abundance, the distances between these zones have only grown more extreme over time, creating a tendency toward spatial and territorial specialization. A figure-ground technique is used here to show that the spatial footprints of productive and residential sites tend toward mutual exclusivity.

**KEY**

- Industrial
- Commercial
- Agricultural
- Residential, Area of Study
- Residential, Context
- Parks and Natural Terrain

**SOURCES**

A3. Municipal Zone. May 22, 2021. Accessed June 15, 2022
B3. San Diego Association of Governments. "SANDAG/SanGIS Regional GIS Data Warehouse Open Data Portal." Accessed September 24, 2021.
C3. "Hardin County Comp Plan, Appendix Maps." Hardin County GIS Department, October 2012.
A4. Municipal Zone. May 22, 2021. Accessed June 15, 2022.
B4. San Diego Association of Governments. "SANDAG/SanGIS Regional GIS Data Warehouse Open Data Portal." Accessed September 24, 2021.
C4. "Hardin County Comp Plan, Appendix Maps." Hardin County GIS Department, October 2012. "Streets." Accessed June 17, 2022.

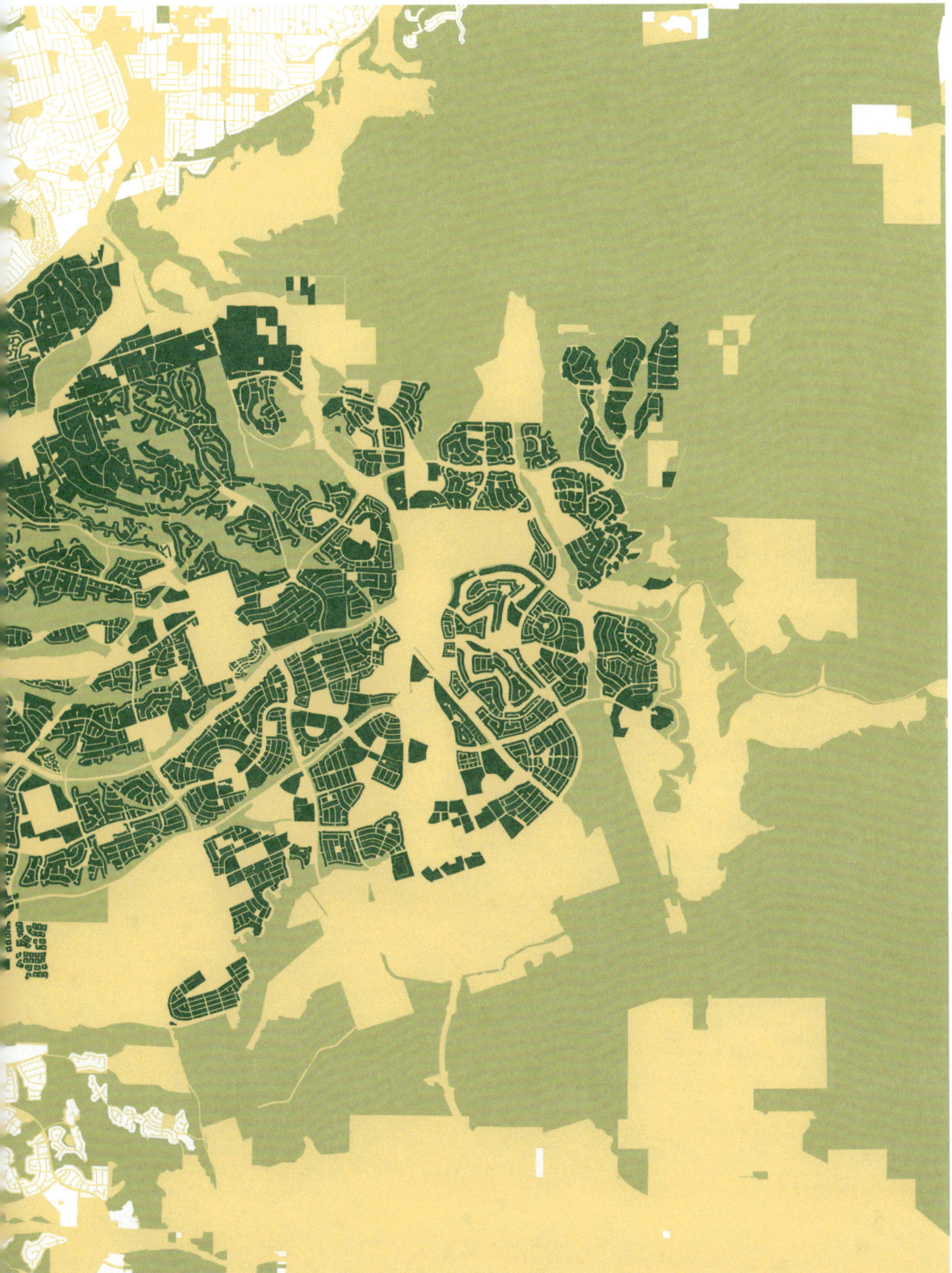

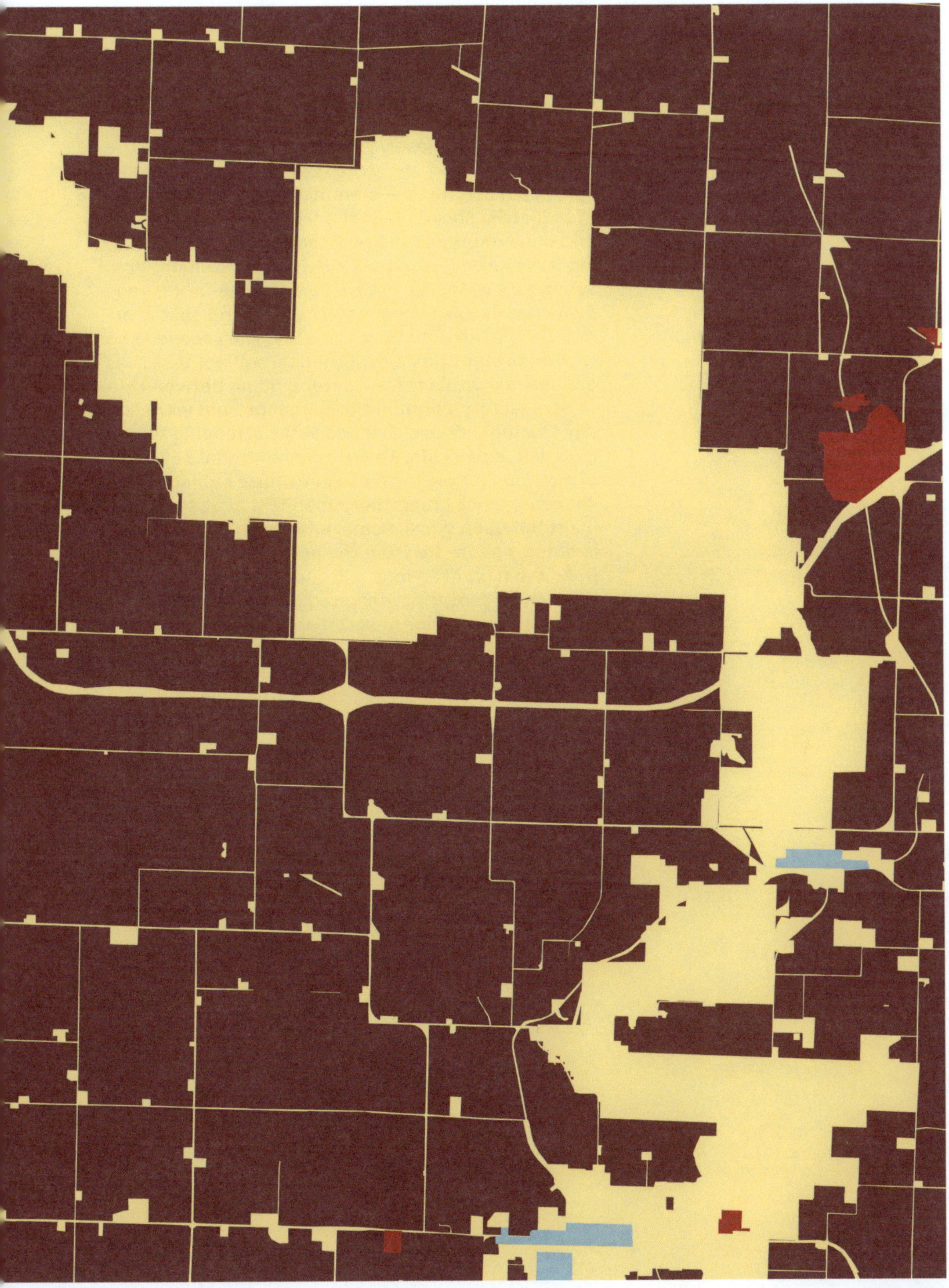

## *Rule*

Carbon form is closely ruled. If the rule of St. Benedict is *ora et labora* (pray and work), then the rule of carbon form — stemming from the demands of industrial society — is the trinity of work, leisure, and consumption. This rule shapes life and, by shaping it, secures its longevity. By tracing primary and secondary roads across these sites, the first three drawings in this set reveal an underlying spatial armature that structures these sites. The second set of drawings identifies a hypothetical subject that lives and moves within this structure, going between sites of domesticity, commercial exchange, and work, each day tracing a figure in space while attending to the logistics of daily life. These are the spatial patterns of a *carbon subject* — a person whose subjectivity is shaped by fossil fuels, here manifested as the movement between work, home, and store, and whose life is notably separate from the production that sustains it. As the next drawings will show, even more clearly, this spatial footprint inhabited by the carbon subject becomes an interior of sorts, defined not only by zoning regulations, but by the very fiction of autonomy from natural and productive processes.

**KEY**

Roads

Routes

**SOURCES**

A5. “Streets.” Accessed June 17, 2022. https://datahub-miamigis.opendata.arcgis.com/maps/streets.
B5. San Diego Association of Governments. “SANDAG/SanGIS Regional GIS Data Warehouse Open Data Portal.” Accessed September 24, 2021.
C5. Microsoft/Building Footprints. 2018. Reprint, Microsoft, 2022.
A6. N/A
B6. N/A
C6. N/A

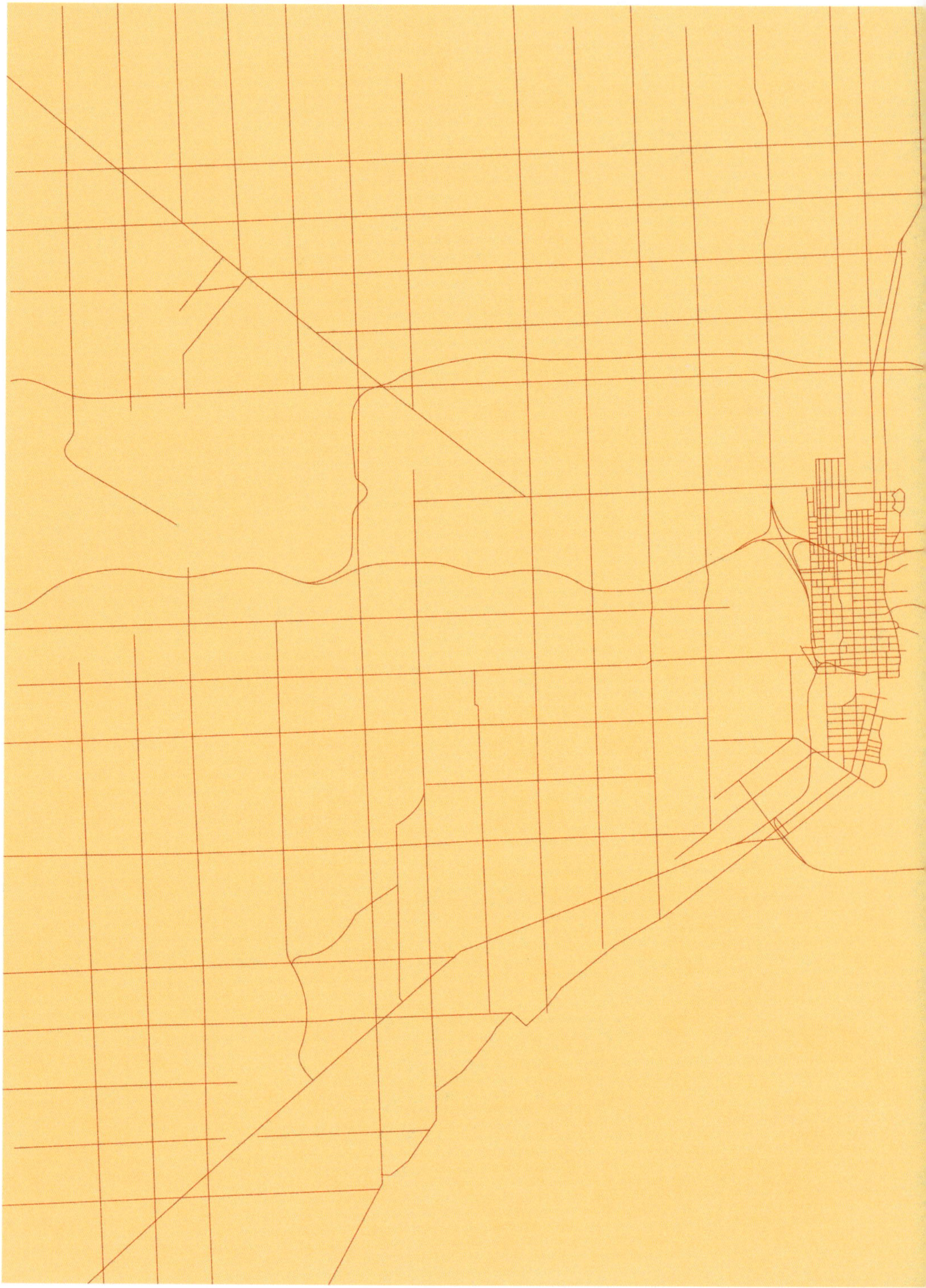

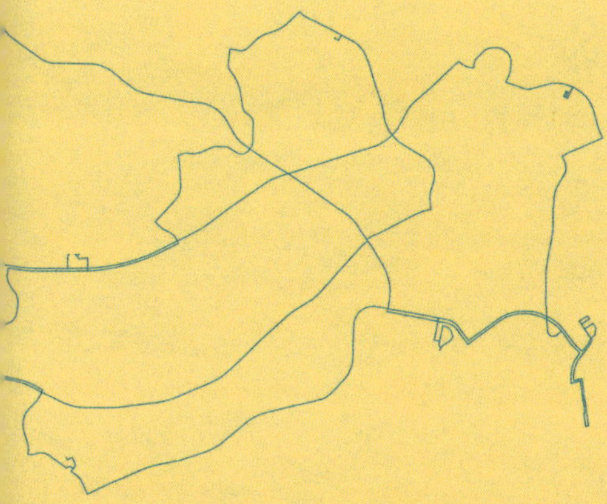

*Logic*

When combined, form, pattern, and rule create a discernible logic: the path of a carbon subject traces lines between home, work, and sites of consumption while distant lands and people deliver energy, food, and commodities. Shown in the *Rule* series as a meandering line, here, that line becomes a solid cyan figure in order to represent the spatial footprint of a life lived within a residential zone. That footprint has hardly any overlap with the global networks of extraction, production, and distribution that sustain that life, as they often occur within distinct spatial fields. In other words, from the perspective of the consumer subject, extraction happens *elsewhere*. Transit networks bring fuel and goods to sites of commodity purchase — stores, gas stations, restaurants, etc. It is those sites that offer the limited interface between consumers and the distant lands that sustain their lives.

This lack of overlap is especially poignant in Bonita, where a large residential field with no mixed use occupies the center of the settlement. Just beyond the limits of the drawing, a port to the northwest brings in goods from Asia and South America; the *maquiladoras* south of the border fabricate machine parts, appliances, and electronics; and the Imperial Valley to the west is an agricultural powerhouse. A suburban subject in Bonita is dependent on these, and many other, distant places, and yet, an entire life might unfold on this site without direct contact with any of them.

***Maquiladoras*** *are manufacturing plants that are located in Mexico but administered by companies located in the United States. A product of free trade agreements between Mexico and the US, they allow American companies to benefit from cheap labor while retaining access to American markets.*

At first glance, Iowa seems to offer a contradictory condition, given that life here unfolds within a productive agricultural landscape. However, a different view emerges if one looks at the movements of a poultry farm worker. Living in the town of Eldora (population 2,600) and commuting to a factory farm that raises chickens for commercial consumption, this worker has no access to the food they help produce. Like the urban and suburban residents in Bonita and Brickell, this rural worker traces a repeating path between home, work, and store. Ultimately, they are just as dependent on the international supply chains that support a consumption-based economy.

Whether dense or sparse, gridded or irregularly parceled, these three sites exhibit a shared spatial logic. One could argue, perhaps, that it has already been identified by economists, who speak of *externalities*, or by critics of capitalism, who denounce the asymmetry between *center* and *periphery* as a significant source of injustice within an industrialized world. Yet the field of architecture has hardly recognized these hierarchies as a property of our dominant spatial order. These drawings aim to do just that, materializing the spatiality of our energy-intensive industrial system, and revealing a shared logic that has, in and of itself, a generic form.

KEY

Carbon Subject

Productive Space

Distribution Point

Residence Location

Work Location

Subject Network

Logistic Network

Unspecified Elsewhere of Production

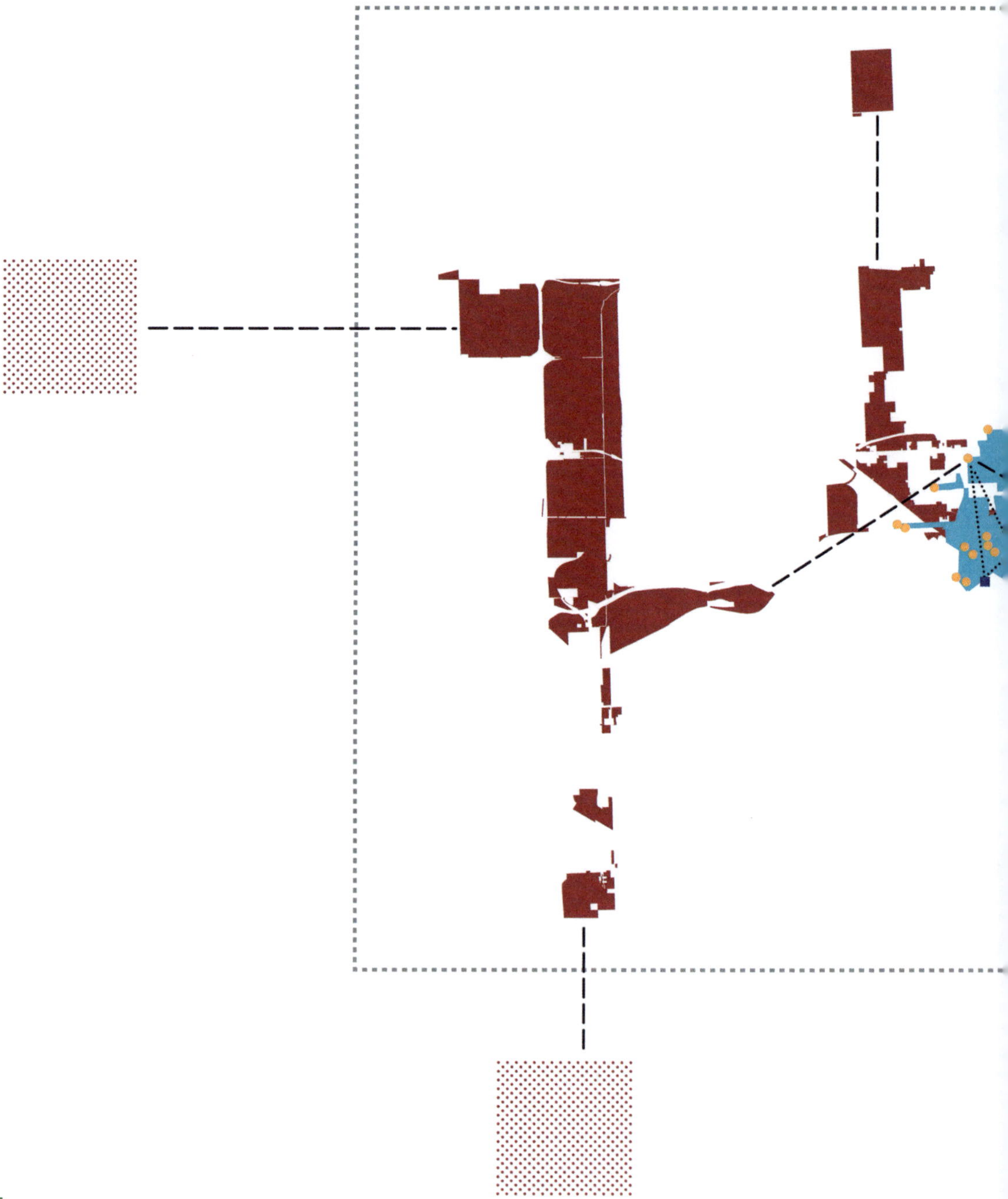

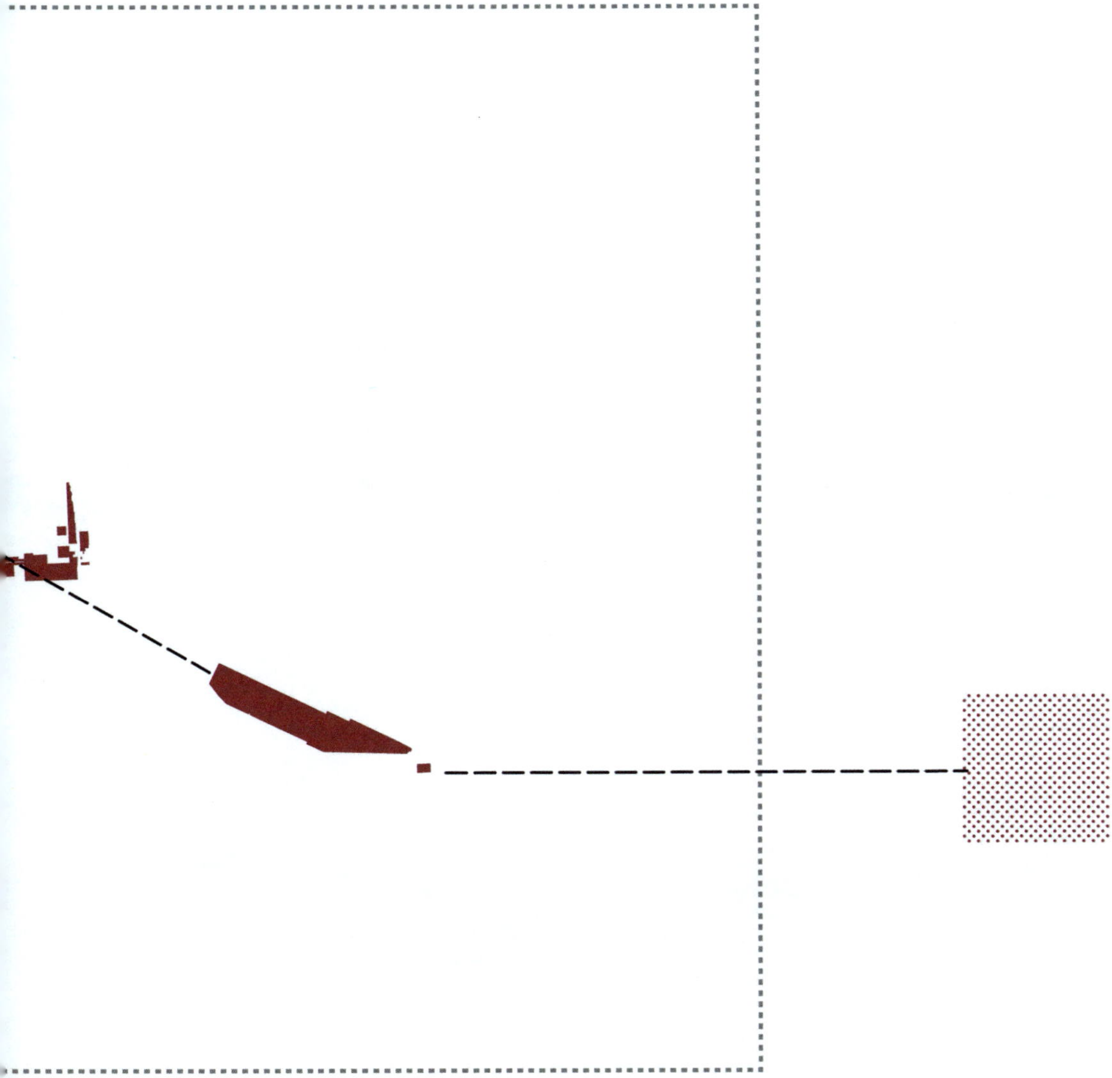

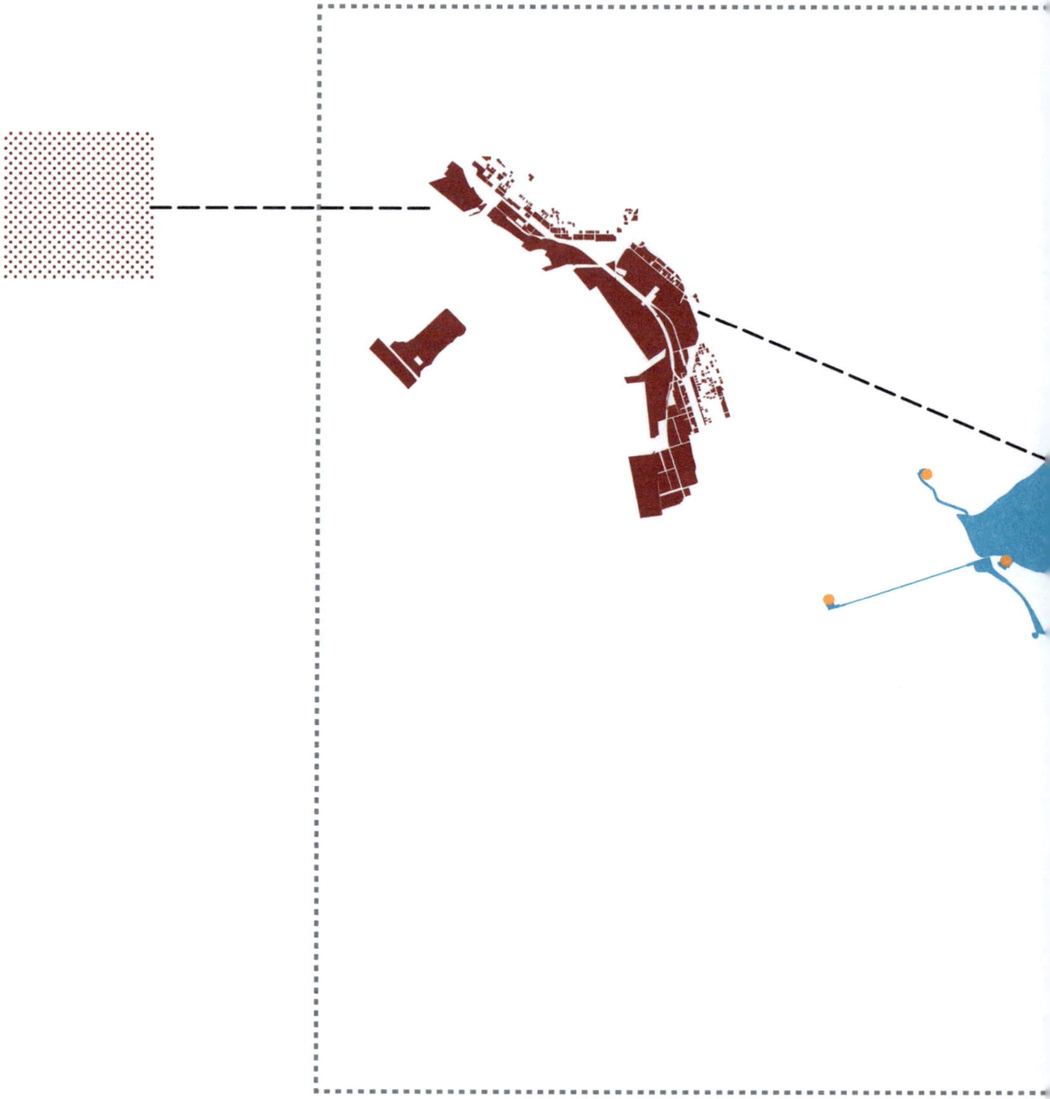

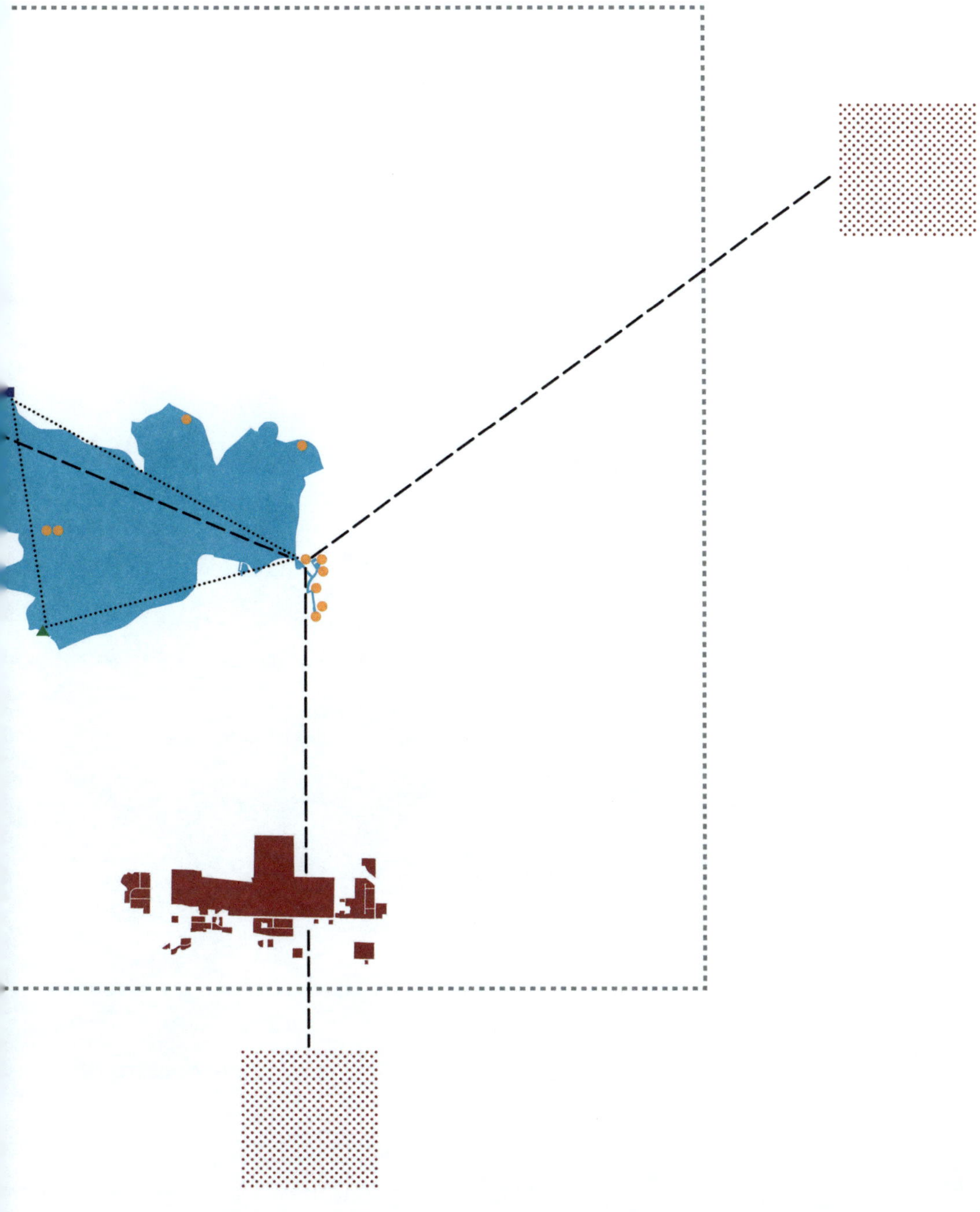

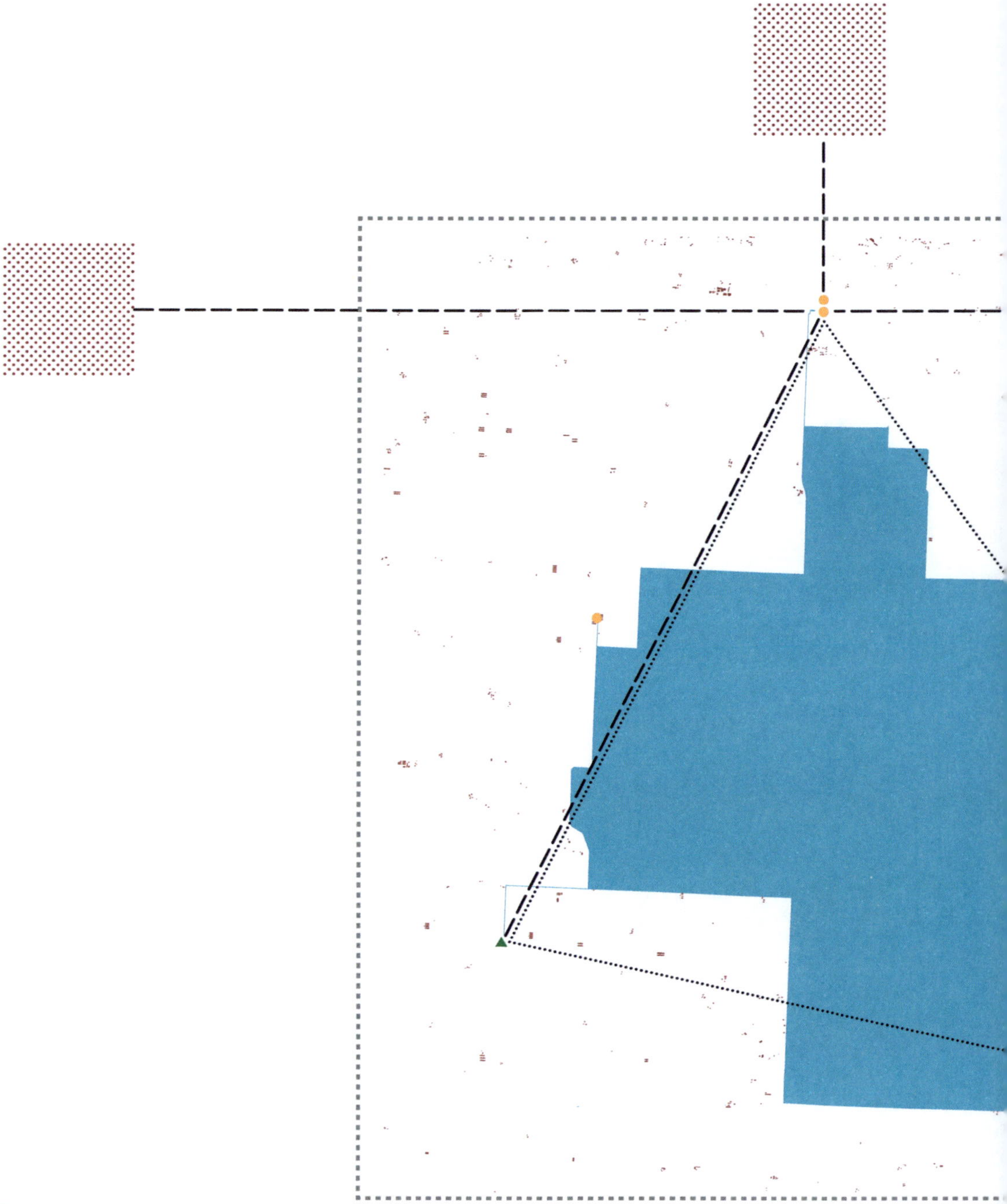

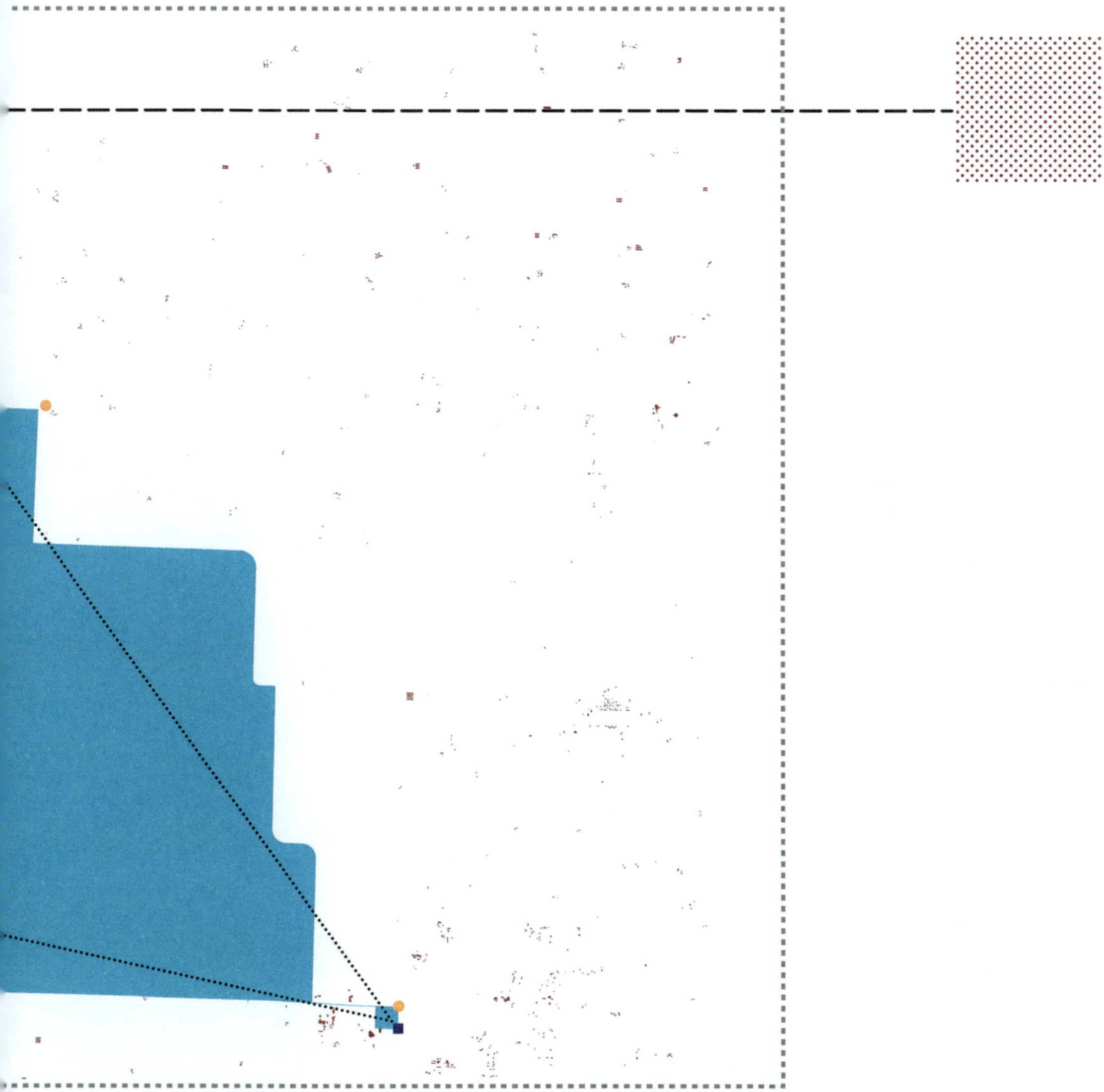

*Territory*

Every life lived within carbon form occurs within territorial networks of power and production. This final set of drawings shifts in scale in order to show the spatial footprint of each carbon subject contextualized within spatial structures so vast that they can never be perceived in their entirety.

**KEY**

Carbon Subject

Electrical Transmission

Industrial Production

Agricultural Production

**SOURCES**

A8. Electric Power Transmission Lines. Homeland Infrastructure Foundation-Level Data, 2022.
B8. "CEC Transmission Lines, California | Data Basin." Accessed October 15, 2021.
"Voltage", San Diego Gas & Electric. San Diego: OpenStreetMap, n.d.
C8. Electric Power Transmission Lines. Homeland Infrastructure Foundation-Level Data, 2022.
A9. Everglades Agricultural Area (EAA) Boundary. South Florida Water Management District, 2018.
B9. Geografía (INEGI), Instituto Nacional de Estadística, "Mapas. Uso de suelo y vegetación." Instituto Nacional de Estadística y Geografía. INEGI Accessed June 13, 2022.
C9. N/A

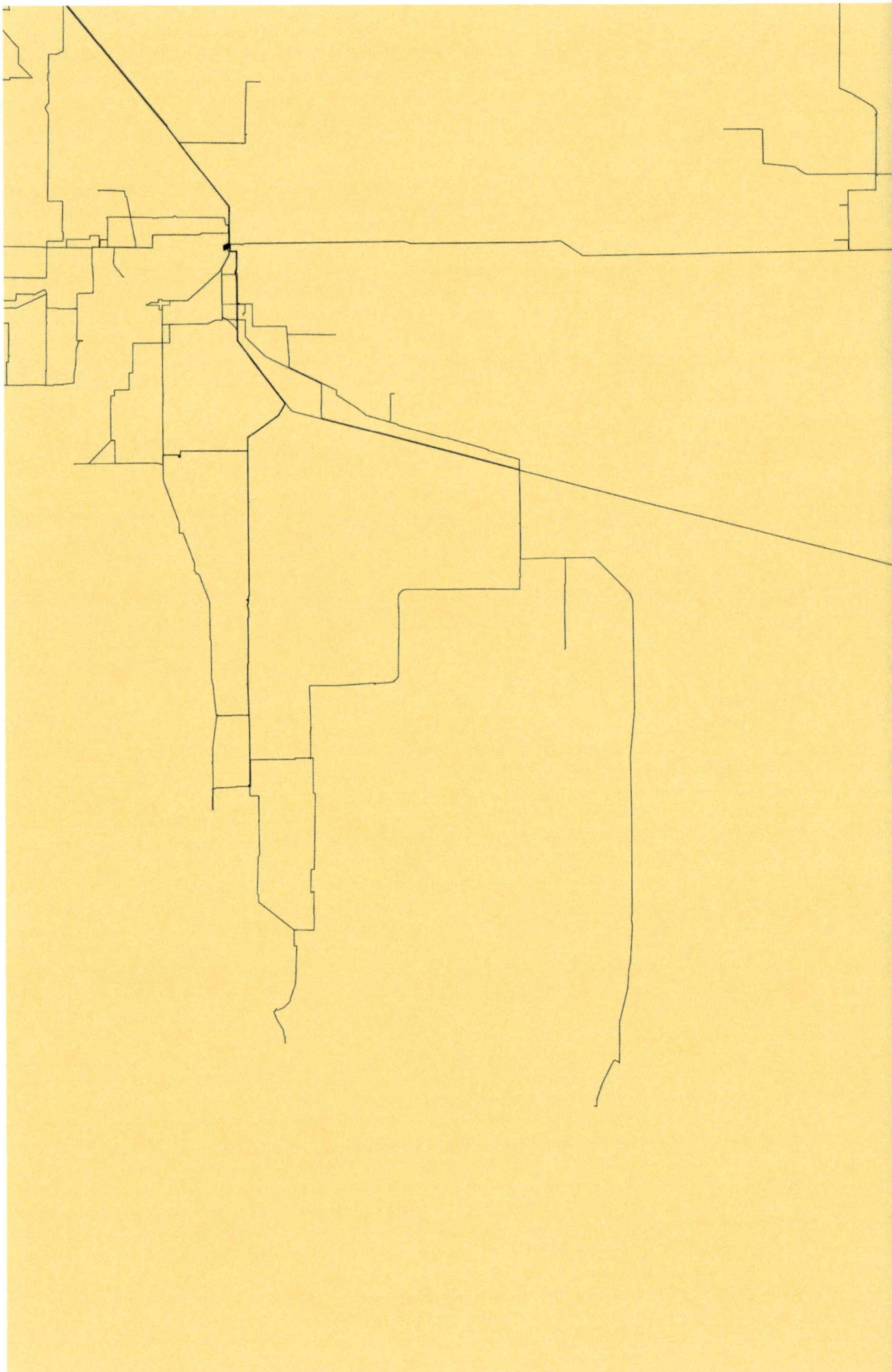

A8 - Electric Power Transmission

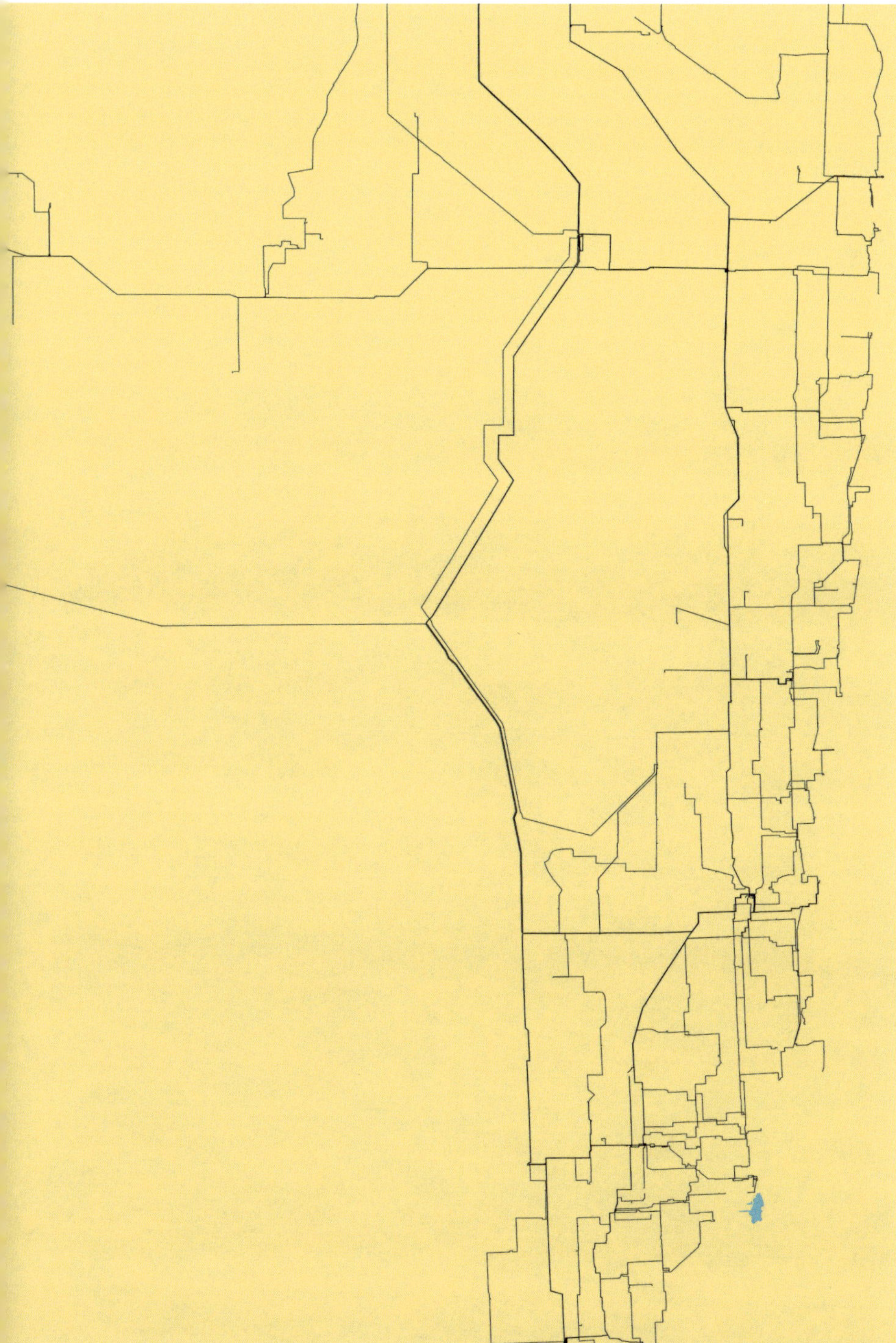

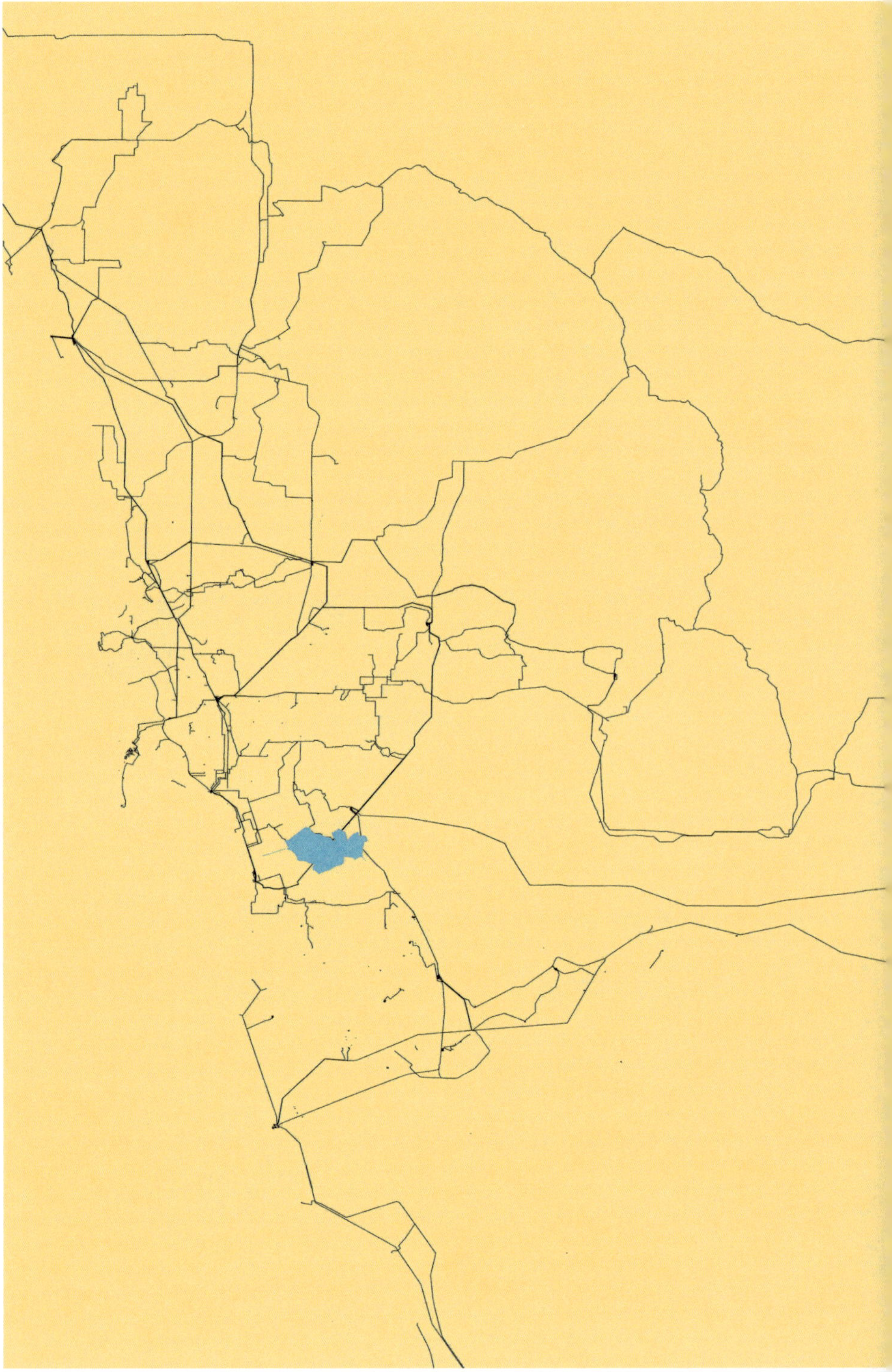

B8 - Electric Power Transmission

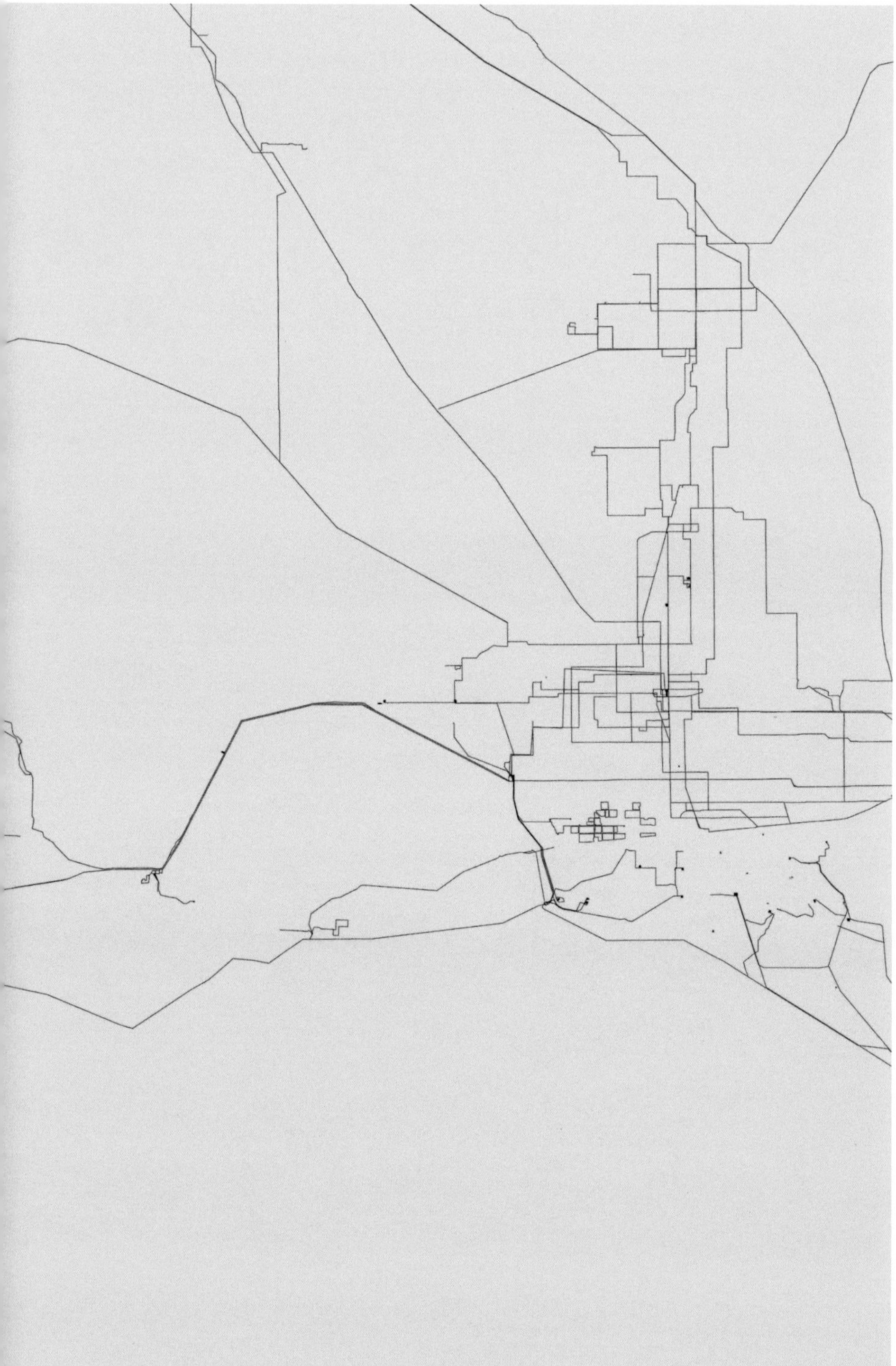

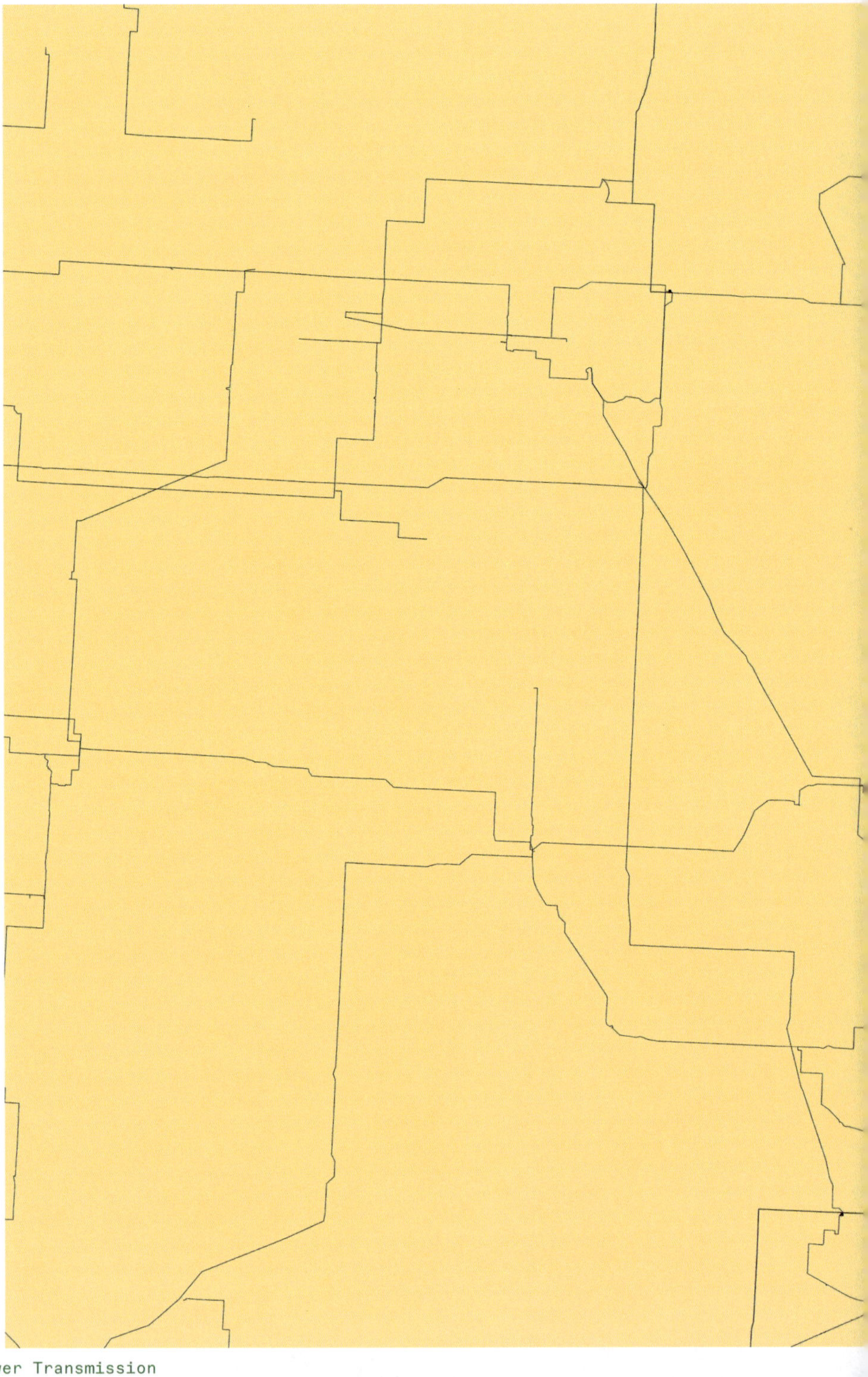

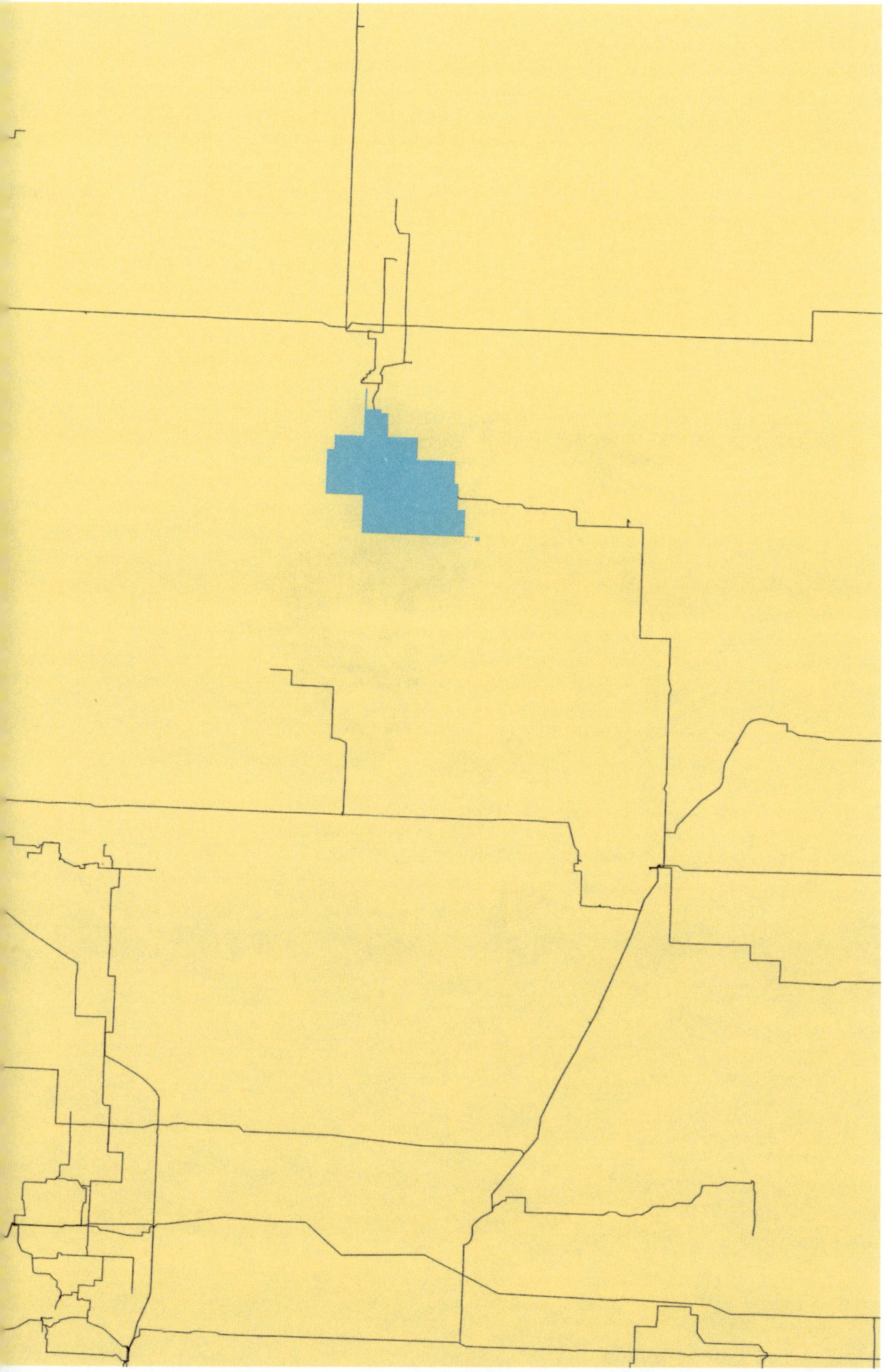

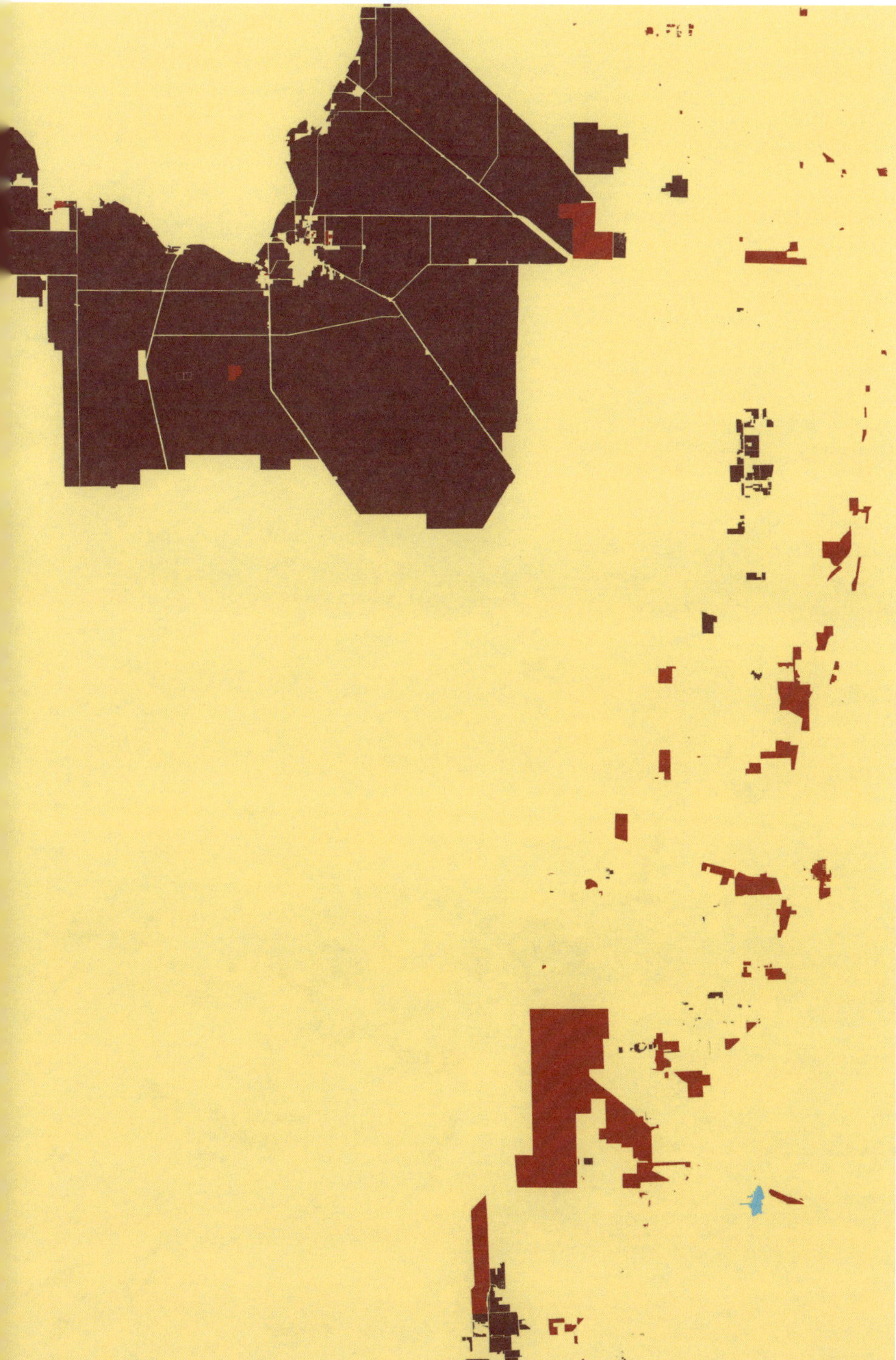

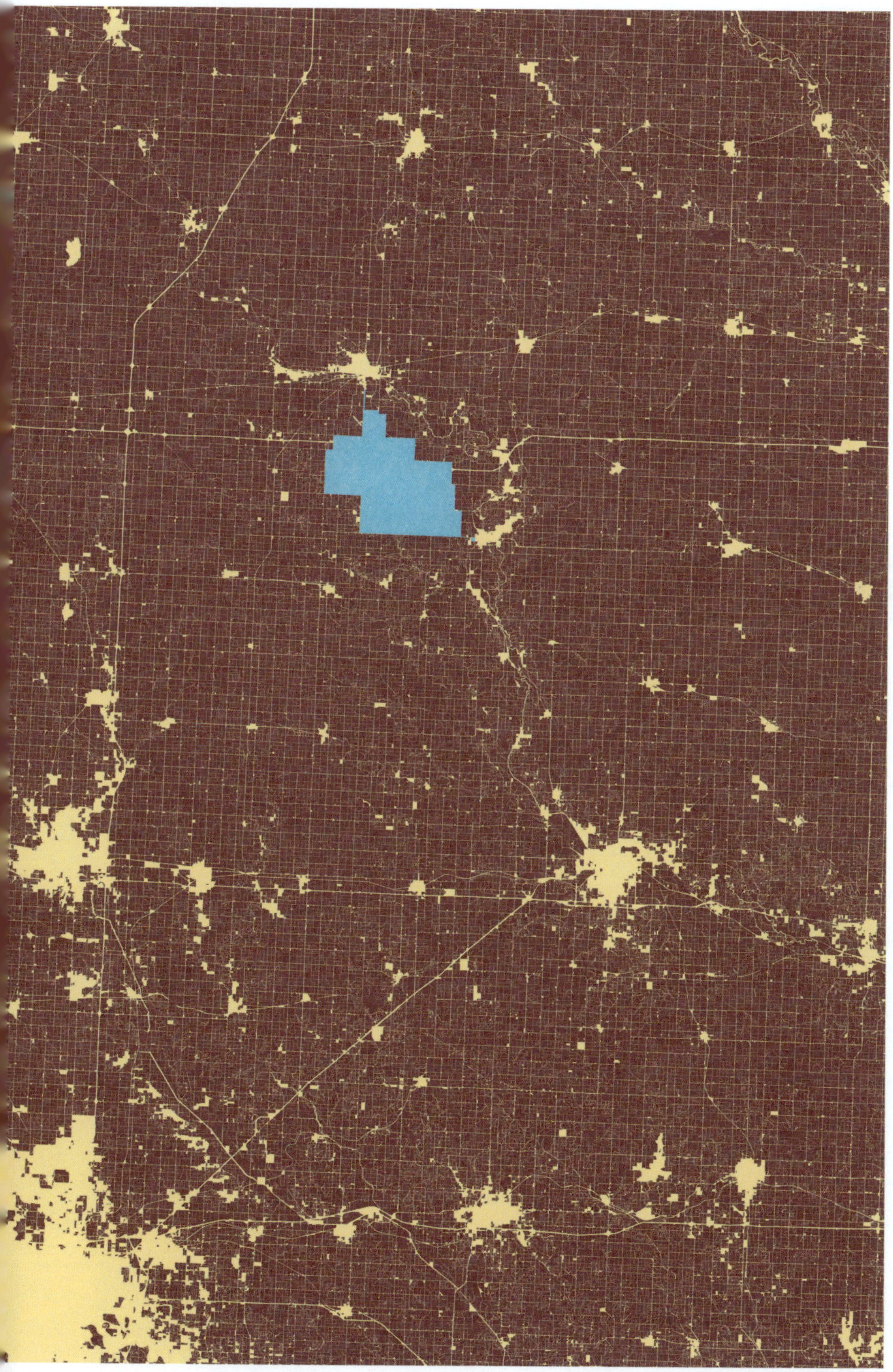

## Conclusions

The editors of *OASE 107* — an issue dedicated to the representation of landscape — argue that drawings at the territorial scale are always "situated in a field of tension between the reduction and multiplication of meaning." ■ This is certainly true of this analysis. Using minimal notation to maximize abstraction, the drawings communicate through their form and composition. This, in some ways, is an act of reduction, yet it multiplies meaning by making visible a common tendency that would otherwise be difficult to see amidst sites that are so different from each other. Comparison and analysis are central to this multiplication, as is the application of the findings beyond these drawings. Ultimately, these drawings tell a story of a metabolic rift, where globalized industrial production produces a contemporary subjectivity that is both disconnected from and deeply embedded within powerful spatio-energetic networks. While the aforementioned locations and their logic seem site specific, the lessons learned are applicable to any site that actively participates in the globalized economy, including the United Arab Emirates.

■

*Frits Palmboom, Bruno Notteboom, Kornelia Dimitrova, Bart Decroos, "The Drawing in Landscape Design and Urbanism,"* ***OASE 107****, (2020), 3.*

# *Seasonal & Local*



Illustrations by Khalid Mezaina

*Chapter* **05**

# Photo Essay 01

Azza Aboualam and Ola Allouz

A collection of images from local farms in the United Arab Emirates (UAE).

***Ingredients***

Shade and Shadow
Conceal and Reveal
Views
Foothills
Paths

Fig. 01: Photo by Ola Allouz.
Fig. 02: Photo by Ola Allouz.
Fig. 03: Photo by Ola Allouz.
Fig. 04: Photo by Azza Aboualam.
Fig. 05: Photo by Ola Allouz.
Fig. 06: Photo by Ola Allouz.
Fig. 07: Photo by Ola Allouz.
Fig. 08: Photo by Ola Allouz.
Fig. 09: Photo by Azza Aboualam.
Fig. 10: Photo by Azza Aboualam.
Fig. 11: Photo by Ola Allouz.
Fig. 12: Photo by Azza Aboualam.
Fig. 13: Photo by Azza Aboualam.
Fig. 14: Photo by Azza Aboualam.
Fig. 15: Photo by Ola Allouz.
Fig. 16: Photo by Azza Aboualam.

01

02

03

04

05

06

07

08

09

10

11

12

13

14

15

16

# Photo Essay 02

Azza Aboualam and Ola Allouz

A collection of images of harvested, picked, and gathered local produce in the United Arab Emirates (UAE) in summer and in fall.

***Ingredients***

Lemons
Mangoes
Okra
Sugarcane
Dates

Fig. 01: Photo by Ola Allouz.
Fig. 02: Photo by Azza Aboualam.
Fig. 03: Photo by Ola Allouz.
Fig. 04: Photo by Ola Allouz.
Fig. 05: Photo by Azza Aboualam.
Fig. 06: Photo by Ola Allouz.
Fig. 07: Photo by Ola Allouz.
Fig. 08: Photo by Azza Aboualam.
Fig. 09: Photo by Ola Allouz.
Fig. 10: Photo by Ola Allouz.
Fig. 11: Photo by Azza Aboualam.
Fig. 12: Photo by Azza Aboualam.

01

02

04

05

06

08

09

11

12

# Photo Essay 03

Azza Aboualam and Ola Allouz

A collection of images of reaped, shared, and sourced local produce in the United Arab Emirates (UAE) in winter and in spring.

***Ingredients***

Corn
Pumpkins
Carrots
Beets
Green Peppers

Fig. 01: Photo by Ola Allouz.
Fig. 02: Photo by Azza Aboualam.
Fig. 03: Photo by Ola Allouz.
Fig. 04: Photo by Azza Aboualam.
Fig. 05: Photo by Azza Aboualam.
Fig. 06: Photo by Azza Aboualam.
Fig. 07: Photo by Ola Allouz.
Fig. 08: Photo by Azza Aboualam.
Fig. 09: Photo by Azza Aboualam.
Fig. 10: Photo by Ola Allouz.
Fig. 11: Photo by Azza Aboualam.
Fig. 12: Photo by Ola Allouz.

01

02

03

04

05

06

07

08

09

10

11

12

# *Epilogue*

Editor's Biography

Writers' Biographies

Bibliography

Illustrations by Khalid Mezaina

# Editor's Biography

**Azza Aboualam** is an Emirati architect and curator of the National Pavilion United Arab Emirates (UAE) for the 19th International Architecture Exhibition – La Biennale di Venezia in 2025. She is an Assistant Professor at the College of Arts and Creative Enterprises at Zayed University, Dubai, UAE, and a Co-Founder and Director of Research at Holesum Studio, an interdisciplinary architecture and design practice based between New York, US, and Sharjah, UAE. In 2021, she co-founded the studio a few years after graduating from the Yale School of Architecture. Her scholarly interests include the intersection of memory, architecture, and society in the Middle East and North Africa. Aboualam worked with the UAE Ministry of Culture's Architecture Initiative, and her field research, sketches, and writing were published in the book *In Search of Spaces of Coexistence: An Architect's Journey* (2019), edited by Dr. Alamira Reem Al Hashimi and Adina Hempel. She also contributed research to *Building Sharjah* (2021), edited by Sultan Sooud Al Qassemi and Todd Reisz, and *Showpiece City: How Architecture Made Dubai* (2020), written by Todd Reisz. While working in Sharjah's Department of Public Works, Aboualam managed the design and construction of large-scale projects such as the Aga Khan Award–winning Wasit Wetland Center. In 2014, Aboualam was a Venice Intern at the National Pavilion UAE's debut participation at the 14th International Architecture Exhibition – La Biennale di Venezia with the exhibition *Lest We Forget: Structures of Memory in the UAE*, curated by Dr. Michele Bambling.

# Writers' Biographies

**Rashed Almulla** is the Founder of MABNAI, Co-Founder of MamarLab, and an independent urban researcher, specializing in urban history and planning. Based in Dubai, Almulla employs multiple mediums focusing on the built environment through exhibitions, symposia, and research contributions. He authored *Spaces that Remain* (2024), directed the *Future of Gulf Housing Symposium* (2023), and curated *Spaces that Remain* exhibition (2022–2023) at Bayt AlMamzar. Almulla has also designed *Nesmah* (SIKKA 2023) and exhibited the *Library Circles* at the Jameel Arts Centre (2022). Almulla holds an MSc in Regional and Urban Planning from the London School of Economics.

**Sarah Saad Alajmi** is a PhD candidate in the History and Theory of Architecture Department at the University of Pennsylvania. Her dissertation examines the interrelationship between architecture and ecology in twentieth-century Arabia, where she focuses on nomadic and modern settlements in the Arabian Desert. Alajmi obtained her professional Bachelor of Architecture from Kuwait University in 2017 and holds a Master of Architecture II from Yale University. She practiced as a junior architect in Kuwait and held teaching positions at Kuwait University, Yale University, and the University of Pennsylvania. Alajmi's work focuses on transience, informality, domesticity, and poetry in the desert environment.

**Dimitri Brand** is a Co-Founder and Director of Built Projects at Holesum Studio. He graduated from the Yale School of Architecture in 2018. Brand was previously a Bass Fellow at the University of Cambridge, where he studied the history of conservatories and greenhouses and their cultural relevance. Focusing on carbon capture and energy efficiency in his design work, and he has integrated greenhouses and their associated technologies into the firm's built projects. In addition, Brand is the Technical Research Consultant and Design-Build Expert of the National Pavilion United Arab Emirates for the 19th International Architecture Exhibition – La Biennale di Venezia in 2025.

**Kit Elsworth** is an Associate and Building Performance Specialist in the transdisciplinary research group at the architecture firm KieranTimberlake. He uses his expertise in building science and building performance modeling to deploy a range of technical analyses on topics of carbon and energy modeling, occupant comfort, and envelope performance. A key aspect of this role is to interpret research and generate actionable design decisions for firm projects and elevate the architecture industry through publications and lectures. Elsworth is a member of ILFI's Energy + Carbon Technical Advisory Group (TAG), the AIA 2030 Commitment Working Group, and ASHRAE Committees. Before working at KieranTimberlake, Kit received his MS in Building Science from the University of California, Berkeley.

**Huma Gupta** is an Assistant Professor in the Department of Architecture at MIT in the Aga Khan Program for Islamic Architecture. She is affiliated with the History, Theory & Criticism of Architecture group and the Leventhal Center for Advanced Urbanism. Dr. Gupta's scholarship deals with the historical emergence of hierarchies and pathways toward dismantling them that span from critique to epistemic interventions. Her research historicizes and theorizes hierarchical systems that span urban housing, the devaluation of rural housing, and the relationship between building materials and the climate crisis. In her archival research that centers other human and more-than-human subjects, she challenges centuries of dehumanizing representation of rural migrants and marsh inhabitants through documentary filmmaking. Dr. Gupta's current book project *The Architecture of Dispossession* theorizes the relationship between state-building and dispossession through architectural transformations of migrant reed and clay dwellings in twentieth-century Iraq. Her scholarship has been published by the *Journal of Architectural Education*, *International Journal of Islamic Architecture*, *Journal of Contemporary Iraq and the Arab World*, MIT Press, and Yale University Press.

**HOME-OFFICE** is a research and design collaborative that explores the reciprocity between architectural types, their technical assemblies, and the environment. HOME-OFFICE was founded by Daniel Jacobs and Brittany Utting in 2017 and is based in Houston, Texas.

**Daniel Jacobs** is an Instructional Assistant Professor in Architecture at the University of Houston. His research and writing centers around labor production and material ecologies of the built environment. He has previously served as the Secretary of the National Organizing Committee of the Architecture Lobby, taught as a Lecturer at Taubman College of Architecture and Urban Planning at the University of Michigan, and practiced as an Associate at SHoPArchitects in New York.

**Brittany Utting** is an Assistant Professor of Architecture at Rice University in Houston, TX. She is the editor of the book *Architectures of Care: From the Intimate to the Common* (Routledge, 2023) and co-editor of *Log 60: The Sixth Sphere* (winter/summer 2024). Utting was a MacDowell Fellow in Architecture and a Willard A. Oberdick Fellow at the University of Michigan. Her work has been supported by the Graham Foundation and the Buell Center.

**Elisa Iturbe** is an Assistant Professor of Architecture at Harvard's Graduate School of Design. Her work studies the relationship between energy, power, and form, with a focus on how the adoption of fossil fuels changed the spatial organization of the built environment, producing an urban and architectural paradigm unique to the carbon age — *carbon form*. This concept was first published in *Log 47*, titled "Overcoming Carbon Form," which she guest-edited in 2019. She also co-curated and co-produced the exhibition *Confronting Carbon Form* at The Cooper Union, which exhibited original works in various media that define the spatial concepts of the carbon age. She has published in journals such as *Log*, *AA Files*, *Perspecta*, and *e-flux*, as well as several essay anthologies. Iturbe previously taught at The Cooper Union, Yale, and Cornell AAP. She is a Co-Founder of Outside Development, a design and research practice.

**Kevin Mitchell** is a Professor of Architecture at the American University of Sharjah (AUS), where he has taught courses in architecture, interior design, and the Foundations Program since 1999. His teaching contributions have been recognized with awards from AUS and the American Institute of Architects. He has served in a number of administrative positions at AUS, including Director of the Foundations Program, Associate Dean of the College of Architecture, Art and Design, Vice Provost for Undergraduate Affairs and Instruction, and Interim Provost. In addition, he led the university as Chancellor from 2019 until 2021. In parallel to ongoing work as a designer, Mitchell continues to write on issues related to education, design, architecture, and urbanism in the Gulf region. In 2022, the AUS Board of Trustees appointed him as the university's first Trustee Professor.

**Faysal Tabbarah** is an Associate Professor of Architecture at the College of Architecture, Art and Design at the American University of Sharjah (AUS), and at Carleton University School of Architecture in Ottawa. He is also a Co-Founder of the architecture and design studio, Architecture + Other Things (A+OT), based in Sharjah. He was the curator for the National Pavilion United Arab Emirates exhibition in the 18th International Architecture Exhibition 2023, La Biennale di Venezia. From teaching, research, and practice, Tabbarah's work explores alternative building practices that are rooted in their surrounding material and cultural environments, with a specific focus on Southwest Asia and North Africa.

# Bibliography

Abdulrahman, A. *Between Sips of Coffee.* Esdarat - Department of Culture and Tourism. 2014.

Ahmar, Abir. "UAE Oil Power Farms the Desert in Quest for Food Security." *Reuters,* February 16, 2023.

"(al-fagʿa).. Nabāt Fiṭrī Tajūd Behe al-Ṣaḥrāʾ Baʿad Mawsim al-Amṭār Wa-Yazkhur Bil-ʿAdīd Min al-ʿAnāṣer al-Ghidhāʾeyah." *Kuwait News Agency (KUNA),* February 4, 2023. https://www.kuna.net.kw/articledetails.aspx?id=3079853.

Al Hashimi, Alamira Reem. *"The Saadiyat Experiment: A Conversation with Dr. Merle Jensen."* In *On Foraging: Food Knowledge and Environmental Imaginaries in the UAE's Landscape,* edited by Dima Srouji, Meitha Almazrooei, and Faysal Tabbarah, 110–117. Beirut, Lebanon: Kaph, 2022.

Al-Himyari, Juma Khalifa Ahmed bin Thalith. *Encyclopedia of the Emirates Wildlife: Part One.* Dubai: Knowledge and Human Development Authority and Emirates Diving Association, 2013. Accessed December 28, 2024. https://altibrah.ae/book/16538.

Alawadhi, Khaled. *Lifescapes Beyond Bigness.* Artifice, 2018.

Alexander, William. "Indoor Farming Is a 'No-Brainer.' Except for the Carbon Footprint." *The New York Times,* June 21, 2002.

Almulla, Rashed. T*he Rise, Demise, and Possible Revival of Al-Hamriyah (Deira), Dubai: Land Policies, Social Cohesion, and Possible Reforms.* Unpublished Thesis. 2021.

Althusser, Louis. *"Ideology and Ideological State Apparatuses."* In *Lenin and Philosophy and Other Essays,* edited by Louis Althusser. New York: Monthly Review Press, 1971.

Al-Qasimi, Sultan Muhammad. *The Myth of Arab Piracy in the Gulf.* 2nd ed. Oxon: Routledge, 1988.

Ammar, Khalil. "Saline/Sea Water Greenhouse." *International Center for Biosaline Agriculture.* Accessed September 3, 2024. https://www.biosaline.org/experiments/experiment-1.

Arabian Gulf Digital Archive. *Internal political situation in Muscat and Oman* (FO 371/120542). 1956. Retrieved from https://www.agda.ae/.

"Architecture as a Science: Is the Scientific Method Applicable to Architectural Design?" *Yale Scientific Magazine,* May 22, 1948, 4.

Bani Hashim, Alamira Reem. *Planning Abu Dhabi: An Urban History.* London: Routledge, 2019.

Basche, Andrea. "Urban Farm-Fed Cities: Lessons from Cuba's Organopónicos." *SAGE Magazine.* Accessed January 19, 2025. https://sagemagazine.org/urban-farm-fed-cities-lessons-from-cubas-organoponicos/.

Bedir, Merve, Ludo Groen, Marten Kuijpers, Victor Muñoz Sanz, and Marina Otero Verzier. "Introduction: Automated Landscapes and the Politics of Collaborative Public Research." *In Automated Landscapes,* edited by Merve Bedir, Ludo Groen, Marten Kuijpers, Victor Muñoz Sanz, and Marina Otero Verzier, 6. Rotterdam: Nieuwe Instituut, 2023.

Bin Darwish, Ahmed. "Residents in Al Twar complain of free roaming livestock." *Emarat Al Youm.* 2013. Retrieved from https://www.emaratalyoum.com/hotline/2013-03-18-1.558327.

Britannica, The Editors of Encyclopaedia. "Quraysh." *Encyclopedia Britannica,* August 6, 2024. https://www.britannica.com/topic/Quraysh.

Britannica, The Editors of Encyclopaedia. "Palace of Versailles." *Encyclopedia Britannica,* October 28, 2024. https://www.britannica.com/topic/Palace-of-Versailles.

Callataÿ, Godefroid de. "The Classification of Knowledge in the Rasā'il." In *Epistles of the Brethren of Purity: The Ikhwān al-Ṣafā' and*
Central Intelligence Agency. "United Arab Emirates." *The World Factbook.* Last updated January 9, 2025. https://www.cia.gov/the-world-factbook/countries/united-arab-emirates/.

Central Intelligence Agency. "United Arab Emirates." *The World Factbook.* Last updated January 9, 2025. https://www.cia.gov/the-world-factbook/countries/united-arab-emirates/.

Chatty, D., & Young, G. eHRAF *World Cultures Summary on Bedouin and Pastoralist Culture in the Middle East.* 2009. Retrieved from https://ehrafworldcultures.yale.edu/cultures/mj04/summary.

Cole, Donald Powell. Nomads of the Nomads: *The Āl Murrah Bedouin of the Empty Quarter.* Arlington Heights, IL: Harlan Davidson, Inc., 1975.

Dal Piaz, Vittorio and Maurizio Rippa Bonati. "The Design and Form of the Padua *Horto Medicinale." The Botanical Garden of Padua 1545-1995.* Venice: Marsilio Editori, 1995. 44, 54.

Damluji, Salma Samar. *The Architecture of the United Arab Emirates.* Reading, UK: Garnet Publishing, 2006.

Davies, Philip, and Charlie Paton. "The Seawater Greenhouse: Background, Theory, and Current Status." *International Journal of Low-Carbon Technologies* 1, no. 2, 2006, 183–190. https://doi.org/10.1093/ijlct/1.2.183.

Deep Roots Project. "Veggie Temperature Tolerances." Accessed January 15, 2025. https://www.deep-roots-project.org/grow-your-own-food-all/veggie-temperature-tolerances#gsc.tab=0.

Deguines, Margot E. J. G. T., et al. "Pollination and Global Change: Examining the Effect of Climate Change on Pollinator-Dependent Crops." *Agriculture, Ecosystems & Environment* 209 (2015): 106–113. https://doi.org/10.1016/j.agee.2015.04.004.

"Development of Agriculture in Trucial States." *The National Archives.* Accessed December 21, 2024. https://www.agda.ae/en/catalogue/tna/fo/371/126956/n/3.

Dickson, H. R. P. *The Arab of the Desert: A Glimpse into Badawin Life in Kuwait and Sau'di Arabia.* London: George Allen & Unwin Ltd., 1967.

Dickson, Violet. *Forty Years in Kuwait.* London: George Allen & Unwin Ltd, n.d.

Dickson, Violet. *The Wild Flowers of Kuwait and Bahrain.* London: George Allen & Unwin Ltd, n.d.

Easterling, Keller. "El Ejido," in *Manual for a Future Desert,* eds. Ida Soulard, Abinadi Meza, and Bassam El Baroni. Milan, Nantes: Mousse Publishing, Beaux-Arts Nantes Saint-Nazaire, 2021, 205.

Early, Evelyn A. Review of *Aesthetics and Ritual in the United Arab Emirates*, by Aida Kanafani. Middle East Studies Association Bulletin 18, no. 2, December 1984, 183–185. Accessed December 28, 2024. https://www.jstor.org/stable/41887992.

Elsheshtawy, Yasser. "Research Materials." In *Transformations: The Emirati National House,* edited by Yasser Elsheshtawy. Abu Dhabi: National Pavillion United Arab Emirates la Biennale di Venezia, 2016.

Elsheshtawy, Yasser. "The Al Meqbali House: A Case Study." In *Transformations: The Emirati National House,* edited by Yasser Elsheshtawy. Abu Dhabi: National Pavillion United Arab Emirates la Biennale di Venezia, 2016.

Elsheshtawy, Yasser, et al. "Transformations: The Emirati National House: Inside UAE's Pavilion at the 2016 Venice Biennale." ArchDaily. 2016.

Epistles of the Brethren of Purity. *On Composition and the Arts.* Edited and translated by Godefroid de Callataÿ and Nader El-Bizri. Oxford: Oxford University Press, 2018.

Fanger, P. O. *Thermal Comfort: Analysis and Applications in Environmental Engineering.* New York: McGraw-Hill, 1970.

Fernandez, Antonio. "La Junta Vigila el Crecimiento de los Invernaderos en Marruecos." *La Voz de Almería.* December 10, 2018.

Food and Agriculture Organization of the United Nations (FAO). "Chapter 2: World Food and Agriculture – Statistical Yearbook 2022." Accessed January 15, 2025. https://www.fao.org/4/s2022e/s2022e02.htm.

Food Tech Valley. "About Food Tech Valley." Accessed January 19, 2025. https://www.foodtechvalley.ae/node/9.

Gabriel, Erhard F. *The Dubai Handbook*. Dubai Petroleum. 1985.

Gillett, Katy. "UAE Primed for Desert Expansion and 15-Minute Cities to Keep Pace with Population Boom." *The National*, December 4, 2024.

Giudici, Maria S. "Cultiver Notre Jardin: On the Park as a Civic Space." *Into the Great Wide Open.* Edited by Andreas Rumpfhuber, 142–165. Barcelona: dpr-barcelona, 2017.

Gospodarek, Ewa, et al. "The Optimal Temperature for the Growth of Blueberry (Vaccinium corymbosum L.)." *Folia Horticulturae* 29, no. 1, 2017, 81–91. https://doi.org/10.1515/fhort-2017-0008.

Government of Dubai and Dubai Municipality. *Public Health and Safety of the Society in the Emirate of Dubai.* Local Order No. (11). 2003. https://www.wkcgroup.com/wp-content/uploads/2023/04/Local-Order-No.-11-of-2003-Concerning-Public-Health-and-Safety-of-the-Society-in-the-Emirate-of-Dubai.pdf.

Hamburgh, Monica. "Get a Pet to Boost Your Child's Immune System." *Orlando Health*. June 17, 2021. Retrieved from https://www.orlandohealth.com/content-hub/get-a-pet-to-boost-your-childs-immune-system.

Horwood, Catherine. *Potted History: How Houseplants Took Over Our Homes*. London: Pimpernel Press, 2020.

Howe, Marvine. "Abu Dhabi Adapting to Modern World." *The New York Times,* January 14, 1972.

Iturbe, Elisa. "Architecture and the Death of Carbon Modernity." *Log* 47. Fall 2019, 10-23.

Jacobs, Daniel, and Brittany Utting. "Life Support: The Greenhouse as an Architecture of Survival." *In Pedagogical Experiments in Architecture for a Changing Climate,* edited by Tülay Atak, Luis Callejas, Jonathan A. Scelsa, and Jørgen Johan Tandberg, 108–22. New York: Routledge, 2024.

James, Barry. "World Uses Ground to Deserts." *The New York Times,* April 5, 2002. https://www.nytimes.com/2002/04/05/news/world-loses-ground-to-deserts.html.

Jamal, Mohamad A. *Aswāq Alkuwait Alqadīmah.* Kuwait City: Center for Research and Studies on Kuwait, 2004.

Janick, Jules, and Harry Paris. "History of Controlled Environment Horticulture: Ancient Origins." *HortScience* 57 (2022): 236–238. https://doi.org/10.21273/HORTSCI16169-21.

Jensen, Merle H. *Zayed: The Saadiyat Miracle.* Abu Dhabi: National Archives, 2021.

Kapp, Paul. "Historic Preservation Design: Using Ethnographic-Based Fieldwork to Introduce Theory and History in the Architecture Studio." *Future Anterior: Journal of Historic Preservation, History, Theory, and Criticism* 17, no. 2 (2020): 17. https://doi.org/10.5749/futuante.17.2.0017.

Khamis, Jumana. "'Grow Your Food Event' Encourages Home Farming." *Gulf News.* October 14, 2016. Retrieved from https://gulfnews.com/going-out/society/grow-your-food-event-encourages-home-farming-1.1912573.

Kohlmaier, Georg H., and Barna von Sartory. *Houses of Glass: A Nineteenth-Century Building Type.* Cambridge: MIT Press, 1991.

Lee, K. 2023. "The Floor: A Reinterpretation of the Korean Home, Focusing on the Ondol." *Space and Culture* 26, no. 4: 505–521. https://doi.org/10.1177/1206331220976486 .

Lee, K. 2023. "The Floor: A Reinterpretation of the Korean Home, Focusing on the Ondol." *Space and Culture* 26, no. 4: 505–521. https://doi.org/10.1177/1206331220976486 .

Lightfoot, Dale R. *"The Origin and Diffusion of Qanats in Arabia: New Evidence from the Northern and Southern Peninsula."* The Geographical Journal 166, no. 3 (2000).

Lokko, Mae-ling. "Hot Air Rising." *e-flux Architecture: Digestion,* September 2022. https://www.e-flux.com/architecture/digestion/487068/hot-air-rising/.

Loos, Adolf. "Someone Is Buried Here: Adolf Loos on Architecture and Death." *Neue Freie Presse.* Accessed November 18, 2024. https://thecharnelhouse.org/2014/03/17/someone-is-buried-here-adolf-loos-on-architecture-and-death/.

Mackay, Charles. *Extraordinary Popular Delusions and the Madness of Crowds.* London: Richard Bentley, 1841. "Tulipomania," 89–97.

Mandaville, James P. *Bedouin Ethnobotany: Plant Concepts and Uses in a Desert Pastoral World.* Tucson: University of Arizona Press, 2011.

Meehan, S. "Urban Farm Coming to Former Sparrows Point Steel Mill Site in Baltimore County." *The Baltimore Sun,* May 8, 2018. Accessed May 10, 2018. http://www.baltimoresun.com/business/bs-md-sparrows-point-farm-20180508-story.html.

Merriam-Webster.com Dictionary. s.v. "fieldwork." Accessed December 20, 2024. https://www.merriam-webster.com/dictionary/fieldwork.

Merriam-Webster.com Dictionary. s.v. "radiant heat." Accessed December 20, 2024. https://www.merriam-webster.com/dictionary/radiant%20heat.

Merriam-Webster.com Dictionary. s.v. "basal metabolic rate." Accessed December 20, 2024. https://www.merriam-webster.com/dictionary/basal%20metabolic%20rate.

Miller, Gordon L. Introduction. *The Metamorphosis of Plants.* Cambridge: The MIT Press, 2009. xxi-xxii.

Mitchell, Kevin. "Privileging the Pragmatic". In: F. Tabbarah and M. Almazrooei (eds) *In Plain Sight: Scenes from Aridly Abundant Landscapes.* Abu Dhabi: National Pavilion UAE La Biennale di Venezia/ Kaph Books, 2023. 300–317.

Müller, Rolf. "Advancing Sustainable Energy Transitions: A Multi-Level Perspective." *Environmental Impact Assessment Review* 110, 2024, 106796. https://doi.org/10.1016/j.eiar.2024.106796.

National Geographic Society. "The Development of Agriculture." *National Geographic Education Resource Library.* Accessed January 27, 2025. https://education.nationalgeographic.org/resource/development-agriculture/.

National Library and Archives of the UAE. "The Civilization of the United Arab Emirates." Accessed December 24, 2024. https://www.nla.ae/en/our-history/historical-periods/the-civilization-of-the-united-arab-emirates/.

Nessim, Marian A., et al. *"The Rise and Evolution of Wind Tower Designs in Egypt and the Middle East." Sustainability* 15, no. 14 (2023). https://doi.org/10.3390/su151410881.

NOAA Science on a Sphere. "ClimateBits: Solar Radiation." Accessed January 15, 2025. https://sos.noaa.gov/catalog/datasets/climatebits-solar-.

Otero Verzier, Marina. "Cartesian Enclosures." *New Geographies* 12: Commons, edited by Mojdeh Mahdavi and Liang Wang. Cambridge, MA: New Geographies Lab, Harvard University Graduate School of Design, 2021, 44.

Oxford English Dictionary. *"Greenhouse, n."* Accessed March 7, 2025.. https://www.oed.com.

Ouis, Pernilla. *"'Greening the Emirates': The Modern Construction of Nature in the United Arab Emirates." Cultural Geographies* 9, no. 3 (2002).

Palmboom, Frits, Bruno Notteboom, Kornelia Dimitrova, Bart Decroos. "The Drawing in Landscape Design and Urbanism." *OASE* 107. 2020. 3.

Phat Beets Produce. "Urban Gardens." Accessed January 19, 2025. https://www.phatbeetsproduce.org.

Power, Timothy, and Peter Sheehan. *"The Origin and Development of the Oasis Landscape of Al-Ain (UAE)." Proceedings of the Seminar for Arabian Studies* 42 (2012).

"ReFarm Global, IGS Break Ground on GigaFarm Project in Dubai." *Oil and Gas News (OGN)* 42, no. 1 (January 2025).

Rogers, Peter. "Water Security: Supplies, Resources, and Uncertainty." *In Water and Food Security in the Arabian Gulf*, 21–36. Abu Dhabi: Emirates Center for Strategic Studies and Research, 2013.

Reisz, Todd. "A Seed Sown in Digdaga for a Stomach in Dubai." In *On Foraging: Food Knowledge and Environmental Imaginaries in the UAE's Landscape*, edited by Dima Srouji, Faysal Tabbarah, and Meitha Almazrooei, 44. Abu Dhabi: Warehouse421 and Kaph Books, 2022.

Reisz, Todd. Showpiece City: *How Architecture Made Dubai.* Stanford, CA: Stanford University Press, 2020.

Saseendran, Sajila. "Top 3 Reasons Why Dubai Residents Complain About Their Neighbours." *Gulf News.* June 14, 2017. Retrieved from https://gulfnews.com/going-out/society/top-3-reasons-why-dubai-residents-complain-about-their-neighbours-1.2043514.

Savoia, Andrea Ubrizsy. "The Botanical Garden of Padua in Guilandino's Day." *The Botanical Garden of Padua 1545-1995.* Venice: Marsilio Editori, 1995. 173.

Scully, Vincent. *"Architecture as a Science: Is the Scientific Method Applicable to Architectural Design?" Yale Scientific Magazine,* May 22, 1948.

Salloum, Habeeb. *"Abu Dhabi Has Been Converted from Desert Land to a Land of Gardens." Washington Report on Middle East Affairs,* December 1995. Accessed March 7, 2025. https://www.wrmea.org/1995-december/abu-dhabi-has-been-converted-from-desert-land-to-a-land-of-gardens.html.

Scott, James C. *Against the Grain: A Deep History of the Earliest States, Yale University Press, 2017. ProQuest Ebook Central,* http://ebookcentral.proquest.com/lib/zu-ebooks/detail.action?docID=6424075. Created from zu-ebooks on 2024-12-23 04:24:02. 5.

Siegner, Alana, Jennifer Sowerwine, and Charisma Acey. "Does Urban Agriculture Improve Food Security? Examining the Nexus of Food Access and Distribution of Urban Produced Foods in the United States: A Systematic Review." *Sustainability* 10, no. 9 (2018): 2988. https://doi.org/10.3390/su10092988.

Smil, Vaclav. *Energy Transition: Global and National Perspectives.* Santa Barbara, CA: Praeger. 2017, ix.

Sowayan, Saad Abdullah. *Al-Ṣaḥrāʾ al-ʿArabiyah: Thaqāfatuhā wa-Shiʿruhā ʿabra al-ʿUṣūr: Qirāʾah Anthrūbūlūjiyah. Beirut:* al-Shabakah al-ʿArabiyah lil-Abḥāth wa-al-Nashr, 2010.

Springstubb, Phoebe. *"A Landscape 'Difficult to Describe': The Model Village and the Capital City." Architectural Theory Review* 26, no. 3 (2022).

Strain, B. R., and E. L. Higginbotham. *"Temperature Acclimation of Mesophyll Conductance in Cowpea." Physiologia Plantarum* 89, no. 2 (1993). https://doi.org/10.1111/j.1399-3054.1993.tb01737.x.

Swaroop, Sangeetha. *"Al Ain Oasis: World Heritage Site Takes a Refreshing Step Back in Time." Gulf News,* September 29, 2019. Accessed March 7, 2025. https://gulfnews.com/travel/al-ain-oasis-world-heritage-site-takes-a-refreshing-step-back-in-time-1.2304600.

"The Cultural Significance of Greenhouses: A Complicated Identity." *ArchDaily,* June 10, 2023. Accessed July 6, 2024. https://www.archdaily.com/996895/the-story-of-greenhouses-a-complicated-identity.

The National Archives. "Development of Agriculture in Trucial States." Accessed December 21, 2024. https://www.agda.ae/en/catalogue/tna/fo/371/126956/n/3.

Tohme Tawk, Salwa, Mounir Said, and Shady Hamadeh. "Urban Agriculture and Food Security in the Middle Eastern Context." *In The Oxford Handbook of Food, Politics, and Society.* Oxford: Oxford University Press, 2014. https://doi.org/10.1093/acprof:oso/9780199361786.003.0007.

Tuson, Penelope, ed. *Records of the Emirates 1820–1960.* Vol. 4, 9, 10, 11, 12. London: Archive Editions, 1990.

UNESCO: Intangible Cultural Heritage. *"Al Aflaj, Traditional Irrigation Network System in the UAE, Oral Traditions, Knowledge and Skills of Construction, Maintenance and Equitable Water Distribution."* 15.COM 8.b.10, 2020. Accessed March 7, 2025. https://ich.unesco.org/en/RL/al-aflaj-traditional-irrigation-network-system-in-the-uae-oral-traditions-knowledge-and-skills-of-construction-maintenance-and-equitable-water-distribution-01577.

Waqas, Muhammad, Xiukang Wang, Syed Zafar, Mehmood Ali Noor, Hafiz Hussain, Muhammad Azher Nawaz, and Muhammad Farooq. "Thermal Stresses in Maize: Effects and Management Strategies." *Plants* 10 (2021): 293. https://doi.org/10.3390/plants10020293.

Wilkinson, Tom. "Gardener's World." *Architectural Review.* Accessed December 22, 2024. https://www.architectural-review.com/essays/ecology/gardeners-world.


Wilkinson, Tom. "Gardener's World." *Architectural Review.* Accessed December 22, 2024. https://www.architectural-review.com/essays/ecology/gardeners-world.


Wilson, Arnold T. The Persian Gulf: *An Historical Sketch from the Earliest Times to the Beginning of the Twentieth Century.* London: Oxford University Press, 1928.

الفلاسي، أمل «حظائر للمواشي في الأحياء السكنية،» صفيحة البيان . ٧ نوفمبر ,٢٠٠٧.

https://www.albayan.ae/across-the-uae/٢٠٠٧-١١-٠٧-١,٨٠٥٧٣٤

الكعبي، كفاح، ويسري يوسف. «غابات وسط الصحراء.. كيف؟» الاتحاد، ٣ مايو ١٩٨٥.

الماحي، سليمان. «تجارب جديدة لزراعة أصناف الفواكه بمشروع الدقداقة.» الاتحاد، ١٧ يناير ١٩٨١.

المنصوري، لولوة. «الحكاية الإيكولوجية للمياه الأحفورية: من أين ينبع الماء في واحتي ليوا والعين؟» تراث: واحات الإمارات جواهر وسط الصحراء، عدد ٢٢٥ (يوليو ٢٠١٨): ٤٥.

النجار، محمود. «ازدياد الطلب على البيوت البلاستيكية يؤكد نجاح هذه التجربة في الإمارات.» الاتحاد، ٢٦ أكتوبر ١٩٨٥.

النجار، محمود. «الزراعة.. وتنمية الإمارات الشمالية.» الاتحاد، ٣- مايو ١٩٧٥.

النجار، محمود. «خطوات هامة لدعم وتطوير القطاع الزراعي في الدولة.» الاتحاد، ١٧ أبريل ١٩٧٦.

المؤسسة الوحدة للنشر والتوزيع. الخليج العربي في مواجهة التحديات: محاضرات الموسمين الثقافيين السابع والثامن ١٩٧٤-١٩٧٥. الكويت: مؤسسة الوحدة للنشر والتوزيع، ١٩٧٥.

نصر، حمدي. «المساحات الزراعية في العين تضاعفت مرتين خلال ٤ سنوات.» الاتحاد، ١٢ أغسطس ١٩٨٥.

رزق، فتحي. «مع الأمواج والرياح في غياب؟ نشرة جوية خاصة بهم.» الاتحاد، ٩ ديسمبر ١٩٨٠.

الخضرجي، إيهاب. «الخضروات المستوردة تملأ الأسواق.» الاتحاد، ١٤ يناير ١٩٨٤.

«الإمارات تحقق الاكتفاء الذاتي من لحوم الدواجن والبيض.» الاتحاد، ٩ نوفمبر ١٩٨٥.

«أول مصنع لتعبئة الخضروات.» الاتحاد، ١٦ يوليو ١٩٨٤.

«تسليم ٧٣ مواطناً مزارع جديدة في منطقتي العراد وأم غافة بالعين.» الاتحاد، ٢٦ مارس ١٩٨٤.

«حديقة فاكهة لكل بيت.» الاتحاد، ١١ فبراير ١٩٨٥.

«زايد يزور المركز التجريبي الزراعي بالعين الذي تقيمه شركة البترول الفرنسية وتقدمه ‹هدية› لأبوظبي.» الاتحاد، ٢٣ مارس ١٩٧٢.

«كانت مزرعة مزيد وكان غيرها من المزارع المنتشرة في العين.» الاتحاد، ٨ يناير ١٩٧٠.

هاني، فادية، «سهيل نجم الأساطير وملهم الأدباء والشعراء،» صحيفة البيان، ٢٣ أغسطس ٢٠٠٤. https://www.albayan.ae/culture-art/culture/٢٠٢٤-٠٨-٢٣-١,٤٩٢٣٠٩٢

***National Pavilion United Arab Emirates 2025***

**Pressure Cooker Recipes: An Architectural Cookbook**

This book is published on the occasion of the National Pavilion United Arab Emirates' exhibition, *Pressure Cooker,* at the 19th International Architecture Exhibition – La Biennale di Venezia from May 10, 2025, to November 23, 2025.

Commissioner: Salama bint Hamdan Al Nahyan Foundation
Supporter: UAE Ministry of Culture
Curator: Azza Aboualam

Editor: Azza Aboualam
Publication Research Assistant: Nujud Alhussain
English Copy Editor: Zeina Assaf
Arabic Translator: Ziad Chakaroun
Arabic Copy Editor: Mohammad Hamdan

Designer: Möbius Design Studio, Sharjah
Publisher: National Pavilion United Arab Emirates
Co-Publisher: Kaph Books
www.kaphbooks.com

**Exhibition Research and Design:**
Exhibition Research and Design: Holesum Studio, New York and Sharjah
Research Director: Azza Aboualam
Technical Research Consultant + Design Build Lead: Dimitri Brand
Exhibition Design Lead and Coordinator: James Coleman

**Research and Design Build Team:**
Senior Researcher and Design Build Coordinator: Noor Hamdan
Nourhan Rahhal

**Research Assistants:**
Alya Al Rushdi
Sara AlMahmoud

**Thermal Modelling Consultant:**
Kit Elsworth

**Exhibition Production:**
Photography: Ola Allouz
Illustration: Khalid Mezaina
Video: Azza Aboualam, James Coleman, and Noor Hamdan
Graphic Design: Möbius Design Studio, Sharjah
Lighting: iGuzzini illuminazione, Recanati
Exhibition Construction: eiletz ortigas | architects, Slovenia

**National Pavilion United Arab Emirates:**
Director: Laila Binbrek
Communications Manager: Dana Al Sadek
Exhibitions Manager: Farah El-Rafei
Programs Manager: Rawan Al Ramahi
Internship Coordinator: Anita Buscaino
Office Coordinator: Jay Yambao
Venice Coordinator: Emanuela Semiani

**Special Thanks:**
International Center for Biosaline Agriculture (ICBA), Dubai
Silal Food and Technology, Abu Dhabi
UAE Ministry of Climate Change and Environment
United Arab Emirates University, Abu Dhabi
Zayed University, Dubai

**Distribution:**

*NORTH AMERICA - LATIN AMERICA - ASIA - AUSTRALIA*
ARTBOOK | D.A.P.
75 Broad Street, Suite 630
New York, NY 10004
www.artbook.com

*FRANCE - SWITZERLAND - BELGIUM - LUXEMBOURG*
Les Presses du Réel
35 rue Colson,
21000 Dijon, France
www.lespressesdureel.com

*REST OF EUROPE*
Idea Books
Nieuwe Herengracht 11
1011 RK Amsterdam, The Netherlands
www.ideabooks.nl

*MIDDLE EAST*
CIEL BOOK DISTRIBUTION
Al Manara Road, Al Quoz 1, P.O.Box 282005
Dubai, United Arab Emirates
www.ciel.me

National Pavilion UAE – La Biennale di Venezia
Studio 19, M_39, Mina Zayed, 7 Al Rutam Street,
Abu Dhabi, United Arab Emirates
www.nationalpavilionuae.org

First Edition, 2025


Printed in March 2025 at die Keure in Belgium
ISBN: 978-614-8035-94-4